Policy and Governance in the Water-Energy-Food Nexus

This book discusses the balance of priorities within the Water-Energy-Food (WEF) nexus and its impact on policy development and implementation, highlighting innovative perspectives in adopting a holistic approach to identify, analyse and manage the nexus component interdependencies.

Due to increasing demands for natural resources, the WEF nexus has emerged as a response to the numerous global challenges. Addressing WEF challenges often involves balancing multiple and competing priorities and identifying and managing interrelations, synergies and trade-offs between the three components of the nexus. In this volume the authors focus on the dynamics between multiple stakeholders, such as governments, businesses, NGOs and local communities, when addressing WEF challenges by adopting a nexus approach. The book argues that effective engagement of multiple stakeholders can address difficulties arising from the introduction of an integrated approach to WEF policy design and implementation, increasing the potential benefits. The book also looks at the effect of international relations and regional power struggles on resolving cross-border WEF nexus issues. Case studies are drawn from Kenya, Central Asia, USA and Peru, highlighting key themes, such as how collaborative governance, enabled and facilitated by relational equity management, can be viewed as an innovative way to reconcile competing priorities.

The combination of theoretical and case study chapters makes the book of interest to a wide audience, including scholars and advanced students of sustainable development, agriculture and food studies, water and energy policy design and governance, as well as to practitioners working in the fields of water, energy and food security.

Anastasia Koulouri graduated from the University of Strathclyde, UK with a PhD in Management Science. Previously she has held posts at the University of Strathclyde, UK, the Technical University of Helsinki, Finland and the Belgian Nuclear Energy Research Centre, Belgium. Currently she is a Lecturer at the School of Business, Law and Social Sciences, Abertay University, UK.

Nikolai Mouraviev is a Senior Lecturer at the School of Business, Law and Social Sciences, Abertay University, UK. Previously he has held teaching positions at KIMEP University, Kazakhstan, Wayne State University, USA and Viterbo University, USA.

Earthscan Studies in Natural Resource Management

For more information on books in the Earthscan Studies in Natural Resource Management series, please visit the series page on the Routledge website: http://www.routledge.com/books/series/ECNRM/.

Agricultural Land Use and Natural Gas Extraction Conflicts
A Global Socio-Legal Perspective
Madeline Taylor and Tina Hunter

Tropical Bioproductivity
Origins and Distribution in a Globalized World
David Hammond

The Commons in a Glocal World
Global Connections and Local Responses
Edited by Tobias Haller, Thomas Breu, Tine De Moor, Christian Rohr, Heinzpeter Zonj

Natural Resource Conflicts and Sustainable Development
Edited by E. Gunilla Almered Olsson and Pernille Gooch

Sustainable Governance of Wildlife and Community Based Natural Resource Management
From Economic Principles to Practical Governance
Brian Child

Sustainability Certification Schemes in the Agricultural and Natural Resource Sectors
Outcomes for Society and the Environment
Edited by Melissa Vogt

Policy and Governance in the Water-Energy-Food Nexus
A Relational Equity Approach
Edited by Anastasia Koulouri and Nikolai Mouraviev

UNESCO Biosphere Reserves
Supporting Biocultural Diversity, Sustainability and Society
Edited by Maureen G. Reed and Martin F. Price

Policy and Governance in the Water-Energy-Food Nexus

A Relational Equity Approach

Edited by
Anastasia Koulouri and Nikolai Mouraviev

Routledge
Taylor & Francis Group

LONDON AND NEW YORK

First published 2020
by Routledge
2 Park Square, Milton Park, Abingdon, Oxon OX14 4RN

and by Routledge
605 Third Avenue, New York, NY 10017

First issued in paperback 2021

Routledge is an imprint of the Taylor & Francis Group, an informa business

© 2020 selection and editorial matter, Anastasia Koulouri and Nikolai
Mouraviev; individual chapters, the contributors

The right of Anastasia Koulouri and Nikolai Mouraviev to be identified as the
authors of the editorial material, and of the authors for their individual
chapters, has been asserted in accordance with sections 77 and 78 of the
Copyright, Designs and Patents Act 1988.

British Library Cataloguing in Publication Data
A catalogue record for this book is available from the British Library

Library of Congress Cataloging-in-Publication Data
A catalog record has been requested for this book

ISBN 13: 978-0-367-78470-6 (pbk)
ISBN 13: 978-1-138-35737-2 (hbk)

Typeset in Sabon
by Taylor & Francis Books

Anastasia Koulouri
To Nikolas, my little star.
You are absolutely amazing!
Always remember, mum loves you to Pluto and beyond!

Contents

List of illustrations   ix
List of contributors   x

1 Introduction: The water-energy-food nexus through the lens of
   relational equity management   1
   ANASTASIA KOULOURI AND NIKOLAI MOURAVIEV

PART I
The nexus in policy and governance   9

2 Governance of the water-energy-food nexus: A relational
   equity approach   11
   ANASTASIA KOULOURI AND NIKOLAI MOURAVIEV

3 Integrating the water-energy-food nexus into policy and
   decision-making: Opportunities and challenges   31
   LIVIA BIZIKOVA

4 Water-energy-food nexus: A property rights approach   48
   CHRISTIAN A. NYGAARD AND ELLIS P. JUDSON

5 The water-energy-food nexus in agricultural policy   64
   JONATHAN C. COOPER

PART II
The nexus in practice   75

6 Water-energy-food nexus and human security in
   northwestern Kenya   77
   JEREMIAH OGONDA ASAKA

7   Relational equity management in water-energy-food nexus
    governance: The case of the Aral Sea Basin restoration programmes   95
    ALIYA TANKIBAYEVA AND AIGUL ADIBAYEVA

8   Using oilfield produced water in agricultural crop irrigation: An
    opportunity for integrative water management for food and
    energy production?   120
    TANJA SREBOTNJAK

9   Integrating the water-energy-food (WEF) nexus in the
    environmental governance of a metropolitan city in a developing
    economy: A case study of Lima, Peru   143
    VIACHASLAU FILIMONAU

PART III
Conclusion   159

10 The water-energy-food nexus: Lessons for governance   161
    NIKOLAI MOURAVIEV AND ANASTASIA KOULOURI

    Index   166

Illustrations

Figures

6.1 Map of Kenya 82
7.1 Map of Central Asia indicating five states – Kazakhstan,
    Kyrgyzstan, Tajikistan, Turkmenistan and Uzbekistan – and the
    Aral Sea between Kazakhstan and Uzbekistan 95

Tables

2.1 Kazakhstan's power generation by source (%) 18
3.1 Framework for selection of the WEF nexus case studies 34
3.2 Overview of the key elements of the reviewed case studies 37
6.1 Overview of human security dimensions 79
7.1 The Aral Sea basin: Application of the relational equity approach
    to the WEF nexus governance 108
7.2 The Aral Sea Basin Programme 1 (ASBP-1): summary of activities 109
7.3 The Aral Sea Basin Programme 2 (ASBP-2): summary of activities 112
7.4 The Aral Sea Basin Programme 3 (ASBP-3): summary of activities 115

Box

4.1 Economic benefits and rights in water, irrigation and energy 54

Contributors

Dr **Anastasia Koulouri** graduated from the University of Strathclyde, UK with a PhD in Management Science. Previously she has held posts at the University of Strathclyde, UK, the Technical University of Helsinki, Finland and the Belgian Nuclear Energy Research Centre, Belgium. Currently she is a Lecturer at the School of Business, Law and Social Sciences, Abertay University, UK. Her research interests include energy security in resource-rich countries and sustainable development of transitional economies.

Dr **Nikolai Mouraviev** is a Senior Lecturer at the School of Business, Law and Social Sciences, Abertay University, UK. Previously he has held teaching positions at KIMEP University, Kazakhstan, Wayne State University, USA and Viterbo University, USA. His research focuses on public-private collaboration in transitional nations. In addition, his research interests include entrepreneurship in cosmopolitan cities and governance of the energy sector.

Aigul Adibayeva is Associate Dean of the College of Social Sciences, KIMEP University, Almaty, Kazakhstan. Her research interests are in the field of politics in Central Asia.

Jeremiah Ogonda Asaka is Assistant Professor of Security Studies at Sam Houston State University, Texas, USA. He holds a PhD in Global Governance and Human Security from the University of Massachusetts, Boston, USA.

Livia Bizikova is a Director at the International Institute of Sustainable Development (IISD) based in Ottawa, Canada. Her expertise focuses on policy implications of and tracking progress on issues such as the water-energy-food nexus, sustainability, the Sustainable Development Goals, food security and climate change.

Dr **Jonathan C. Cooper** is Senior Lecturer in Sustainable Technology and Geography at Harper Adams University, Shropshire, United Kingdom. His research interests include energy policy, especially related to on-farm installations, agricultural innovation and sustainable development.

Viachaslau Filimonau is Principal Lecturer in Hospitality Management in the Faculty of Management at Bournemouth University, Bournemouth, United Kingdom. His academic interests include sustainable mobilities, food systems research and environmental management in tourism and hospitality enterprises.

Dr Ellis P. Judson is Postdoctoral Researcher in the Centre for Urban Transitions, Swinburne University of Technology, Melbourne, Australia. Her research interests centre on the socio-technical change within infrastructure systems, the interactions between people, technology and the environment, and governance for energy efficiency.

Dr Christian A. Nygaard is Associate Professor and social economist at the Centre for Urban Transitions, Swinburne University of Technology, Melbourne, Australia. His research centres on the long-term urban change and the institutional drivers of governance adaptations in resource-rich economies.

Tanja Srebotnjak is the Hixon Professor of Sustainable Environmental Design at Harvey Mudd College in California, USA. Her research involves the environmental and health risks of unconventional oil production. She received her PhD in environmental statistics and policy from Yale University.

Dr Aliya Tankibayeva is Lecturer of Public Administration at KIMEP University, Almaty, Kazakhstan. She earned her PhD from the University of Northampton, United Kingdom.

1 Introduction

The water-energy-food nexus through the lens of relational equity management

Anastasia Koulouri and Nikolai Mouraviev

Over the past ten years, the water-energy-food (WEF) nexus has emerged as a response to numerous challenges. The rapidly increasing demand for natural resources stems from exponential population growth and is exacerbated by urbanisation with the associated resource intensive lifestyles, concentrated consumption, and ever-expanding middle-classes characterised by avid consumerism. Further, globalisation – despite its positive impact on the world's economic development by enhancing economic links, creating employment opportunities and bringing resources to regions which experience scarcity – has also exposed countries to market volatility. This development has been inequitable, leaving a large portion of the world population without adequate access to food, clean water and/or modern energy sources. In addition, climate change operates as a threat multiplier, exacerbating the already significant burden on natural resources and deepening the vulnerability of human and ecological systems.

The WEF nexus could support the transition to sustainable development by providing a framework for a holistic approach to (1) the intersectorality of resource management; (2) the interdependencies and interdisciplinarity of resource management decisions; and (3) the interactionality of resource management decisions and their impacts (Al-Saidi and Elagib, 2017). Such integration across sectors, institutions and scales entails increased tensions between the stakeholders and actors involved compounded by institutional inertia, path dependence and a natural tendency to sectoral and/or linear thinking (Hoff, 2011). This necessitates an improved conceptualisation of governance frameworks that would permit the effective application of the WEF nexus in framing and addressing resource management problems. In achieving this, relational equity management may be a suitable perspective to adopt.

The book aims to discuss balancing priorities within the WEF nexus and its impact on policy development and implementation through the lens of relational equity management (Sawhney and Zabin, 2002). It highlights innovative perspectives in adopting a holistic approach to identify, analyse and manage the nexus component interdependencies. Looking beyond interdisciplinarity, to intersectorality and interactivity of policies and the impact of their implementation, the WEF nexus should be viewed as an approach that offers a tool for balancing trade-offs, enhancing synergies and promoting effective resource management. The book features creative solutions aiming to harmonise the multiple and (often) competing priorities of the WEF sectors through enhancing the relational equity of all stakeholders/agents. It further discusses how nexus thinking materialises in policy and governance in the three sectors – water, energy and food – within different contexts. Developing and implementing policies within sectoral silos and/or without the engagement of local communities typically faces a multiplicity of barriers that drastically reduce the efficacy of resource management. In these sectoral policies, externalities are often unacknowledged and/or inappropriately handled.

The book's thematic focus is relational equity management as part of the governance framework applied to the WEF nexus. Relational equity management refers to the government's efforts to identify the relationships of all actors within the nexus, and manage those that it considers critical. Specifically, relational equity is the value that a stakeholder derives from interacting with a group of other stakeholders, rather than from individual, one-to-one interaction with each actor, pursuing the goal of solving a common (e.g. regional or national) problem, and the value that a stakeholder contributes to nexus problem-solving. These relationships include those between government organisations, as well as those between the government, businesses, NGOs, interest groups and the community. Is the onus of managing these relationships and the responsibility for doing so productively solely a government duty? Can nexus governance be more effectual if each stakeholder and actor accepts part of this duty? Through the legal and regulatory frameworks the government defines the boundaries within which these relationships operate. However, other stakeholders/agents should be invited to contribute and actively participate in developing these frameworks.

The book pays special attention to under-researched topics that form its main themes including:

- The dynamics between policy makers, sectoral experts and researchers when undertaking a WEF nexus analysis to address specific problems and the impact of those dynamics on policy and governance decision-making;
- The role of business elites in framing and addressing WEF nexus challenges;
- The impact of politics, political systems and power holders on designing and implementing suitable policies to address WEF nexus problems;
- The influence of corruption on prioritising WEF nexus problems and formulating solutions;
- The effect of international relations and regional power struggles on resolving cross-border WEF nexus issues.

This is a non-technical book. Rather, it looks at the WEF nexus through the lens of policy and governance. Although affordable and cutting-edge technological solutions are essential for underpinning the efficient management of resources, often the focus on technology does not lead to suitable policy solutions. The development of fitting technological and engineering solutions, on its own, is insufficient, as each policy has to be supported by organised actors, institutions, funding, tools, procedures and mechanisms (i.e. governance) to ensure successful implementation.

This book draws on many years of the editors' work experience in resource-rich Kazakhstan. Initially, this work focused on energy policy with particular emphasis on renewables (Koulouri and Mouraviev, 2018; Mouraviev and Koulouri, 2018, 2019b). The thematic focus later evolved to embrace energy security, its understanding by the majority of people and its conceptualisation by the government as reflected in the nation's energy policy (Koulouri and Mouraviev, 2019; Mouraviev and Koulouri, 2019a, 2019c). Nonetheless, focusing on energy policy and energy security has been insufficient, as challenges, relating directly or indirectly to the energy field, cannot be addressed in isolation. Some examples of problems with significant spill-over effects beyond one or two sectors include: the use of scarce water resources for hydropower generation and the multiple negative impacts on the local populations, as was the case with the change of operations in the Toktogul reservoir in neighbouring Kyrgyzstan (UNDP, 2004); or, the water quality degradation due to extracting and refining of fossil fuels (UNDP, 2003), which provided 88 per cent of Kazakhstan's total electricity generation in 2017 (EIA, 2019) and which are a key revenue source for the country's economy. These and many other examples brought to the fore the need for an integrative approach that would permit the holistic consideration of interlinkages, interdependencies, synergies and trade-offs in policy and governance of the WEF sectors. This edited collection offers insights into the application of the WEF nexus into policy and governance of these sectors from the perspective of relational equity management as an enabler. Therefore, it would be of interest to readers who live, work and/or study in both resource-rich and resource-poor nations.

The book's main argument is that relational equity management may efficaciously address and overcome the limitations set by sectoral approaches to the governance of the water, energy or food sectors. Further, it may provide a way to create governance structures, processes and tools necessary to solve problems within the WEF nexus. Moreover, the case studies show that relational equity management can be viewed as an innovative way to reconcile competing priorities, such as the goal to increase food production and the need to protect freshwater sources. The book argues that successful policy interventions for the efficient holistic management of the WEF nexus require the impactful engagement of multiple stakeholders including governmental agencies, international and national non-governmental institutions, businesses and civil society. In this collaboration, a critical dimension is the management of stakeholders' relational equity.

This novel conceptualisation of the governance approach to the WEF nexus is the book's distinctive and original element. The conceptualisation of nexus to model the interrelationships of the water, energy and food sectors was developed about a decade ago. Since then, researchers have looked into interrelations, synergies and trade-offs between the three nexus elements from a number of perspectives (e.g. technological innovation to address nexus challenges, the nexus in the light of climate change, in dyads). However, none of these contributions has looked into the integration of the nexus concept into policy and governance of the water, energy and food sectors through the lens of relational equity management. This book views the latter as an enabler of successful collaborative policy design and implementation, a way to create and implement appropriate interventions and address issues of environmental and economic sustainability.

The book offers a blend of theoretical/conceptual chapters and case studies, organised in three parts. The first part includes conceptual chapters discussing the management of relational equity as part of the WEF nexus governance framework; the challenges and opportunities in integrating a WEF nexus approach in policy and decision-making; the use of a property rights approach in considering the nexus; and the application of the nexus approach in agricultural policy.

The second part includes case studies in relation to how the nexus concept is implemented to manage WEF issues in Kenya, Central Asia, USA and Peru, highlighting the importance of relational equity management in policy design and implementation. Discussing the application of a WEF nexus approach to address different problems, these case studies offer insights into the challenges and opportunities in adopting a cooperative approach, rather than pursuing national, regional, local or sectoral interests, and into the role of community engagement in WEF nexus policy and governance decision-making within varying contexts. This explains the choice of the cases presented in this edited collection. The case study from northwestern Kenya links nexus governance to human security. The case study from Central Asia details the efforts for the transnational management of the Aral Sea. The case study from the USA analyses the integrative management of water in food and energy production in California. Finally, the case study from Peru discusses the integration of WEF nexus thinking in the environmental governance of a metropolitan area, Lima.

The chapters/cases demonstrate the significance of managing relational equity in governing the WEF sectors in different economic conditions and at different levels – the international level (the Aral Sea in Central Asia), the regional level (northwestern Kenya, California in USA), and the local level (Lima in Peru). Irrespectively of the variety and number of selected cases, it is impossible for any book to capture all perspectives and examples of WEF nexus integration in policy and governance. With this in mind, this edited collection attempts to showcase examples that afford the reader significant breadth of perceptive.

The third part of this edited collection compares and contrasts theoretical perspectives as well as the implementation of a nexus approach elucidated in the book's chapters and offers conclusions. This part also draws insights into the role relational equity management may play in governing the WEF nexus by discussing implications for policy-making and implementation.

Academics, students and practitioners may equally benefit from the blend of chapters (conceptual as well as practice-oriented) that reinforces the book's main argument that relational equity management is critically important for applying WEF nexus thinking in policy and governance. To this end, this edited collection provides a novel outlook at the application of the WEF nexus in policy and governance and explores the substantial benefits brought by the holistic consideration of the WEF sectors, offering readers insights into the integrated evaluation of water-energy-food interrelations, interactions, synergies and trade-offs.

As the ultimate purpose of nexus governance is to ensure environmental and economic sustainability, this edited collection is likely to be of interest to scholars concerned with sustainable development and the efficient utilisation of resources from the policy and governance perspectives. Further, the book may be of interest to: staff members in companies, across the globe, in the water, energy and food sectors; government experts involved in the regulation of those sectors; experts in international and national, governmental and non-governmental agencies involved in policy research on water, energy and food; and staff and volunteers in NGOs and consultants working on sustainable development and resource efficiency.

These practitioners may find the book useful as it highlights an array of challenges and opportunities that governments of industrialised and developing countries may face in designing policy and governing the water, energy and food sectors. The analysis of enablers of and barriers to resource management, followed by critical appraisal, will be of interest to practitioners across the globe allowing them to compare and contrast the narrative with their own understanding of the issues associated with developing and implementing policies for sustainable environmental and socio-economic development. Practitioners may identify differences and commonalities regarding how policy for the WEF sectors is developed and implemented in comparison to their experience where they live/work, permitting them to analyse best practice and/or borrow from the experience of other nations.

Researchers and students may also benefit from reading this book, as it offers insights into the implementation of WEF nexus thinking into policy and governance that are not yet commonly shared. The book explores resource management through the application of WEF nexus thinking to policy and governance and argues that successful implementation rests on engaging all stakeholders/actors and drawing on equity mobilisation in managing relationships. By reading this book, academics and students may identify commonalities and differences between developing and industrialised nations regarding how nexus thinking informs, or could inform, policy development and implementation in the three sectors. Readers will have the opportunity to draw comparisons on a broad range of particularities and draw their own insights into the experience of different nations, the opportunities they have and the challenges they face in the nexus governance.

In summary, this book shows WEF nexus governance in action and departs from merely theoretical considerations. The discussion of relational equity management in governing the WEF nexus and integrating it in policy and decision-making, the analysis of the nexus from a property rights perspective and the integration of the nexus into the UK and the European Union agricultural policies as well as the adoption of an integrative approach by developing and industrialised nations, in rural and urban contexts, create a unique blend of practice and theory that may attract a wide spectrum of readers who are interested in the application of WEF nexus to policy and governance, aiming, ultimately, to ensure sustainable resource management.

References

Al-Saidi, M. and Elagib, N.A. (2017). "Towards understanding the integrative approach of the water, energy and food nexus". *Science of the Total Environment*, vol. 574, pp 1131–1139.

EIA (U.S. Energy Information Administration). (2019). *Country Analysis: Kazakhstan.* [Online] [Accessed 7 February 2019] Available from: www.eia.gov/beta/international/a nalysis.php?iso=KAZ.

Koulouri, A. and Mouraviev, N. (2018). "Governance of the clean energy sector in Kazakhstan: Impediments to investment". *International Journal of Technology Intelligence and Planning*, vol. 12, no. 1, pp 6–23.

Koulouri, A. and Mouraviev, N. (2019). "Energy security through the lens of renewable energy sources and resource efficiency". In N. Mouraviev and A. Koulouri (eds) *Energy Security: Policy challenges and solutions for resource efficiency*. London: Palgrave Macmillan.

Mouraviev, N. and Koulouri, A. (2017). "Public-private partnerships as a policy tool for the sustainable utilisation of renewable energy sources: The case of Kazakhstan". In N. Mouraviev and N. Kakabadse (eds) *Public-Private Partnerships in Transitional Nations: Policy, governance and praxis*. Newcastle upon Tyne: Cambridge Scholars Publishing.

Mouraviev, N. and Koulouri, A. (2018). "Clean energy and governance challenges". *International Journal of Technology Intelligence and Planning*, vol. 12, no 1, pp. 1–5.

Mouraviev, N. and Koulouri, A. (eds) (2019a). *Energy Security: Policy challenges and solutions for resource efficiency*. London: Palgrave Macmillan.

Mouraviev, N. and Koulouri, A. (2019b). "Enabling green energy production: Implementing policy by using public-private collaboration". In N. Mouraviev and A. Koulouri (eds) *Energy Security: Policy challenges and solutions for resource efficiency*. London: Palgrave Macmillan.

Mouraviev, N. and Koulouri, A. (2019c). "Renewable energy and resource efficiency: Governance is key". In N. Mouraviev and A. Koulouri (eds) *Energy Security: Policy challenges and solutions for resource efficiency*. London: Palgrave Macmillan.

Sawhney, M. and Zabin, J. (2002). "Managing and measuring relational equity in the network economy". *Journal of the Academy of Marketing Science*, vol. 30, no. 4, pp 313–332.

Hoff, H. (2011). *Understanding the Nexus. Background paper for the Bonn 2011 Nexus Conference: The water, energy and food security nexus.* Stockholm: Stockholm Environment Institute.

UNDP. (2003). *National Human Development Report.* New York: United National Development Programme. [Online] [Accessed 31 March 2019]. http://waterwiki.net/images/6/64/KazakhstanHDRWater.pdf.

UNDP (2004). *Water Resources of Kazakhstan in the New Millennium.* New York: United National Development Programme. [Online] [Accessed 31 March 2019]. Available from: http://waterwiki.net/images/a/ad/KazakhstanWater.pdf.

Part I

The nexus in policy and governance

2 Governance of the water-energy-food nexus

A relational equity approach

Anastasia Koulouri and Nikolai Mouraviev

Introduction

This chapter focuses on the need to adopt a novel approach to governance of the water-energy-food (WEF) nexus. It argues that successful integration of the nexus conceptualisation – in order to address holistically the challenges in the WEF sectors and take cognisance of their interdependencies – is contingent on the effective management of the relational equity of all stakeholders/actors. Adopting a view on collective governance as an arrangement that brings various actors, public and private, together in collective forums with public agencies to engage in consensus-oriented decision-making (Ansell and Gash, 2008), the chapter further contends that collaborative approach is one of the most impactful means of nexus governance, enabled and facilitated by effective relational equity management. By emphasising the significance of effective relational equity management to enable and facilitate higher levels of integration across sectors, institutions, levels and scales, leading to more impactful policy design and implementation, this chapter lays the foundation for further debate in the book.

Following the introduction, the chapter outlines the concept of WEF nexus, its genesis and evolution and the main benefits it brings to policy design and implementation. The chapter further discusses the concept of relational equity, placing it in the context of governance theories. It argues that relational equity is critical in enabling and facilitating a collective approach for the effective governance of the nexus and compares and contrasts relational equity management and stakeholder theory. Using the case of Kazakhstan, the chapter illustrates the importance of a collective approach to governance, enhanced by the effective management of the relational equity of all stakeholders/agents. The chapter concludes by discussing the implications for governing the WEF nexus.

The WEF nexus

The water-energy-food and climate nexus was first discussed at the World Economic Forum in Davos in 2011. This led to the publication of the book *Water Security: The water-food-energy-climate nexus* (Waughray, 2011). Recognising the importance of moving away from a sectoral approach to policy design and implementation, science and practice, the German Federal Government in November 2011 organised the international conference "The Water, Energy and Food Security Nexus – Solutions for the Green Economy", the Bonn 2011 Nexus Conference. The aim was to contribute to the United Nations (UN) Conference on Sustainable Development (Rio+20) (Endo et al., 2017). In 2013, the Asian Development Bank (2013) stressed that the worldwide debate should not consider water security in isolation but through the lens of the WEF nexus, considering the interlinkages between the water, energy and food sectors. The inextricable link between the three sectors was further highlighted by the UN in their 2014 World Water Development Report (UN, 2014).

There is no commonly accepted, clear definition of the nexus and no consistent way of operationalising, facilitating and implementing the nexus conceptualisation (Endo et al., 2017). In this book, we consider the WEF nexus as an approach that enables the analysis of the interrelations between water, energy and food, identifying synergies, trade-offs and potential conflicts emerging from the management of each of these resources with the view to achieve various socio-economic and environmental goals (FAO, 2014). The nexus is therefore closely aligned with water, energy and food security, the UN Sustainable Development Goals (UN, 2019), and policy design and implementation for the water, energy and food sectors. It is also linked to Integrated Water Resource Management (IWRM), with the main difference between the two being that the IWRM focuses on the water sector.

The main benefit of the nexus approach is that it enables the analysis of the complex and dynamic interrelations between the three sectors by lending a dynamic and holistic perspective and by promoting a multi-sectoral and multi-stakeholder collaborative engagement, involving governmental institutions/agencies, development organisations, funders, NGOs, local communities, business and industry, media, science-policy interface and academics (Endo et al., 2017). In doing so, the nexus enhances the sustainable management of limited resources and, as a consequence, water, energy and food security.

From a policy and governance perspective, there are multiple advantages in adopting the nexus approach in policy design and implementation for the water, energy and food sectors. These include: increased policy coherence, effective operationalisation and implementation of policy through appropriate governance instruments and institutions and decrease of the impact of the most influential stakeholders/agents and their vested interests. Critical for the materialisation of these benefits is the existence of political will – locally, regionally and internationally – to engage across sectors and levels, both within, across and outwith governmental agencies and institutions and to coordinate this collaborative effort (Hoff, 2017). Further, the development of institutional capacity is necessary to facilitate integrative analysis, joint planning and the development and implementation of policies and legal and regulatory frameworks informed by the analysis of their cumulative and interrelated impacts (Lindberg and Leflaive, 2015). Lastly, it is important to consider political and market forces and their influence on the nexus (Allan and Matthews, 2016).

Nonetheless, the adoption of a nexus approach in policy design and implementation is more complex and resource intensive than sector-focused approaches and requires greater capacity. As noted in Chapter 3, there is a balance to be found between the level of complexity of the WEF analysis and the associated time and resource cost and allowing sufficient time for the development of partnerships and for collaborative working.

Relational equity and nexus: setting the scene

This book adopts the concept of relational equity as a means for mobilising participation of various actors in solving WEF nexus problems. The concept serves as a foundation for dealing with complex, multi-dimensional aspects of the three sectors embracing water, energy and agriculture, particularly once the policy for each sector has been set. It is not uncommon that policy may be designed at the national level as this is where most policy-making takes place. Many policies are high-order, that is setting just the general policy objectives and lacking specifics of what needs to be done and how. Whilst this book does not engage with in-depth policy analysis and related political and economic discourse, it focuses on existing policy and, importantly, on the WEF nexus governance. This chapter elucidates the book's key concepts – relational equity and governance – and positions them within a range of available theories and approaches in the literature, as well as highlights how they apply to the nexus.

What is relational equity?

In reference to the WEF nexus, relational equity refers to the willingness and ability of various actors to make a contribution to problem-solving within the nexus agenda, rather than within an actor's sole sector. This way each participant's benefits are maximised through the common good (i.e. for the nexus), rather than from some isolated improvements within a certain sector. By contributing to each nexus project, an actor pursues the nexus improvement goals, which means that its own interests give way to broader societal interests. Each actor contributes and expects other actors to contribute to the nexus problem-solving. At the same time, each actor expects to receive benefits from the joint effort, and each actor is aware that all other actors expect to maximise their benefits as well.

In the concept, the word *relational* refers to the network of relationships between actors, whilst *equity* refers to two perspectives (or dimensions): (a) value embedded in the ownership of the process by all actors via their contribution (i.e. each actor's contribution carries value and signifies the actor's engagement in the nexus problem-solving) and (b) fair, rather than equal, contribution by each actor. As each actor may have varying levels of capacity (i.e. vastly different human, financial, technological and all other tangible and intangible resources), it is unrealistic to expect equal contribution from each participant in the network. Rather, contribution has to be fair, given the capacity and the volume of resources available to the participant. For example, a small local community typically does not have any financial resources and is unable to make investment in building a pipeline system for potable water. Nonetheless, a local community can make a significant improvement to water utilisation, for instance, by not using potable water for agricultural needs. Rational use of potable water, which will reduce its volume and the cost of water supply, forms a fair contribution of the local community to the nexus governance.

An additional note should be made regarding conceptualising a *fair* contribution. Contributions have to be sustainable, that is they need to be made in a manner that the current input does not compromise the actor's ability to contribute in future years. This means that a relational equity approach does not require maximising actors' contributions. Rather, it focuses on sustainability in management, as well as in its outcomes for the WEF nexus.

To summarise, relational equity means an approach to governance, in which problem-solving is addressed by a network of multiple actors who put aside their competing interests and adopt a different stance: everyone contributes and everyone, therefore, benefits. It is worth emphasising that in the case of the WEF nexus the sectoral benefits are likely to have significant spill over effects for other sectors, within the nexus and beyond. Due to the high value of potential societal benefits (such as reduced pollution, improved water supply for many regions, job creation through sustainable agriculture), the active role in network formation and mobilising actors' resources belongs to the government. This does not mean that the government agency leads the network. Rather, the government, by providing financial resources and administrative support, might sponsor one of the network participants who will assume the project and network leadership. The relational equity approach, therefore, does not necessarily require direct government intervention. In many cases it will require government input in the form of setting legal, regulatory and/or institutional frameworks, providing incentives and/or financial support.

Relational equity approach and governance theories

As this book aims to identify how the problems of three sectors could be effectively dealt with through the prism of the nexus, the concept of governance comes to the fore. Governance is defined differently by different academics (see, for example, Kooiman, 1993; Rhodes, 1997; Stoker, 1998; Pierre and Peters, 2000; Osborne, 2010; Klijn and Koppenjan, 2012; Fukuyama, 2013; Rose-Ackerman, 2017). This book adopts a stance that at governance's core is execution of policy goals (Fukuyama, 2013). In a more detailed way, governance can be defined as "a government's ability to make and enforce rules, and to deliver services regardless of whether that government is democratic or not" (Fukuyama, 2013, p. 350). How and why the goals were set is largely irrelevant when the quality of governance is considered; quality of governance is defined as the government's ability to get things done (Fukuyama, 2013). Hence, this book investigates *execution* of the policy goals in relation to the WEF nexus, rather than the goals themselves.

Within the adopted framework that views governance as execution a natural question has to be addressed: what can make governance effective? A search for appropriate tools has led to the emergence of a broad range of concepts, such as collaborative governance, network management, network governance, governance networks, coordinating mechanisms in networks, process management, direct participation and governance of governance, among others. A large number of overlapping concepts and terminology is a clear indication that governance theories, focusing on networks, are rapidly developing.

Despite significant diversity of governance concepts, there is at least one element that is embedded in most, if not all, approaches. It is the acknowledgement of horizontal interactions among actors and of understanding that these interactions need to be managed (see, for example, Marin and Mayntz, 1991; Mandell, 2001; Meier and O'Toole, 2007; Lewis, 2011). A broader reflection of this need is the concept of collaborative governance (see, for example, Skelcher et al., 2005; Sørensen and Torfing, 2009; Mesquita et al., 2017). Whilst the focus on collaboration in the networks is undoubtedly useful, the framework draws criticism due to its breadth and inherent lack of details as collaboration between actors in the network may have multiple forms and manifestations. Furthermore, in almost all types of collaboration, the participants tend to negotiate their roles and their input, which may result in varying degrees of contribution and, ultimately, effectiveness. In addition, by itself collaboration may or may not lead to the desired outcomes. To mitigate this vagueness, the relational equity approach aims to serve as a more specific method to exercise collaborative governance. Therefore, relational equity management could be viewed as a subset of collaborative and/or network governance and an attempt to make governance more effective by setting the principles that guide actors' contributions to nexus problem-solving and sketch their expectations of anticipated benefits. The latter are derived from the application of the WEF nexus perspective and related departure from the sector-focused approach.

Why is relational equity useful for nexus governance?

Positioning the relational equity approach within collaborative governance theory also sheds light on why and how this approach could be useful particularly for the WEF nexus. Owing to the nature of the WEF nexus, which is multi-sectoral (i.e. involving many sectors) and inter-sectoral (i.e. dealing with problems that exist in or have impact on more than one sector and reach even beyond the scope of all three sectors), nexus governance inevitably should include a network of actors not only from the water industry, energy sector and agriculture, but also participants from business associations, governments at various levels, international development agencies, local communities, NGOs and interest groups. Within a network, this multiplicity and diversity of actors presents a challenge to governance in the form of a need to manage a network, participants' roles and contributions and their expectations of the outcomes. This is when and where the requirement for guiding principles of network governance becomes apparent, and relational equity management serves this need. In the light of the nexus complexity and its significant impact on society, which stretches far beyond the three sectors, the framework offered by relational equity is based on societal values (e.g. sustainable economic and social development supported by clean energy, reduction of waste and pollution and by resilient agriculture), rather than sectoral interests.

The relational equity management vs. stakeholder theory

In stakeholder theory, the underlying assumption is that a corporation needs to provide balanced benefits to all stakeholders, for example employees, shareholders, the government, the private sector partners, local communities and citizens (Freeman, 1984; Mitchell et al., 1997; Carroll, 1999; Freeman et al., 2010). In his seminal text, Freeman (1984) argues that stakeholder management as a concept refers to the necessity for an organisation to manage the relationships with its specific stakeholder groups in an action-oriented way. Whilst academics contend that a company has to be responsive to external demands in a variety of ways (e.g. Freeman, 1984; Clarkson, 1995; Jones, 1995; Carroll and Buchholtz, 2008), most researchers have adopted the key notion that stakeholder theory is far more effective in managing an organisation rather than ensuring its survival (Donaldson and Preston, 1995; Philips, 2003; Fassin, 2009; Freeman et al., 2010). Over more than three decades stakeholder theory has been well developed and applied to many contexts and sectors and the use of the term *stakeholder* is common in business and management, as well as in the discussion of governance. Despite the widespread use of stakeholder as a term that technically requires the proper application of a theory, this is often not the case. Stakeholder theory has been designed and is for a corporation's strategy, which means that its use for network governance is highly problematic. Although this book occasionally makes use of the term stakeholder, this has no connection to corporate strategies. Rather, stakeholders are typically network participants and the book investigates how that network aims to solve WEF nexus problems and how that network could be effectively managed via the application of the relational equity approach, which is underpinned by network management theories (see, for example, Koppenjan and Klijn, 2004; Klijn, 2008; Considine et al., 2009; Hwang and Moon, 2009; Klijn et al., 2010; Akkerman and Torenvlied, 2011).

The water-energy-food nexus: the case of Kazakhstan

This section discusses an example of a country in which nexus thinking is just emerging and the relational equity approach is yet to be implemented. An ex-Soviet nation, Kazakhstan faces dramatic challenges in each of the three nexus sectors. The energy sector enjoys significant resources of fossil fuels (oil, gas and coal), which constrains the growth of renewable energy generation. At the same time, the nation's agriculture experiences lack of water resources that are also required by the energy facilities. To date, competing priorities in the three sectors and isolated, industry-focused decision-making has not yielded satisfactory results for the actors, or for society at large. A close look at the water, energy and agricultural profiles of this economy enables the identification of issues where a nexus approach might be particularly useful for delivering plausible outcomes for all nexus network participants, rather than selected actors. Furthermore, as this chapter shows, nexus thinking, although advantageous for a comprehensive assessment of WEF interdependencies, by itself would not suffice. The benefits are likely to be significantly enhanced when the nexus enjoys network governance in a collaborative fashion, which is yet to be developed in Kazakhstan.

Kazakhstan is located in Central Asia bordering Russia to the north, China to the east, and Kyrgyzstan, Uzbekistan and Turkmenistan to the south, and adjoining the Caspian Sea to the west. It is the ninth largest nation in the world and the largest landlocked country with an area of 2.72 million km^2 (Worldatlas, 2019). It has a population of 18.52 million (Worldometers, 2019) and one of the lowest population densities worldwide, approximately seven people per km^2, with 49.9% of the population living in urban areas (Worldometers, 2019).

The land is primarily steppe with some oases and deserts to the south. The climate is continental with cold winters and hot summers, and arid to semi-arid conditions.

Kazakhstan has the largest gross domestic product (GDP) in Central Asia amounting to USD 162.887 billion in 2017 (World Bank Group, 2019), representing 61.4% of the GDP of Central Asia. The nation's economy is export-oriented, and energy is the largest sector accounting for 21% of the country's GDP and approximately 62% of its exports in 2017 (World Bank Group, 2018), rising to 73% as of February 2019 (Trading Economics, 2019).

The water, energy and food sectors: profiles

Water profile

Kazakhstan is one of the most arid countries in Central Asia. Both its surface and ground water resources are "extremely unevenly distributed" across the country (FAO, 2012, pp. 4 and 6), with surface water affected by "perennial and seasonal dynamics" (FAO, 2012, p. 4) and with parts of its groundwater resources being of "variable quality that prevents its exploitation ... for economic activity" (FAO, 2012, p. 6). Furthermore, the pattern of water resource availability does not reflect that of population dispersion and economic development and, hence, demand. For example, the Nura-Sarysu and Tobol-Torgai river basins account for 3% of the country's total water resources but are home to 21% of its population and include 35% of its total cultivable and cultivated land (Karatayev et al., 2017a). Uneven water availability and consumption across the nation and above-the-norm water losses give rise to water scarcity. For example, losses related to water transportation/delivery (approximately 70% in agriculture and 40% in industry); open and under-ground water pollution; deteriorating infrastructure; antiquated irrigation practices; and excessive water consumption (Karatayev et al., 2017a; Zhupankhan et al., 2018; UN-Water, 2008).

These challenges are compounded by the fact that 45% of the annual river flow in the country comes from transboundary inflows from other Central Asian countries, as well as Russia and China (Lioubimtseva and Henebry, 2009).

Water withdrawals increased steadily until the mid-1980s. However, since then they have decreased slightly due to the adoption of water conservation measures in the agricultural sector and the nation's post-independence decline in industry. In 2010, 66% of water withdrawals were for agriculture, farming and aquaculture purposes, 30% for industrial use (including central heating, energy enterprises, metallurgy and the oil industry) and 4% for public supply/municipalities (FAO, 2012).

Although 56% of Kazakhstan's annual river flow is formed within the country (Sievers, 2002), spatial and temporal distribution particularities as well as numerous factors impacting negatively mean that the core issue is ineffective water management with future impacts dependent not only on the current and future water supplies but on water management systems (including institutions, processes and regulatory and legislative frameworks). In addition, decrease of transboundary inflows due to neighbouring nations' water claims combined with increased water demand due to population growth, urbanisation and expansion of the middle-income class with the subsequent impact on lifestyles present challenges that compound the existing water stress.

Energy profile

Kazakhstan ranks amongst the largest energy producers in Central Asia, being a resource-rich country in both traditional (oil, gas, coal, uranium) and renewable (solar, wind, biomass, hydro) energy sources (IEA, 2015). Despite its significant renewable energy sources (RES) generation potential (estimated at over 1

Table 2.1 Kazakhstan's power generation by source (%)

	2015	2016
Fossil fuels	81.6	79.4
Hydro	10.2	12.3
Gas turbine	8.0	7.9
Solar and wind	0.2	0.4
Total	100	100

Source: Kazakhstan Electricity Grid Operating Company (KEGOC, 2017).

trillion kWh/year), which for wind and solar power generation is deemed technically and economically viable (Energy Charter Secretariat, 2013; REEEP, 2014), fossil fuels dominate Kazakhstan's energy mix (see Table 2.1).

In terms of total energy consumption (in Mtoe) by sector, in 2016, industry was responsible for 54.3% of it, transport for 14.7% and other sectors for 30.9% (IEA, 2015). The overall energy consumption in the country shows significant fluctuations: between 1990 and 2001, there was a decrease of almost 80% (from 179Mtoe in 1992 to 35Mtoe in 2001), followed by an increase of more than 50% to 80Mtoe in 2017 (Enerdata, 2018). Similar fluctuations were observed in energy production: between 1990 and 1996, there was a decrease of about a third, from 91Mtoe in 1990 to 64Mtoe in 1996, followed by a more than 200% increase to 178Mtoe in 2017 (Enerdata, 2018). Importantly, Kazakhstan's energy intensity, despite its steady decline since 1992, remains one of the highest in the world at 0.175koe/$2015p (calculated as the ratio of total energy consumption, over the nation's GDP in 2015) (Enerdata, 2018).

The energy sector and the nation's economy are dominated by fossil fuels with oil and gas being the most significant contributors to the nation's budget. As a result, despite the Kazakhstani government's efforts to achieve economic diversification and the pursuit of a green development path (e.g. Kazakhstan 2050, 2012) – including increasing the share of renewable sources in the country's energy mix – results have been limited (Koulouri and Mouraviev, 2018). Furthermore, a legacy of low electricity tariffs, high transmission and distribution losses (due to antiquated infrastructure) and inefficient technologies, as well as a lack of awareness by the population at large, have meant that there are significant barriers to pursuing resource use efficiency.

Despite the abundance of traditional and renewable energy sources and considering Kazakhstan's low levels of renewables utilisation, the nation faces energy security challenges due to its long-term reliance on non-renewable sources for both energy generation and revenue for the government budget. This is aggravated by poor resource efficiency. Energy security is defined as the ever-increasing utilisation of renewables and improved resource efficiency, whilst the latter is understood as deriving the most value from resource inputs for energy production (Mouraviev and Koulouri, 2019). In summary, clean energy generation has stalled despite the country's ambitious targets for renewable energy power generation (50% of the country's total power generation by 2050) and energy efficiency (decrease of energy intensity of GDP by 25%, in relation to the 2008 baseline, by 2020) (Kazakhstan 2050, 2012).

Food profile

In 2016, an estimated 80.38% of Kazakhstan's land was agricultural including arable land (13.55%), land under permanent crops (0.06%) and land under permanent meadows and pastures (86.39%) (FAO, 2019b). The country is endowed with fertile land but faces significant challenges in relation to water availability and climatic conditions, including droughts, hot winds, late spring and early autumn frosts and other conditions damaging to agriculture. In addition, there has been extensive desertification of the Aral Sea, Ili-Balkhash and Ural-Caspian Sea basins.

Kazakhstan's agricultural sector endured a challenging transition to a market economy following the declaration of independence in 1991. Changes included land and farm ownership reforms with significant changes to the farm structure (FAO, 2019a). There was also a decline of agricultural output, although since 2000 there has been a steady growth of about 62% (Kazakhstan's National Statistics Agency, 2016). The country has been a net importer of agricultural food products since the mid-2000s (FAO, 2019a).

In addition to challenges arising from water availability and the prevailing climate conditions, Kazakhstan's agriculture sector faces structural challenges, including the domination of subsistence-supported production, weakly integrated domestic food chains, problematic access to external markets, lack of qualified labour, and limited credit markets increasing reliance on state provision (FAO, 2019a). This is compounded by a number of factors. Firstly, there is lack of training and knowledge exchange on new irrigation methods and technologies and water conservation practices, which characterises Central Asian countries. This results in farmers either paying for consultancy services themselves or relying on old-fashioned, inefficient irrigation and agronomic methods/ practices and sub-optimal crop choices (for example, using crops with development requirements mismatched with local water availability) (Karatayev et al., 2017b; Rakhmatullaev et al., 2017). Secondly, there is high inefficiency in water usage due to low water tariffs, which makes water in essence almost a free resource, and deteriorating infrastructure and considerable water wastage due to leakages in irrigation networks and lack of modern irrigation practices. Thirdly, increased demand in areas with high soil salination (e.g. Ural-Caspian basin) should be noted.

Similar challenges are faced by sheep and cattle husbandry, which are the main livestock sectors in Kazakhstan, with acute water shortage due to lack of pools and watering holes and the complete state of disrepair of over 60,000 shaft and tube wells that pumped water up (National Human Development Report, 2008).

Nonetheless, Kazakhstan has made significant progress in addressing food (in)security. Here, food security is understood as "all people, at all times, hav(ing) physical and economic access to sufficient, safe and nutritious food that meets their dietary needs and food preferences for an active and healthy life" (World Food Summit, 1996). The number of undernourished people in the country (three-year average) has decreased from 0.9 million (in 1999–2001) to 0.5 million (in 2010–2012) and the prevalence of undernourishment (three-year average) has fallen from 5.9% of the total population (in 1999–2001) to 2.7% (in 2010–2012) (FAO, 2019a). Conversely, the prevalence of severe food insecurity in the total population (three-year average) has slightly increased from 0.9% (in 2014–2016) to 1.4% (in 2015–2017) (FAO, 2019a).

The Kazakhstani government wishes to develop the agricultural sector as part of its wider economic diversification efforts, whilst protecting natural resources and addressing structural constraints and other challenges (FAO, 2019a). Grain plays a key role in Kazakhstan's food security policy (National Human Development Report, 2008). This continues to be the case as Kazakhstan is one of the top wheat producers in the world (as of 2017, FAO, 2019b) and one of the top grain exporters (export.gov, 2018).

Water-energy-food interlinkages

The water, energy and food sectors are closely interlinked. Water is required for resource extraction, cooling purposes during power generation, fossil fuel processing and biofuel irrigation. In 2014, water usage in the energy sector represented 8.5% of the total use across various economy sectors (Karatayev et al., 2017b) and, in 2016, hydropower accounted for 12.3% of the nation's power generation (KEGOC, 2017). Correspondingly, energy is needed for the treatment, pumping and distribution of water as well as irrigation; whilst food production requires both water and energy. Population growth, urbanisation and middle-class expansion with the associated changes to more resource-consuming lifestyles would lead to increased water, energy and food demand and, hence, increased challenges to Kazakhstan's water, energy and food security.

Impact of climate change

Challenges faced by the water, energy and food sectors in Kazakhstan are compounded by the impact of climate change, which is expected to lead to a decrease in precipitation by 0.5mm per decade and to a temperature increase of 1.4°C by 2030 and 2.7°C by 2050, the latter leading to increased evaporation and water demand (Salnikov et al., 2015).

Projected temperature increase and precipitation decrease might lead to intensified water shortages in western Kazakhstan, impacting on food production, and increased glacier melting in the mountain areas in the southeast resulting in mudflows and avalanches (Lioubimtseva and Henebry, 2009). Moreover, projected changes in temperature and precipitation, and the associated increases in demand and natural evaporation will further exacerbate the existing water stress (Rakhmatullaev et al., 2017). However, the impact of climate change on agriculture and livestock husbandry could be mixed, including both negative impacts (such as soil moisture decrease; expansion of weeds, pests and diseases; biodiversity decrease; lack of winter fodder; longer periods of hot weather; and the expansion of animal diseases) and positive impacts (such as extended growing seasons; improved production conditions for certain crops; and improved livestock husbandry conditions in winter) (National Human Development Report, 2008).

Nonetheless, land use change, compounded by desertification (with overgrazing one of the main causes of the latter), and ineffective water management systems present a greater threat to human and ecological systems than the potential impact of climate change (Lioubimtseva and Henebry, 2009).

Legal and regulatory frameworks

Water

During Soviet times, the 1970 Law of "Basics of water legislation of the USSR and Union Republics" and the 1972 Water Code of the Kazakh SSR provided the legal framework for water management. Following independence, the 1993 Water Code of the Republic of Kazakhstan was adopted, with many of its provisions over time becoming obsolete and impeding necessary market reforms (UNDP, 2004). A new Water Code was adopted in 2003 based on the international principles of fair and equitable access to water with priority given to the supply of potable water. It provided the framework for establishing relations within the water sector and between the water sector and agriculture. It also introduced water management at basin level. The 2003 Water Code was amended and supplemented in 2009.

In addition, as of June 2004, aiming at improving water resource management and underpinning the nation's approach with international practice and norms, the Kazakhstani government started developing a national International Water Resource Management and Water Efficiency Plan (IWRM), a draft of which was adopted in 2005. This was further developed to include an IWRM National Roadmap and proposed project outlines to accelerate the implementation of the IWRM 2005 plan.

In addition to these provisions, the special chapter on water fund land in the Land Code, the Code on "Administrative Offences" of 2001 and the 2003 "Law on rural consumer cooperative of water users" provide the legal framework in relation to land serving the use and protection of water, the responsibilities of individuals and legal entities for violations of the water legislation of Kazakhstan, and the rights and responsibilities of water users, respectively.

Despite the existence of legislative and regulatory frameworks pertaining to all major aspects of water resource management in the country, legislative provisions remain inadequate with, in some cases, an unclear legal nature and regulatory provisions that are weak whilst the implementation of both is inconsistent (Karatayev et al., 2017a).

Energy

Kazakhstan has long recognised the necessity of transitioning to a more sustainable development model by reducing its reliance on exhaustible resources, hence its long-term exposure and vulnerability to energy security threats and market fluctuations. Since 2006, Kazakhstan has been making significant efforts to develop the renewable energy sources (RES) sector by introducing a number of key policy instruments including:

> The Sustainable Development Concept (Decree of the President of the Republic of Kazakhstan (RK) On the Concept of Transition of the RK to

sustainable development, 2006); the Kazakhstan 2050 Strategy (Kazakhstan 2050, 2012); and the "Green Economy" Concept (Decree of the President of the RK on the Concept of Transition of the RK to "Green Economy", 2013).

(Mouraviev and Koulouri, 2019)

Parallel to delineating a policy framework, Kazakhstan has been establishing a legal framework to underpin its policy actions for developing and enhancing the RES sector. Numerous legislative and regulatory provisions govern the power sector including RES. Furthermore, Kazakhstan's Law on Support of the Use of Renewable Energy Sources (2009; adopted in 2009, amended in 2013) provides the legal foundations and support mechanisms for expanding the utilisation of RES.

Food

Acknowledging the importance of the agriculture sector for diversifying the nation's economy and enhancing its food security, the Kazakhstani government has sought to support it through numerous policy provisions and government programmes. Key policy documents – the Kazakhstan-2030 Strategy (introduced in 1997), the Strategic Plan for the Development of the Republic of Kazakhstan until the Year 2020 (approved in 2010) and the Kazakhstan-2050 Strategy (adopted in 2012) – make provisions for the sector. In addition, a host of sector specific programmes have been introduced: the Agricultural Development Programme 2013–2020 (also known as Agrobusiness-2020) (adopted in 2013); the Agro-industrial Development State Programme for 2017–2021 (adopted in 2017) and the State Programme on Forced Industrial-Innovative Development of Kazakhstan for 2010–2015 (SPFIID) and SPFIID 2015–2019. Moreover, at a regional level the Concept on Food Security of the Commonwealth of Independent States (CIS) was introduced in 2010.

Between 2007 and 2017, Kazakhstan's key agricultural policies aimed to decrease the nation's dependence on food imports and to increase its domestic food production by supporting the development of the national agro-industrial complex and promoting the agriculture sector overall. To achieve this, the Kazakhstani government introduced numerous producer-oriented measures, such as increased production subsidies, incentives to improve efficiency, enhanced crop diversification and increased access to credit and financial services with the establishment, in 2006, of KazAgro which is the leading agency responsible for financing and support services to the sector. These measures were accompanied by trade-oriented and macroeconomic policy decisions, such as measures to promote agricultural exports; regulations for the import and export of livestock; signing the Treaty on the Creation of a Single Customs Territory and the Formation of the Customs Union between the Russian Federation, Belarus and Kazakhstan (in 2007); creating the Eurasian Economic Union (in 2012) and becoming a member of the World Trade Organisation (in 2015).

The basis of the nation's agrarian legislative framework is the 1991 Law "About the priority of an aul, a village and an agrarian and industrial complex development". In 2002, in the annual Message of the President of the Republic of Kazakhstan, the Kazakhstani government was given the task to develop a suite of laws focusing on enhancing the nation's food security and addressing related challenges. This was followed by the Decree of the President of the Republic of Kazakhstan, in 2002, approving the "Government Agriculture and Food Programme of the Republic of Kazakhstan for the years 2003–2005". In 2015, a Law was adopted "On Agricultural Cooperatives", aiming at facilitating the creation of large producer units. In addition, legislation relating to land use includes: the 1995 Law "On Land" underpinned by the principles of state ownership of land with private use rights under 99-year leases; the 2003 Land Code; and the Rules of Use of Agricultural Land, adopted in 2012.

The Kazakhstani government has stated intentions to develop the agriculture sector as one of the key pillars of its economy and introduced relevant policies and programmes to that effect. However, the associated regulatory and legislative frameworks appear to be a mixture of legislative acts and Presidential Decrees, which are executive orders to be implemented by the executive branch of the government with the freedom to contextualise and interpret them. Moreover, the regulatory and legislative frameworks do not appear to coherently flow from the policies they aim to operationalise and facilitate. There are even cases of provisions made that seem counter-intuitive (e.g. the law for the development of cooperatives which is reminiscent of instruments of Soviet times) (Petrick and Pomfret, 2016).

The WEF nexus in Kazakhstan

During the Soviet era, with water considered a common good to be used for reaching centrally set production targets (Black et al., 1991), Central Asian water resources were developed and managed centrally (O'Hara, 2000). Centralised water resource management together with a unified (i.e. countrywide) energy system that was able to operate fuel and hydropower energy stations (Rakhmatullaev et al., 2017) meant that a quasi-nexus approach was applied to managing the WEF sectors in the area. An example of the implementation of this quasi-nexus approach is the development of the Toktogul Dam in Kyrgyzstan, designed as an irrigation and hydropower facility. The modus operandi, in the summer, involved the generation of hydropower, distributed through the united energy grid system. In the winter, water was collected in reservoirs and used for downstream irrigation in the summer with the produce entering the Soviet economy (Stucki and Sojamo, 2012). Following the collapse of the Soviet Union and the emergence of the independent Central Asian nations, this arrangement collapsed. A number of bilateral and regional agreements were made between the nations aimed at strengthening regional cooperation for the collaborative management of water resources. However, the operation of the Toktogul Dam has caused serious disagreements between Kazakhstan,

Kyrgyzstan and Uzbekistan, with Kazakhstan and Uzbekistan interested in water storage for summer irrigation and Kyrgyzstan interested in winter hydropower generation.

More broadly, considering Kazakhstan's laws and regulations pertaining to the three sectors —water, energy and food – it becomes clear that despite the Kazakhstani government's stated intention to ensure effective water use and preserve potable water, to increase the utilisation of renewable energy sources and improve resource efficiency, to develop the agriculture sector and enhance the nation's food security, pursuing these objectives has been disjointed and informed by sectoral rather than nexus thinking. Moreover, decision-making has been heavily influenced by dominant stakeholders, such as the oil and gas sector, resulting in policies and governance measures impeding rather than enabling and in little progress being made (see, for example, Koulouri and Mouraviev, 2018, on impediments to investment in the renewable energy sector).

Conclusion

In many countries across the globe problems related to energy, water and food most often are dealt with within the boundaries of one sector only and the decisions are typically driven by one or few major stakeholders that tend to pursue their own, not even industry-wide, agendas. In these conditions, decision-making becomes constrained and framed by the narrative of major industry players who would not want their interests influenced by smaller, less powerful industry participants and by actors from other industries. Part of this picture stems naturally from the way most organisations work and how their performance is assessed: unless an organisation is a public agency with a broad mandate, its performance indicators do not include targets beyond the organisation's scope (i.e. industry-wide or those embracing a few industries). However, another part of the picture relates to social responsibility and business ethics, and this is where the WEF nexus approach becomes not only useful, but necessary, given the interconnections between the three sectors. Whilst nexus thinking has emerged in response to multiple challenges that extend beyond the boundaries of one sector, it has also developed as part of growing pressure on businesses and various types of organisation to act in a socially responsible way.

Nexus thinking involves consideration of intersectorality, interdependencies and trans- and inter-disciplinarity. Whilst the benefit in the form of integrated, rather than disjointed, decisions is apparent, there are also benefits to society. In a broad form, these can be described as contribution to sustainable development in each of its three dimensions – economic, social and environmental. This chapter discussed the example of Kazakhstan, where nexus thinking is at a nascent stage. Other chapters in this book offer a detailed discussion of how nexus thinking has been embedded (or not) in decision-making and policy implementation in a range of contexts, be it urban (e.g. the chapter on Lima, Peru) or rural (e.g. the chapter on the challenges in north-western Kenya), and a range of scales, be it international (e.g. the chapter on the Aral Sea) or regional (e.g. the chapter on the WEF nexus problems in California).

By itself, the nexus approach does not guarantee good results. It requires governance. As many actors – including the government – are involved, multiple organisations and citizens interested in the nexus (or part of it) form networks, and the governance of these networks presents a challenging task in itself. This chapter emphasised the need for a certain framework that would set the guiding principles for network governance. This is the area where relational equity management becomes useful by offering clarity regarding each participant's contribution and their expectations of results and benefits. Other chapters in this book show whether relational equity management has been used in a variety of cases, to what extent its implementation has been successful and what the improvement opportunities are.

References

Akkerman, A. and Torenvlied, R. (2011). "Managing the environment effects of network ambition on agency performance". *Public Management Review*, vol. 13, no. 1, pp 159–174.

Allan, T. and Matthews, N. (2016). "The water, energy and food nexus and ecosystems: The political economy of food and non-food supply chains". In F. Dodds and J. Bartram (eds) *The Water, Food, Energy and Climate Nexus: Challenges and an agenda for action*. Oxford: Routledge.

Ansell, C. and Gash, A. (2008). "Collaborative governance in theory and practice". *Journal of Public Administration Research and Theory*, vol 18, no 4, pp 543–571.

Asian Development Bank. (2013). *Thinking about water differently: Managing the water-food-energy nexus*. Mandaluyong City, Philippines: Asian Development Bank. [Online] [Accessed 31 March 2019]. Available from: https://waterfootprint.org/media/downloads/ADB-2013-Thinking-about-water-differently_1.pdf.

Black, C.E., Dupree, L., Endicott-West, E., Matuszewski, D.C., Naby, E. and Waldron, A.N. (1991). *The Modernization of Inner Asia*. Armonk, New York: M.E. Sharpe.

Carroll, A.B. (1999). "Corporate social responsibility: The evolution of a definitional construct". *Business and Society*, vol 38, no 3, pp 268–295.

Carroll, A.B. and Buchholtz, A.K. (2008). *Business and Society: Ethics and stakeholder management*, 7th edn. Nashville: South Western Educational Publishing.

Clarkson, B.E. (1995). "A stakeholder framework for analyzing and evaluating corporate social responsibility". *Academy of Management Review*, vol 20, no 1, pp 92–117.

Considine, M., Lewis, J. and Alexander, D. (2009). *Networks, Innovation and Public Policy*. Basingstoke: Palgrave Macmillan.

Decree of the President of the Republic of Kazakhstan. (2006). *On the Concept of Transition of the Republic of Kazakhstan to Sustainable Development for the Period 2007–2024, Presidential Decree*. (No 216, 2006). [Online]. [Accessed 22 October 2017]. Available from: http://climatepolicydatabase.org/index.php?title=The_Concept_of_Transition_of_the_Republic_of_Kazakhstan_to_Sustainable_Development_for_the_Period_2007-2024,_Presidential_Decree_No_216_of_2006_Kazakhstan_2006.

Decree of the President of the Republic of Kazakhstan. (2013). *On the Concept of Transition of the Republic of Kazakhstan to "Green Economy".* (No 577, 2013). [Online]. [Accessed 19 October 2017]. Available from: http://gbpp.org/wp-content/up loads/2014/04/Green_Concept_En.pdf.

Donaldson, T. and Preston, L.E. (1995). "The stakeholder theory of the corporation: Concepts, evidence, and implications". *The Academy of Management Review*, vol 20, no 1, pp 65–91.

Endo, A., Tsurita, I., Burnett, K. and Orencio, P.M. (2017). "A review of the current state of research on the water, energy, and food nexus". *Journal of Hydrology: Regional Studies*, vol 11, pp 20–30.

Enerdata. (2018). [Online]. [Accessed 14 February 2019]. Available from: www.enerdata.net.

Energy Charter Secretariat. (2013). *Investment Climate and Market Review in the Energy Sector of Kazakhstan.* [Online]. [Accessed 5 January 2017]. Available from: www.ene rgycharter.org/what-we-do/investment/investment-climate-and-market-structure/invest ment-in-kazakhstan-2013/.

Export.gov. (2018). *Kazakhstan Country Commercial Guide – Agricultural sector.* [Online]. [Accessed 24 March 2019]. Available from: www.export.gov/article?id=Kaza khstan-Agricultural-Sector.

FAO (Food and Agricultural Organisation of the United Nations) (2012). *AQUASTAT – Kazakhstan, Water Report 39.* [Online]. [Accessed 21 February 2019]. Available from: www.fao.org/nr/water/aquastat/countries_regions/KAZ/KAZ-CP_eng.pdf.

FAO (Food and Agricultural Organisation of the United Nations) (2014). *The Water-Energy-Food Nexus. A new approach in support of food security and sustainable agriculture.* Rome: FAO. [Online] [Accessed 31 March 2019]. Available from: www.fa o.org/3/a-bl496e.pdf.

FAO (Food and Agricultural Organisation of the United Nations) (2019a). *FAOSTAT – Kazakhstan.* [Online]. [Accessed 23 March 2019]. Available from: www.fao.org/faosta t/en/#country/108.

FAO (Food and Agricultural Organisation of the United Nations) (2019b). *FAOSTAT – Crops: Production quantities of wheat by country.* [Online]. [Accessed 23 March 2019]. Available from: www.fao.org/faostat/en/#data/QC/visualize.

Fassin, Y. (2009). "The stakeholder model refined". *Journal of Business Ethics*, vol 84, no 1, pp 113–135.

Freeman, R.E. (1984). *Strategic Management: A stakeholder approach.* Marshfield, Massachusetts: Pitman Publishing.

Freeman, R.E., Harrison, J.S., Wicks, A.C. et al. (2010). *Stakeholder Theory: The state of the art.* Cambridge: Cambridge University Press.

Fukuyama, F. (2013). "What is governance?". *Governance: An International Journal of Policy, Administration, and Institutions*, vol 26, no 3, pp 347–368.

Hoff, H. and Ulrich, A. (2017). *Mainstreaming the Water-Energy-Food Security Nexus into Sectoral Policies and Institutions in the Arab Region.* Hamburg/Cairo: GIZ/GFA. [Online] [Accessed 31 March 2019]. Available from: www.water-energy-food.org/filea dmin/user_upload/files/documents/giz/nexus-mainstreaming/1_Final_report_NEXUS-fi nal.pdf.

Hwang, S. and Moon, I.C. (2009). "Are we treating networks seriously? The growth of network research in public administration and public policy". *Connections*, vol 29, no 2, pp 4–17.

IEA (International Energy Agency). (2015). *Eastern Europe, Caucasus and Central Asia. Energy policies beyond IEA countries.* [Online]. [Accessed 15 February 2019].

Available from: www.iea.org/publications/freepublications/publication/IDR_EasternEu
ropeCaucasus_2015.pdf.

IEA (International Energy Agency). (2017). *World Energy Statistics and Balances Data Service*. [Online] [Accessed 31 March 2019]. Available from: http://data.iea.org/paym
ent/products/103-world-energy-statistics-and-balances-2018-edition.aspx.

Jones, T.M. (1995). "Instrumental stakeholder theory: A synthesis of ethics and economics". *Academy of Management Review*, vol 20, no 2, pp 404–437.

Karatayev, M., Kapsalyamova, Z., Spankulova, L., Skakova, A., Movkebayeva, G. and Kongyrbay, A. (2017a). "Priorities and challenges for a sustainable management of water resources in Kazakhstan". *Sustainability of Water Quality and Ecology*, vols 9–10, pp 115–135.

Karatayev, M., Rivotti, P., Sobral Mourão, Z., Konadu, D.D., Shah, N. and Clarke, M. (2017b). "The water-energy-food nexus in Kazakhstan: Challenges and opportunities". *Energy Procedia*, vol 125, pp 63–70.

Kazakhstan 2050. (2012). *Strategy Kazakhstan – 2050: New political course of the established state. Address by the President of the Republic of Kazakhstan, Leader of the Nation, N. Nazarbayev on 14 December 2012*. [Online]. [Accessed 5 January 2017]. Available from: https://strategy2050.kz/en/multilanguage/.

Kazakhstan's National Statistics Agency (2016). *Kazakhstan Socio-economic Outcome for 1991–2015*. [Online]. [Accessed 31 March 2019]. Available from: http://stat.gov.kz/
faces/mobileHomePage/mobileHomePage3?_adf.ctrl-state=16ud528s7k_25&_afrLoop=
5279140941075940.

KEGOC (Kazakhstan Electricity Grid Operating Company). (2017) [Online]. [Accessed 19 October 2017]. Available from: www.kegoc.kz/en/company/national-power-system.

Klijn, E.H. (2008). "Governance and governance networks in Europe". *Public Management Review*, vol 10, no 4, pp 505–525.

Klijn, E.H. and Koppenjan, J.F.M. (2012). "Governance network theory: Past, present and future". *Policy and Politics*, vol 40, no 4, pp 187–206.

Klijn, E.H., Steijn, B. and Edelenbos, J. (2010). "The impact of network management strategies on the outcomes in governance networks". *Public Administration*, vol 88, no 4, pp 1063–1082.

Kooiman, J. (ed.) (1993). *Modern Governance. New government–society interactions*. Newbury Park, California: Sage.

Koppenjan, J.F.M. and Klijn, E.H. (2004). *Managing Uncertainties in Networks: A network approach to problem solving and decision making*. London: Routledge.

Koulouri, A. and Mouraviev, N. (2018). "Governance of the clean energy sector in Kazakhstan: Impediments to investment". *International Journal of Technology Intelligence and Planning*, vol. 12, no. 1, pp 6–23.

Lewis, J. (2011). "The future of network governance: Strength in diversity and synthesis". *Public Administration*, vol 89, no 4, pp 1221–1234.

Lindberg, C. and Leflaive, X. (2015). "The water-energy-food nexus: The imperative of policy coherence for sustainable development". *Coherence for Development, Organisation for Economic Development and Co-operation*, Issue 6, December 2015.

Lioubimtseva, E. and Henebry, G.M. (2009). "Climate and environmental change in arid Central Asia: Impacts, vulnerability, and adaptations". *Journal of Arid Environments*, vol 73, pp 963–977.

Mandell, M.P. (ed.). (2001). *Getting Results through Collaboration: Networks and network structures for public policy and management*. Westport, Connecticut: Quorum Books.

Marin, B. and Mayntz, R. (eds). (1991). *Policy Networks: Empirical evidence and theoretical considerations*. Boulder, CO: Westview Press.

Meier, K. and O'Toole, L.J. (2007). "Modelling public management: Empirical analysis of the management-performance nexus". *Public Administration Review*, vol 9, no 4, pp 503–527.

Mesquita, L.F., Ragozzino, R. and Reuer, J.J. (eds). (2017). *Collaborative Strategy: Critical issues for alliances and networks*. Cheltenham: Edward Elgar Publishing.

Mitchell, R., Agle, B. and Wood, D. (1997). "Toward a theory of stakeholder identification and salience: Defining the principle of who and what really counts". *Academy of Management Review*, vol 22, no 4, pp 853–886.

Mouraviev, N. and Koulouri, A. (eds). (2019). *Energy Security: Policy challenges and solutions for resource efficiency*. London: Palgrave Macmillan.

National Human Development Report. (2008). *Climate Change and Its Impact on Kazakhstan's Human Development*. [Online]. [Accessed 29 March 2019]. Available from: http://hdr.undp.org/sites/default/files/kazakhstan_nhdr_2008.pdf.

O'Hara, S.L. (2000). "Lessons from the past: Water management in Central Asia". *Water Policy*, vol 2, pp 365–384.

Osborne, S.P. (2010). *The New Public Governance: Emerging perspectives on the theory and practice of public governance*. London: Routledge.

Petrick, M. and Pomfret, R. (2016). *Agricultural Policies in Kazakhstan*. Discussion Paper, Leibniz Institute of Agricultural Development in Transition Economies, No. 155. Halle (Saale): Leibniz Institute of Agricultural Development in Transition Economies (IAMO). [Online] [Accessed 31 March 2019]. Available from: www.econstor.eu/bitstream/10419/130714/1/857482297.pdf.

Pierre, J. and Peters, B.G. (2000). *Governance, Politics and the State*. Basingstoke: Macmillan.

Philips, R. (2003). *Stakeholder Theory and Organizational Ethics*. Oakland, California: Berrett-Koehler Publishers.

Rakhmatullaev, S., Abdullaev, I. and Kazbekov, J. (2017). "Water-energy-food-environmental nexus in Central Asia: From transition to transformation". In S.S. Zhiltsov et al. (eds) *Water Resources in Central Asia: International context*. Basel: Springer.

REEEP (Renewable Energy and Energy Efficiency Partnership). (2014). [Online]. [Accessed 2 February 2019]. Available from: www.reeep.org/kazakhstan-2014.

Republic of Kazakhstan. (2009). *Law of the Republic of Kazakhstan "On Support of the Use of Renewable Energy Sources" of 4 July 2009*, No. 165-IV ZRK. [Online]. [Accessed 5 January 2017]. Available from: http://cis-legislation.com/document.fwx?rgn=28433.

Rhodes, R.A.W. (1997). *Understanding Governance*. Milton Keynes: Open University Press.

Rose-Ackerman, S. (2017). "What does 'governance' mean?" *Governance: An International Journal of Policy, Administration, and Institutions*, vol 30, no 1, pp 23–27.

Salnikov, V., Turulina, G., Polyakova, S., Petrova, Y. and Skakova, A. (2015). "Climate change in Kazakhstan during the past 70 years". *Quaternary International*, vol 358, pp 77–82.

Sievers, E.W. (2002). "Water, conflict, and regional security in Central Asia". *New York University Environmental Law Journal*, vol 10, pp 356–403.

Skelcher, C., Mathur, N. and Smith, M. (2005). "The public governance of collaborative spaces: Discourse, design and democracy". *Public Administration*, vol 83, no 3, pp 573–596.

Sørensen, E. and Torfing, J. (2009). "Enhancing collaborative innovation in the public sector". *Administration and Society*, vol 29, no 2, pp 115–138.

Stoker, G. (1998). "Governance as theory: Five propositions". *International Social Science Journal*, vol 50, no 155, pp 17–28.

Stucki, V. and Sojamo, S. (2012). "Nouns and numbers of the water–energy–security nexus in Central Asia". *International Journal of Water Resources Development*, vol 28, no 3, pp 399–418.

Trading Economics. (2019). *Kazakhstan Exports*. [Online]. [Accessed 29 March 2019]. Available from: https://tradingeconomics.com/kazakhstan/exports.

UN (2014). *World Water Development Report*. Paris, France: United Nations Education, Scientific and Cultural Organisation. [Online] [Accessed 31 March 2019]. Available from: www.unesco.org/new/en/natural-sciences/environment/water/wwap/wwdr/2014-water-and-energy/.

UN (2019). *Sustainable Development Goals*. UN Knowledge Platform. [Online] [Accessed 31 March 2019]. Available from: https://sustainabledevelopment.un.org/?menu=1300.

UNDP (2004). *Water Resources of Kazakhstan in the New Millennium*. New York: United National Development Programme. [Online] [Accessed 31 March 2019]. Available from: http://waterwiki.net/images/a/ad/KazakhstanWater.pdf.

UN-Water (2008). *Status Report on Integrated Water Resources Management and Water Efficiency Plans. Prepared for the 16th Session of the Commission on Sustainable Development (CSD16)*. [Online]. [Accessed 21 February 2019]. Available from: www.unwater.org/publications/status-report-integrated-water-resource-management-water-efficiency-plans-csd-16/.

Waughray, D. (ed.). (2011). *Water Security: The water-energy-food-climate nexus*. Washington, DC: Island Press.

Worldatlas. (2019). [Online]. [Accessed 13 February 2019]. Available from: www.worldatlas.com/articles/the-largest-countries-in-the-world-the-biggest-nations-as-determined-by-total-land-area.html.

World Bank Group. (2018). *The World Bank in Kazakhstan Country Snapshot*. [Online]. [Accessed 13 February 2019]. Available from: http://pubdocs.worldbank.org/en/530541539098312156/Kazakhstan-Snapshot-Oct2018.pdf.

World Bank Group. (2019). *Data: GDP current (USD)*. [Online]. [Accessed 13 February 2019]. Available from: https://data.worldbank.org/indicator/NY.GDP.MKTP.CD?view=map.

World Food Summit. (1996). *Rome Declaration on World Food Security*. [Online]. [Accessed 24 March 2019]. Available from: www.fao.org/3/w3613e/w3613e00.htm.

Worldometers. (2019). [Online]. [Accessed 13 February 2019]. Available from: www.worldometers.info/world-population/kazakhstan-population/.

Zhupankhan, A., Tussupova, K. and Berndtsson, R. (2018). "Water in Kazakhstan, a key in Central Asian water management". *Hydrological Sciences Journal*, vol 63, no 5, pp 752–762.

3 Integrating the water-energy-food nexus into policy and decision-making

Opportunities and challenges

Livia Bizikova

Introduction

For close to a decade, the water-energy-food (WEF) nexus has had strong policy and societal underpinnings. WEF research has been highlighted in a number of global initiatives and forums of international agencies focusing on that nexus. For example, global forums such as the World Economic Forum, Rio+20, the Bonn Climate Change Conferences in 2011 and 2017, the Dresden Nexus Conference in 2017 and the World Water Week 2012 have all strongly advocated integrative frameworks that address the interlinked nature of WEF security. The definition of the WEF nexus originates from the Bonn 2011 WEF Nexus Conference: "enhance water, energy and food security by increasing efficiency, reducing trade-offs, building synergies and improving governance across sectors" (Hoff, 2011, p. 4). This early definition provides a comprehensive understanding of the WEF nexus by connecting science and policy development and implementation. The improved understanding of the relationships within the WEF nexus and its elements would arguably lead to the improved management of the water, food and energy sectors through governance and policy changes (Bazilian et al., 2011; Bizikova et al., 2014; Lawford, 2016).

Building on the WEF nexus definition by Hoff (2011), early research focused on creating methodologies to assess synergies and trade-offs between the WEF sectors – water, energy and food. While aiming to cover all three, water has often received greater attention and has been given a central role in the modelling efforts through using hydrological and other models at a basin-wide and/or watershed level (e.g., Keskinen and Varis, 2016; Hermann et al., 2012; Riegels et al., 2013). In addition to a focus on WEF nexus elements, many of the modelling approaches added other critical dimensions, such as greenhouse gas emission changes (Howells et al., 2011), climate change adaptation and resilience (Cervingni et al., 2015), natural resource extraction (Huppé et al., 2015) and local livelihoods (Biggs et al., 2015; Johnston, de Silva and Try, 2014). These studies advanced the understanding of the nexus through its quantitative representation and, despite data availability and quality challenges to enable the detailed modelling of all three WEF sectors (Endo et al., 2015; Weitz et al., 2017), they have been able to make policy recommendations.

Given the progress in research methods advancing the understanding of the WEF nexus, the next step is ensuring that the formulated recommendations are being effectively integrated into policy and decision-making. Hoff's early definition of the WEF nexus (Hoff, 2011) emphasised the importance of improving governance across the WEF nexus elements in order to address pressing WEF security concerns. Many WEF nexus assessments – for example, by Bazilian et al. 2011; Beck and Walker, 2013; Pittock, Hussey and McGlennon, 2013 – concluded with a number of policy and governance recommendations to reduce trade-offs and maximise synergies within the WEF nexus elements. These recommendations include, for example, explicitly addressing resource conflicts in the policy process (Bizikova et al., 2014), using costing methodologies for better integration of the WEF nexus elements into strategic planning (Ringler, Bhaduri and Lawford, 2013), and revising institutional agreements for rights to land, water and other resources to minimise trade-offs (Pittock et al., 2013). Recently, Lawford (2016) and Weitz et al. (2017) emphasised the WEF nexus as a useful framework to advance policy coherence in the context of the UN's Sustainable Development Goals, a number of which relate to the nexus (UN, 2015).

Governance and policy recommendations identified in WEF nexus assessments also list critical issues necessary for the overall improvement of their relevance for decision-making. For example, Bizikova et al. (2014) and Pittock et al. (2013) stress that policy recommendations need to be highly specific, covering both institutional and policy processes to improve the management of the WEF elements in a concrete (local) context. Such recommendations should also aim to deepen collaboration, policy integration and coherence and monitoring across sectors relevant for the nexus (Bizikova et al., 2014; Pittock et al., 2013; Mohtar, Assi and Daher, 2015). These types of recommendation are often very challenging to address in a WEF nexus assessment as the strong focus on quantitative modelling often leaves less capacity for the required collaboration with policy-makers to ensure that WEF assessment recommendations are policy relevant (Howells et al., 2011; Moser and Luers, 2007; Waldick et al., 2016).

This chapter focuses on the policy-relevance of WEF nexus assessments. The definition of WEF nexus adopted here is that given by Hoff (2011) indicating that improving governance across the WEF sectors is the goal of WEF assessments. Using this definition, WEF nexus assessments and/or case studies encompass the systematic exploration of WEF linkages including both trade-offs and synergies by using quantitative and/or qualitative methods with specific recommendations to improve governance by changes in public policy and decision-making. In this context, public policy and decision-making mean policies and other strategies developed and implemented by all levels of government from the local to national levels as well as public decision-making institutions and their structures that facilitate the design, implementation and review of these public policies.

The next section outlines a framework for the comparative review of WEF nexus case studies, from diverse sectors and geographical areas. The aim is to explore how and to what extent policy-makers effectively integrate identified policy recommendations into policy design and implementation. Based on this framework, the WEF nexus case studies are then compared along a number of dimensions: (1) the focus on local and regional challenges in the context of the nexus; (2) the use of diverse research methods to assess WEF linkages; (3) the activities used to integrate findings/recommendations into policy design and decision-making institutions; and (4) their overall policy relevance. Building on the outcomes of the comparative analysis, key opportunities and barriers to improve the integration of the WEF nexus assessments into public policy design and implementation are identified. The conclusion outlines actions to mitigate barriers in conducting WEF nexus assessments in order to improve their relevance to and effectiveness in contributing to policy and governance.

Methodology

This section offers an overview of the methodological approach to the comparative analysis of the WEF nexus case studies with the aim to explore barriers and opportunities in improving governance by informing the design and implementation of public policy and by implementing institutional changes. The section focuses on defining a framework (and its constituent dimensions) to guide the selection of the case studies to be analysed. It then provides a summary of the comparative analysis process of the selected WEF nexus case studies. This section is followed by an overview of the selected cases.

Framework for the WEF nexus case studies selection

Completed WEF nexus case studies can be used to inform policy and governance based on their findings. They can also provide information about: (1) the collaboration between policy-makers and researchers conducting the case studies; (2) how they consider policy and institutional issues; and (3) how they integrate outcomes into the policy process. To collect this information, a framework was defined to guide the selection and analysis of WEF nexus case studies based on the methodology described by Martinez et al. (2011). The framework specifically aims to cover critical areas by examining whether explicit policy questions were considered to instigate the case study, how critical local and regional challenges are incorporated into the analysis, methods used to assess WEF linkages, the interactions between researchers and policy-makers during the assessment and how effectively recommendations were integrated into policy and decision-making. For details on the framework, see Table 3.1.

Table 3.1 Framework for selection of the WEF nexus case studies

Criteria	Description of the criteria for the case study
Policy relevance	Explicitly identified policy and/or institutional challenges/ questions in the context of the WEF nexus.
Science and policy linkages	Involvement of policy-makers in the research design as well as consideration of their needs by researchers in selecting methods and developing recommendations for the WEF nexus assessment.
Enabling conditions influencing the case study outcomes	Identified any local and regional conditions that contributed and/or influenced the outcomes of the case study such as previous collaborations with researchers, pressing/well-known WEF challenges in the area, planned policy/strategy review, new strategy development and other policy opportunities.
Policy changes based on the outcomes	Availability of information on how the outcomes and/or recommendations were integrated into the policy process and changes were planned or actually made to move towards implementing the outcomes of the WEF nexus assessment.

Source: Adapted by the author from Martinez et al. (2011).

Comparative analysis of the case studies

In total, six case studies were analysed. They have all been published after 2015 and cover both developed and developing countries. The case studies were analysed using Microsoft Excel spreadsheets. First, the key characteristics of each case study were summarised by considering their sectorial focus; their geographical scale; the representation of the WEF nexus and whether any of the three nexus dimensions were prioritised; and the types of method, both quantitative and qualitative, used. Second, the collected information was analysed using the framework dimensions (using a separate spreadsheet for each dimension). A simple coding system was used to indicate the strength of the presence of the dimension in each case study: "1" for weak or barely included, "2" well covered and "3" core dimension of the case study. In addition to the coding, a descriptive note supported by citations from the case studies to provide additional details on the analysed dimensions was provided, including identified barriers and opportunities for each dimension.

In the findings section, the outcomes of the comparative analysis are presented, organised by framework dimension.

Overview of the case studies

This section provides a brief overview of the case studies that were analysed. Using the selection criteria and focusing on both developed and developing countries, six case studies were identified for this review. The following countries were covered: Canada, United States, Japan, Ecuador, Chile and Suriname.

Canada – eastern Ontario agricultural landscape (Waldick et al., 2015, 2016)

This case study focused on the agricultural communities in the Province of Ontario in Canada. It aimed to identify specific challenges of mostly plant production in the context of the WEF sectors to address other pressing challenges such as climate change and increasing competition from regional and global producers. The case study combined quantitative landscape-level modelling with qualitative methods and active participation of policy-makers from local to national level. Often these policy-makers are already organised in cross-sectorial committees and groups such as farmers' groups, agricultural boards, conservation groups and other stakeholders, to co-produce knowledge and recommendations at each step of the assessment.

Suriname – Competing priorities for resources in the context of mining (Huppé et al., 2015; Roy et al., 2015, 2016).

This case study primarily focused on water resources and the impacts of planned mining development on water availability for mining, local communities and local food production. It developed and applied a quantitative mapping tool to aggregate availability and demand for water and then made linkages to food production and energy. It examined the availability and needs for water and energy infrastructure as well as transportation to assess the existing and potential accessibility of the mining site and of goods and services for the mine's employees and communities. The case study was developed in collaboration with national and regional policy-makers and mining companies in the region. Secondary data were used to describe the needs of the communities.

United States – climate change impacts and WEF nexus in California (Liu, 2016)

This case study explored the role of climate change as the driver of major changes in water availability and its impacts on the WEF nexus elements, considering water availability for agricultural production and ecosystems. It used quantitative estimates from completed studies on linkages between the WEF nexus and climate change. It also provided a detailed account of existing policies, strategies and specific mitigation measures of relevance to the WEF nexus and with the potential to reduce trade-offs between the nexus elements. The case study was developed in collaboration with national and regional policy-makers.

Japan – effects of groundwater changes on fisheries in coastal areas
(Endo et al., 2015)

This case study explored the impacts on groundwater used as a source of drinking water and energy and in agricultural production in three coastal communities in Japan. Pollution of the groundwater from these activities can significantly affect valuable fishery resources close to the coastal areas. The study included a cost-benefit analysis of different policy options and the availability of decision-making structures at city level with the aim to reduce the negative impacts of the evaluated activities which use groundwater on fisheries within the WEF framework. It was developed in collaboration with city-level policy-makers and completed by an interdisciplinary research team using diverse methodological approaches such as system mapping and quantitative and qualitative methods to assess linkages, synergies and trade-offs between WEF sectors.

Ecuador – investing in natural infrastructure in water and energy (IUCN and IWA, 2015b; Echavarria et al., 2004)

This case study focused on addressing the challenge of meeting the water needs of Ecuador's capital, Quito. Unsustainable water use and changes in land use in upstream regions reduce the water quantity and quality for Ecuador's capital city. Furthermore, the capital's water needs are increasing due to population and economic growth. The case study team used a system-mapping approach to identify up-stream measures that provide significant benefits to water resources in downstream areas, including to the capital city. Such measures included, for example, the reduction of the destruction of natural vegetation and the restriction of timber production, the revision of grazing rules and practices, and the regulation of agricultural production. In collaboration with the capital city authority, local utility companies and an international non-governmental organisation, a water protection fund was established to support the implementation of the identified upstream measures. The city mandated that utilities should contribute financially to the fund. Moreover, additional water monitoring and surveillance programmes by the city were established as a result of the stablished trust fund.

Chile – water management in the Huasco River Basin (IUCN and IAW, 2015a)

This case study focused on water resources to optimise irrigation in an agricultural area. Other priorities included managing water availability for hydro-electricity, mining and ecosystems. The region had been affected by dry seasons and thus water availability had been critical at that time. The case study used modelling to optimise the water allocation system. It was developed in close collaboration with already existing committees and groups such as water users' associations, the water allocation regulating and granting body and managerial bodies of the river basin. A new volumetric allocation and management system was adopted based on the outcomes of the modelling effort. In addition, the city also created and financially supported a water fund to improve irrigation practices and infrastructure to optimise the hydroelectric and irrigation infrastructure.

For an overview of the key elements of the case studies in this review, see Table 3.2.

Table 3.2 Overview of the key elements of the reviewed case studies

Case study	Sectorial focus	Geographical scale	Representation of the WEF nexus	
			Prioritised WEF element	Other issues included
Canada	Agriculture Rural development	Province	Food and land	Climate change impacts and adaptation
Suriname	Mining Local development Agriculture	Regional	Water and energy	Climate change adaptation
United States	Agriculture Water resources	State	Water and food	Climate change impacts and adaptation
Japan	Fisheries Municipal water use	Regional	Water (groundwater)	-
Ecuador	Water resources Municipal use Natural resources	Regional	Water	-
Chile	Agriculture Water resources Energy and mining	Regional	Water and food	Climate change adaptation

Source: Compiled by the author.

Findings

This section summarises the outcomes of the comparative analysis of the case studies on the basis of the adopted analysis framework. The results are grouped by the framework's dimensions. The case studies share several similarities in terms of the ways of working with policy-makers and using diverse qualitative and quantitative approaches to address pressing local and regional issues. Furthermore, all aimed to feedback their outcomes into the policy process and decision-making by recommending policy revisions, promoting collaboration across different sectors and improving established and/or introducing new decision-making processes.

Policy relevance

One of the important criteria for selecting the case studies was an explicit aim to be policy relevant. The reviewed case studies achieved this by addressing local and regional challenges that required a comprehensive approach and improved policy and governance, as suggested in the WEF nexus' definition. For example, Chile, Ecuador and the United States aimed to address water availability conflicts for different uses, such as agriculture, energy and drinking water for the local population.

In the case studies conducted in Canada and Suriname, the research focused more on helping policy-makers anticipate future policy and other challenges because of changing local conditions. This included assessing the impacts of climate change, mostly on agriculture (in Canada) and potential conflicts over water and energy resources in the context of new mining operations (in Suriname).

In all the analysed case studies, the lack of integration and coherence between different sectorial policies, as well as the limited coordination between key stakeholders, presented a challenge in addressing the issues faced. This led to the involvement of policy-makers in all six case studies, often in their early phases, to define the problem and to provide information about the relevant policy documents. Policy-makers became involved based on their expertise and not as representatives of their departments and agencies. This meant that the participating policy-makers had no mandate to commit to the implementation of the outcomes and they mostly provided comments and suggestions based on their experience and expertise. A notable exception was the case study from Ecuador, in which the city administration took an active role in the development of the case study and were very involved in integrating the case study findings into policies and leading the latter's implementation.

Science and policy linkages

Given the strong involvement of policy-makers and pressing local and regional challenges, the case studies have strong science–policy linkages. Even in studies that were primarily initiated by researchers, such as Canada, Japan and the United States, the policy-makers played an active role in defining the problem, interpreting the results and helping with data gathering. However, in the case studies in Canada and Japan a clear separation can be recognised between research and policy during the assessment of linkages between the WEF nexus elements. This indicates that the researchers guided the modelling approaches used in the assessment with relatively minimal (if any) involvement of policy-makers. To some extent, this is understandable, as the quantitative models used to assess the relationships within the WEF nexus need in-depth, up-to-date scientific expertise and policy-makers may have neither the interest nor the capacity/time to effectively participate.

However, the research teams carrying out the case studies in Canada and Japan made efforts to engage policy-makers by incorporating qualitative data collection approaches, such as conducting interviews to collect policy-makers' views on topics such as types of WEF benefit needed; most feasible ways of integrating the outcomes of the WEF assessment into the policy process; and insights about data availability and quality used in modelling.

Regular interactions with policy-makers occurred in the case studies from Ecuador, Suriname and Chile, where no in-depth quantitative modelling was performed, but rather a simpler system-mapping approach was used to assess

WEF linkages. The outcomes of these case studies suggest that conducting integrated modelling requires a considerable effort and that this was not possible when a case prioritised regular collaborations with policy-makers (Roy et al., 2016 for the case study in Suriname).

Finally, the modelling efforts required creating multidisciplinary teams that bring together scholars and researchers from specific disciplines with experience in multidisciplinary projects. Liu (2016) and Endo et al. (2015) stress that involving diverse researchers can in itself require considerable effort, particularly into managing the project prior to embarking on the modelling. Here, previous collaboration and research team development can be useful supports in conducting a WEF case study. However, in the case studies considered, the specific WEF assessment was often the first and most significant collaboration effort of the involved researchers and policy-makers.

Enabling conditions influencing the case study outcomes

In all the case studies analysed, researchers and policy-makers had very little experience in collaborating to address pressing local and regional issues. In most cases, the collaboration with researchers was instigated by a clear need for assistance in quantifying and addressing complex problems such as those in the WEF nexus. The collaboration was not based on previous experience so much as the willingness of policy-makers to engage in such a project with researchers. For their part, the researchers involved recognised the importance of incorporating the policy perspective and were interested in engaging with policy-makers to create opportunities for the implementation of the WEF case study findings. It would be interesting to know if this collaborative work between policy-makers and researchers continued in other areas and sectors, but the case studies did not conduct follow-up assessments.

Based on the case studies reviewed, WEF assessments were not enabled by the need to provide inputs to specific policy/strategy reviews or to new strategy development. However, the case studies provided inputs in new policy development, for example, in the cases of Canada and the USA, the case studies informed policy development for the allocation of water resources and climate change adaptation planning.

Policy changes based on the outcomes of the WEF case studies

Unless changes on the ground are made, for example, through changes in the management and allocation of resources in the WEF nexus to exploit synergies and reduce trade-offs, one can conclude that the case studies had limited impact. The case studies contribute in other ways, such as learning and awareness-raising through improved understanding of the WEF nexus elements and their interactions within the local system.

The case studies were primarily aimed at addressing local challenges, thus the question remains: did they succeed in achieving this aim? In the case of Ecuador and Chile, their very practical focus on the local challenge likely contributed to a policy-action-driven approach. This approach led to practical actions such as the revision of the water allocation rules and the financial support for upstream natural infrastructure to improve WEF synergies and benefits. Furthermore, these cases not only identified these measures, but also developed new means of implementation, such as creating a water protection fund in Ecuador and a fund to support the modernisation of irrigation in Chile. The implementation in Ecuador also engendered institutional reform resulting in the transformation of the former river management association into an oversight board with expanded jurisdiction and representation covering the whole river basin and gathering the necessary technical expertise (IUCN and IWA, 2015b).

The case studies in Japan and Canada focused more on understanding the water resource and climate change impacts of agriculture and fisheries, rather than on developing actual policies and strategies. This led to outcomes that were strongly research focused such as peer-reviewed journal articles. Consequently, additional efforts, such as creating briefing materials for policy-makers, would have been necessary to make the case study findings easily usable for policy design and implementation.

Finally, in the case studies in the United States and Suriname, the policy focus served only as an input to inform the design of the research; there was no documented contribution to policy processes by for example revising current policies and/or modifying the management of the WEF nexus elements. These two case studies left it to the policy-makers to interpret the results in a policy-relevant manner and to draw specific policy recommendations.

Discussion

Through the comparative analysis of the selected case studies, a number of insights and implications have been identified impacting on the policy relevance and overall uptake of WEF nexus assessments by public policy and decision-making institutions. In this chapter, the focus is specifically on how to foster collaboration between researchers and policy-makers as a means to increase the uptake of the WEF case studies' recommendations. In this section, an overview is provided of major barriers and challenges limiting the policy relevance of the WEF nexus assessments.

As was found by other authors (Johnston et al., 2014; Karlberg et al. 2015; Leck et al., 2015), the case studies reviewed reinforced that urgent local issues instigated the work on the WEF nexus. As a result, the case studies did not treat all the elements of the nexus equally but rather prioritised them based on the local context and needs. Keskinen and Varis's (2016) work suggests that a more balanced approach to project design covering all WEF nexus elements could increase buy-in by the less represented sectors. However, based on the reviewed case studies the stronger focus on one or two sectors was problem-driven and extending the focus to address the rest of the sectors may not be in line with the policy-makers' priorities and interests.

To address the issues initiating WEF nexus studies, policy actions need to follow. However, it seems that the implementation of policy recommendations in the form of changing/revising policies and/or changing governance systems and management of and allocations to the WEF nexus elements were limited in the reviewed case studies. A number of barriers can be identified that prevented such policy uptake, including limited capacity to establish extensive collaboration with policy-makers, including cross-sectorial collaboration (Bizikova et al., 2014); lack of effort to ensure policy coherence and integration of WEF assessment recommendations with existing policies and strategies (Leck et al., 2015; Weitz et al. 2017; de Roo et al., 2014); and limited mandates of the policy-makers involved for the required changes to be implemented.

The case studies showed strong collaboration between actors in the science and policy domains. The findings further show that there is a link between the extent of policy-makers' involvement and the use of case study findings to inform policy design and implementation. Similar to Endo et al. (2015), the case studies that had policy-makers involved in the co-design and co-production from conception to completion had findings/outcomes that were more relevant to policy. At the same time, Biggs et al. (2015) stressed that perhaps researchers need to be more strongly involved in some stages of the WEF nexus assessment, such as during model development and application. As previously discussed, the case studies analysed show that those that maintained strong collaboration between policy-makers and researchers had outcomes that led to implementation. However, even though this strong collaboration existed in some of the case studies, there was limited comprehensive modelling of the WEF nexus. The outcomes of this review, like Liu (2016) and Howells et al. (2011), indicate that in-depth modelling of the WEF linkages is a significant research effort and once the researchers focus on the modelling, policy-maker engagement is often significantly reduced and this in turn diminishes the relevance of the outcomes to policy design and implementation.

Often multiple sectors were included in the reviewed case studies, such as water, agriculture, mining and infrastructure; all operating at national to local levels, involving a series of agencies and departments. This not only necessitated collaboration with policy-makers, but required that these policy-makers represented all critical sectors that may need to be involved in designing and/or implementing policy. The analysis of the selected cases studies showed that several sectors were represented, however often on an ad hoc basis rather than after conducting stakeholders' analysis to identify all relevant sectors and agencies representing them. Some of the case studies, for example Canada and Chile, aimed to tap into sectorial and cross-sectorial partnerships and committees that brought together already identified relevant agencies. But overall, given the broad range of the WEF nexus elements, a number of agencies need to be involved early on during the assessment design when its focus and the key questions surrounding it are defined.

In addition to the policy-makers' participation, it is also critical that the participating policy-makers represent their agencies/departments having a mandate to commit to the uptake of the WEF nexus assessment outcomes. However, with the exception of the case studies in Chile and Ecuador, the policy-makers involved participated as experts rather than representatives of their agencies, with mandates to make changes to policies and governance systems. The case study in Ecuador in particular showed strong institutional commitments of a number of sectorial agencies to participation in the study, resulting in revised governance systems and a more effective decision-making framework to implement the outcomes of the study. A major cause of the limited institutional commitments is the existence of often strongly hierarchical systems within the public policy agencies/departments leading to complicated and/or lengthy approval procedures. In the case studies in Chile and Ecuador, this was overcome by enlisting leaders of the sectorial agencies that had the mandate to undertake institutional commitments. Without such partnerships, WEF case studies provide more of an awareness-raising and learning opportunity for policy-makers rather than an opportunity for policy and governance change. Finally, taking a more institutional-level approach to partnerships allows a better coordinated approach for selecting the policy-makers to participate in a WEF assessment, as the agencies involved can nominate policy-makers based on their expertise and capacity needed for the specific WEF assessment.

Furthermore, in addition to ensuring the participation of policy-makers with institutional commitment representing all critical sectors, it is also necessary to ensure policy coherence and integration. This is because the major focus of a WEF nexus assessments is to improve synergies and reduce trade-offs between the nexus sectors. Policy coherence and integration is required for example to reduce water use in several sectors such as environment, agriculture, infrastructure and industry. As Weitz et al. (2017) noted, policy coherence requires negotiations among the involved stakeholders and their agencies, and this is not possible if the participating policy-makers have no power to make and implement decisions and action change, and are not representative of the relevant sectors. There therefore needs to be a stronger focus on creating institutional partnerships, with key agencies, ensuring that policy design and implementation are coordinated and thus can be brought to successful completion.

Achieving much needed policy changes identified by a WEF assessment, often requires changes in the governance systems relevant for the WEF nexus sectors and the effective coordination of these systems. This could mean, for example, bringing together agencies and departments that manage critical WEF nexus sectors and/or implement well-defined changes in a governance system to streamline coordination and decision-making procedures across several WEF sectors. For example, to maximise synergies of water use between different users an effective governance system needs to be in place to ensure timely and science-based decisions involving all critical agencies. In practice, this could mean revising existing governance systems by, for example, including additional agencies and/or creating processes to make and implement decisions.

So far, the focus has been on discussing how to strengthen the policy-relevance of the WEF assessments and, consequently, improve the potential benefits policy and governance change/improvement might bring to better address the allocation of scarce WEF resources. A potentially significant enabler in terms of improving policy relevance is to look at the relational equity between the involved researchers and policy-makers, policy-makers representing diverse sectors as well as researchers coming from diverse fields in multi-disciplinary assessments. The nature of each of these relationships could potentially improve the assessment in terms of bringing change and improving existing policy and governance systems.

One critical relationship is between scientists and policy-makers. This relationship is often the most unequal in terms of both groups accessing financial resources from the WEF assessment, gaining recognition in their workplaces for participating in it and this participation being recognised at the participants' performance reviews. In terms of financial resources, funding for the WEF assessments reviewed was almost exclusively awarded to the research institutions and the researchers were their main beneficiaries. This is because the research institutions are often the primary recipients of such funding whereas policy-makers tend to participate on a voluntary basis. Creating agreements between the research institutions and the departments and agencies representing policy-makers and providing access to funding could possibly reduce inequality and thus increase the level of commitment by all involved. This was successfully implemented in the case study focusing on Chile with funding shared between the city government and the researchers involved.

Another important dimension in ensuring relational equity between researchers and policy-makers is the contribution to their performance review of their participation in a WEF assessment. In other words, the perceived value that participating in a WEF assessment has for them and their careers. For the researchers, participation in WEF assessment is often seen as an activity that meets many of their performance priorities such as getting project funding, conducting multidisciplinary research and consulting with stakeholders. Additionally, many WEF assessments result in peer-reviewed articles published in scientific journals directly relevant for researchers. From the policy-makers' point of view, participation in WEF assessments has often been encouraged, but working with the research community has neither been linked directly to their "job" nor has led to a reduction of their other activities to enable them to participate in the WEF assessment. This lack of parity between researchers and policy-makers increases the researchers' contributions to the WEF assessments by feeding into their job priorities while this is only the case for policy-makers to a very limited extent.

The other two types of interaction amongst researchers from different fields and amongst policy-makers from different sectors appear more balanced as in both cases each group will have to negotiate internally, among peers, work allocation, participation in different activities and outcomes.

Finally, the reviewed case studies paid little attention to the continuous monitoring and evaluation of the implementation efforts. Monitoring has been suggested by Ringler et al. (2013), Beck et al. (2013) and Bizikova et al. (2014)

as an important tool to keep track of the performance of the implemented actions and other factors influencing the WEF nexus over time. Only two of the case studies reviewed attempted to develop a monitoring system to track changes aiming to improve synergies and reduce trade-offs within the WEF nexus elements. Out of these cases, one took a narrow approach only on water availability and the other looked at a broader indicator system tracking rural well-being and environment. Developing monitoring and evaluation systems is critical in assessing progress in achieving synergies and reducing trade-offs between the WEF nexus sectors. At the same time, establishing impact monitoring and assessment mechanisms depends on the relationships between researchers and policy-makers and the commitments they made. This is because continuous monitoring is often operated by policy-makers who are also responsible for linking the collected data to policy development.

Conclusion

This section summarises potential opportunities to address identified challenges and encourage using WEF nexus assessment outcomes in policy and governance.

Overall, the WEF nexus provides an approach appropriate to bringing together three critical areas, food, energy and water, connected by complex relationships and stakeholders' interests that could lead to deepening trade-offs, but also to exploiting synergies. To be able to focus on the emergent synergies, the WEF nexus should be solution-centred in order to identify specific actions to address and mitigate against WEF challenges such as the overuse of water, pollution and other impacts of food production and conflicts relating to water availability for energy production and for other activities. Such solution-centred approaches can also instigate and guide necessary changes in policy and governance as they provide details not only on what changes are required (e.g. policy change), but also on the relevant institutions and the necessary governance structures to make effective and timely decisions.

Considering the actual WEF assessment, it is critical to balance the needs of policy-makers against those of researchers. This includes using quantitative modelling of the WEF linkages only as required to identify information needed in order to identify synergies between the WEF elements and formulate appropriate solutions to address specific challenges. Often using a simpler model can be more effective in that it shifts the focus from extensive modelling and leaves time for collaboration with policy-makers. Moreover, it can considerably reduce model development and testing efforts (and time required to complete these activities) and may fit better with shorter policy development cycles and the often-competing priorities of policy-makers. Using a simpler, conceptual model and/or several sectorial models would not detract from the value of the analysis as − if applied as intended when designed − such model(s) can provide an insight into WEF synergies and trade-offs and lead to findings and recommendations relevant for policy-making.

The findings of the comparative analysis of the selected WEF case studies suggest that success in designing a policy-relevant WEF nexus assessment depends on the extent to which individual policy-makers and relevant institutions and agencies representing critical sectors have opportunities for collaboration and involvement in the research design. This requires establishing partnerships and/or collaborative agreements with institutions and agencies involved in policy and decision-making to create a basis for shaping the focus of the assessment that would later underpin its findings and recommendations and the latter's uptake. Involvement in a WEF nexus assessment thus becomes part of the participating policy-maker's "job" with an expectation for active policy action to follow.

Finally, it could be argued that the relational equity perspective allows a better balance of policy-makers' and researchers' needs and gains from WEF assessments and thus potentially increases their relevance for policy-making. Such a perspective permits the establishment of a negotiated agreement between research and policy-focused agencies regarding each partner's contribution, including funding and other resource allocation and the explicit commitment to actively participate in the assessment. Finally, adopting a relational equity perspective will likely help in building trust and can encourage future collaborations that are critical in overcoming or mitigating against many sustainability challenges that necessitate addressing trade-offs and identifying and enhance synergies in socio-ecological systems.

References

Bazilian, M., Rogner, H., Hoells, M., Hermann, S., Arent, D. and Yumkella, K.K. (2011). "Considering the energy, water and food nexus: Towards an integrated modelling approach". *Energy Policy*, vol 39, no 12, pp 7896–7906.

Beck, B. and Walker, R.V. (2013). "On water security, sustainability, and the water–food–energy–climate nexus". *Frontiers of Environmental Science and Engineering*, vol 7, no 5, pp 626–639.

Biggs, E.M., Bruce, E., Boruff, B., Duncan, J.M.A., Horsley, J. and Imanari, Y. (2015). "Sustainable development and the water–energy–food nexus: A perspective on livelihoods". *Environmental Science and Policy*, vol 54, pp 389–397.

Bizikova, L., Roy, D., Venema, H.D. and McCandless, M. (2014a) *The Water-Energy-Food Nexus and Agricultural Investment: A sustainable development guidebook*. Winnipeg: International Institute for Sustainable Development.

Cervingni, R., Liden, M.J.R., Neumann, J.L. and Strzepek, K.M. (2015). *Enhancing the Climate Resilience of African Infrastructure: The power and water sectors*. [Online]. Available from: www.worldbank.org/content/dam/Worldbank/Feature%20Story/Afric a/Conference%20Edition%20Enhancing%20Africas%20Infrastructure.pdf.

de Roo, A., Burek, P., Bouraoui, F., Reynaud, A., Udias, A., Pistocchi, A., Lanzanova, D., Trichakis, I., Beck, H. and Bernhard, J. (2014). *Large Scale Hydro-economic Modelling for Policy Support*. EGU General Assembly Conference Abstracts. pp 2951.

FAO, F. and A.A., n.d. GAEZ: Global Agro-Ecological Zones [Online]. Available from: www.fao.org/nr/gaez/en/#.

Echavarria, M., Vogel, J., Alban, M. and Meneses, F. (2004). *The Impacts of Payments for Watershed Services in Ecuador. Emerging lessons from Pimampiro and Cuenca.* [Online]. Available from: http://pubs.iied.org/9285IIED/.

Endo, A., Burnett, K., Orencio, P., Kumazawa, T., Wada, C., Ishii, A., Tsurita, I. and Taniguchi, M. (2015). "Methods of the water-energy-food nexus". *Water*, vol 7, no 10, pp 5806–5830. DOI: doi:10.3390/w7105806.

Hermann, S., Welsch, M., Segerstrom, R.E., Howells, M.I., Young, C., Alfstad, T., Hans-Holger, R. and Steduto, P. (2012). "Climate, land, energy and water (CLEW) interlinkages in Burkina Faso: An analysis of agricultural intensification and bioenergy production". *Natural Resources Forum*, vol 36, no 4, pp 245–262.

Hoff, H. (2011). "Understanding the nexus". Background Paper for the Bonn 2011 Conference: The Water, Energy and Food Security Nexus; Stockholm Environment Institute: Stockholm, Sweden.

Howells, M., Hermann, S., Welsch, M., Bazilian, M., Segerström, R., Alfstad, T., Gielen, D., Rogner, H., Fischer, G., van Velthuizen, H., Wiberg, D., Young, C., Roehrl, R.A., Mueller, A., Steduto, P. and Ramma, I. (2013). "Integrated analysis of climate change, land-use, energy and water strategies". *Nature Climate Change*, vol 3, no 7, pp 621–626.

Howells, M., Rogner, H., Strachan, N., Heaps, C., Huntington, H. and Bazillian, M. (2011). "OSeMOSYS: The open source energy modelling system: An introduction to its ethos, structure and development". *Energy Policy*, vol 39, pp 5850–5870.

Huppé, G.A., Bizikova, L., Roy, D., Borden, C. and Swanson, D. (2015). *Water-Energy-Food Resource Book for Mining.* [Online]. Available from: www.iisd.org/publications/water-energy-food-resource-book-mining.

IUCN and IWA (International Union of Conservation of Nature and International Water Association). (2015a). *Water Management in the Huasco River Basin: Huasco, northern Chile.* [Online]. Available from: www.waternexussolutions.org/ContentSuite/upload/wns/file/Case%20study_Huasco_FINAL.pdf.

IUCN and IWA (International Union of Conservation of Nature and International Water Association). (2015b). *Financing Natural Infrastructure: Quito, Ecuador.* [Online]. Available from: www.waternexussolutions.org/ContentSuite/upload/wns/all/Case%20study_FONAG.pdf.

Johnston, R., de Silva, S. and Try, T. (2014, 7–9 May). "Investing in water management to improve productivity of rice-based farming systems in Cambodia". In Robins, L. (ed.), *A Policy Dialogue on Rice Futures: Rice-based farming systems research in the Mekong Region.* ACIAR Proc No. 142. Australian Centre for International Agric Res, Canberra, Proceedings of a dialogue held in Phnom Penh.

Karlberg, L., Hoff, H., Amsalu, T., Andersson, K., Binnington, T., Flores, F., de Bruin, A., Gebrehiwot, S.G., Gedif, B., zur Heide, F., Johnson, O., Osbeck, M. and Young, C. (2015). "Tackling complexity: Understanding the food-energy-environment nexus in Ethiopia's Lake Tana sub-basin". *Water Alternatives*, vol 8, no 1, pp 710–734.

Keskinen, M. and Varis, O. (2016). "Water-energy-food nexus in large Asian river basins". *Water*, vol 8, no 10, pp 446.

Lawford, R. (2016). *The WEF Nexus and SDGs.* 4th Regional WEF Nexus Workshop. [Online]. Available from: http://water-future.org/wp-content/uploads/2016/12/Introduction-No.-4-R.-Lawford-Discussion-Paper.pdf.

Leck, H., Conway, D., Bradshaw, M. and Rees, J. (2015). "Tracing the water–energy–food nexus: Description, theory and practice". *Geography Compass*, vol 9, no 8, pp 445–460.

Liu, Q. (2016). "Interlinking climate change with water-energy-food nexus and related ecosystem processes in California case studies". *Ecological Processes*, vol 5, p 14.

Martinez, G., Bizikova, L., Blobel, D. and Swart, R. (2011). "Emerging climate change coastal adaptation strategies and case studies around the world". In G. Hofstede Schernewski and J.T. Neumann (eds) *Global Change and Baltic Coastal Zones*. Coastal Research Library, Vol. 1. Berlin: Springer-Verlag.

Mohtar, Rabi H., Assi, Amjad T. and Daher, Bassel T. (2015). *Bridging the Water and Food Gap: The role of the water-energy-food nexus*. UNU-FLORES Working Paper Series 5, edited by Hiroshan Hettiarachchi. Dresden: United Nations University Institute for Integrated Management of Material Fluxes and of Resources (UNU-FLORES).

Moser, S.C. and Luers, A.L. (2007). "Managing climate risks in California: The need to engage resource managers for successful adaptation to change". *Climatic Change*, vol 87, pp 309–322.

Pittock, J., Hussey, K. and McGlennon, S. (2013). "Australian climate, energy and water policies: Conflicts and synergies". *Australian Geographer*, vol 44, no 1, pp. 3–22. doi:10.1080/00049182.2013.765345.

Riegels, N., Kromann, M., Karup Pedersen, J., Lindgaard-Jørgensen, P., Sokolov, V. and Sorokin, A. (2013). "Basin Economic Allocation Model (BEAM): An economic model of water use developed for the Aral Sea Basin". *Geophysical Research Abstracts*, vol 15, p 8608.

Ringler, C., Bhaduri, A. and Lawford, R. (2013). "The nexus across water, energy, land and food (WELF): Potential for improved resource use efficiency?". *Current Opinion in Environmental Sustainability*, vol 5 no 6, pp 617–624. doi:10.1016/j.cosust.2013.11.002.

Roy, D., Bizikova, L., Huppé, G.A., Borden, C. and Swanson, D. (2015). *WEFsat-Mining Tool User – Guidance Manual: Water, energy and food security analysis tool for mining*. [Online]. Available from: www.iisd.org/sites/default/files/publications/WEFsat-mining-tool-user-guidance-manual.pdf.

Roy, D., Swanson, D., Borden, C., Crawford, A., Bizikova, L. and Huppé, G. (2016). "A water-energy-food security analysis tool for mining in Suriname: Operationalizing the mining policy framework of the intergovernmental forum on mining, minerals, metals and sustainable development". *Water International*, vol 41, no 6, pp 1035–1043.

UN (United Nations) (2015). *Sustainable Development Goals (SGDs)*. [Online]. Available from: https://sustainabledevelopment.un.org/topics/sustainabledevelopmentgoals.

Waldick, R., Bizikova, L., Bolte, J., MacDonald, D., Zaytseva, A. and Swanson, D. (2015). *Mainstreaming Climate Change Integrated Landscape Assessment. Decision-support process and tool kit: Guidebook to implementing the quantitative and qualitative aspects of the assessment*. [Online]. Available from: www.iisd.org/sites/default/files/publications/mainstreaming-climate-change-toolkit-guidebook.pdf.

Waldick, R., Bizikova, L., White, D. and Lindsay, K. (2016). "Integrated regional assessment and decision-support process for strategic approach to adaptation planning to climate change". *Regional Environmental Change*, pp 1–14.

Weitz, N., Stramboa, C., Kemp-Benedicta, E. and Nilsson, M. (2017). "Closing the governance gaps in the water-energy-food nexus: Insights from integrative governance". *Global Environmental Change*, vol 45, pp 165–173.

4 Water-energy-food nexus

A property rights approach

Christian A. Nygaard and Ellis P. Judson

Introduction

The water-energy-food nexus (WEF) is an analytical perspective that seeks to highlight the complexity and interdependencies between the WEF sectors themselves and their relation to wider economic and ecological sustainability issues. The need for such an approach arises from the inequitable global use of resources and failure to coordinate sectoral activities – lack of access to adequate resources in some areas and over-consumption of resources in other areas; increasing demand due to population growth and deepening economic prosperity, including continued urbanisation and globalisation; and climate change – that affects the availability and distribution of natural resources (Hoff, 2011). However, finding mutually acceptable decisions to trade-offs resulting from competing demands is often inhibited by informational deficiency and the capacity of institutions, ownership and governance structures to manage collaboration and benefits-enhancing initiatives (Pittock et al., 2015). In such a context prices can no longer be relied on to provide efficient signals to guide resource allocation, coordination and use.

This chapter adopts an economic property rights perspective as a means of mapping who owns what in the WEF nexus *and* on what basis. The chapter argues that mapping property rights is an important tool for understanding motivations and behaviours that characterise the relationships between different actors in the WEF nexus. It is also an important tool for establishing functional coordination mechanisms for scarcity and competition in the WEF nexus. These coordination mechanisms can be either market based, or other forms for collaborative governance.

In the economic property rights perspective, rights are sometimes divided into economic rights and legal rights (Barzel, 1997). Economic right is the ability to receive income (benefit), either through use of trade, from economic activity, assets and resources.[1] Legal right is the right that is recognised and enforced by a third party (e.g. a state or supra-national institution). Legal rights enhance the value of economic rights (Barzel, 1997). The alignment of economic and legal right, for instance through trade or collaborative governance mechanisms, can serve to enhance the value and productivity of a natural resource in the WEF nexus. But the relationship between economic and legal rights is in itself complex. For instance, perceptions of moral legitimacy can affect the intentions and behaviours of individuals and firms separately from the self-interest that might otherwise guide the maximisation of economic rights (Hodgson, 2015).

An important related concept here is that of residual claimancy (Barzel, 1997). In a WEF nexus that is characterised by a range of externalities, where use of resources can be based on a range of (sometimes co-existing) traditions (e.g. legal contracting, common use, traditional/customary use) residual claimancy is the ownership of benefits and costs that remain after the different claims have been met. Population growth, economic modernisation and climate change often bring this issue into particular focus by reducing residual benefits, or increasing costs, and by exacerbating the variability of outcomes over time. For instance, use traditions may have emerged in an environment of seeming abundance that, in an environment of scarcity are wasteful and unproductive. New economic activity or additional users can bestow significant costs on other users of the same resource. Coordination of competing claims in the WEF nexus requires effective institutions and/or third-party enforcement mechanisms. However, such institutions are missing, ineffective or biased in many countries; and, even where existing, they often become weakened during periods of particular resource stress (Hughes, 2015).

In this chapter we aim to highlight how a mapping of property rights can be instrumental in enhancing the efficacy of a relational equity and collaborative governance approach. In particular we focus on the delineation of attributes of natural resources and residual claimancy to highlight how a mapping of property rights can be instrumental in enhancing relational equity and collaborative governance approaches. To operationalise delineation and residual claimancy issues in the WEF nexus this chapter focuses on property rights traditions, interactions and interdependencies in river systems. River systems are central to the management of water, but also energy and food production. Moreover, river systems clearly exemplify spatial interdependencies.

Following this introduction, the chapter provides a brief background to the evolution of the WEF nexus "thinking". It then offers additional details on the economics property rights perspective and its application to the WEF nexus and distils key insights from a property rights perspective for relational equity and collaborative governance approaches. It finally provides concluding remarks.

Background of the WEF nexus thinking evolution

The WEF nexus has gained analytical and policy traction following the 2011 Bonn conference on "The water, energy and food security nexus: Solutions for the green economy". According to Hoff (2011) the nexus concept enables more integrated cross-sectoral and cross-scale management and governance of resource use, which in turn can support transitioning to a green economy, climate change resilience and greater resource efficiency (productivity).[2]

While there have been repeated calls for more integrated and efficient use of natural resources for some time, Wichelns (2017) describes and details the evolution of the post-war debate; it is argued by others that unlike earlier calls and approaches the nexus concept is multi-centric. That is, it stresses the most critical inter-linkages on an equitable basis (e.g. Liu et al., 2017). Integrated resource management, in this view, is a three-sector system optimisation – or more efficient use of resources to ensure increased resource productivity, enabling more water, energy and food to be consumed with the same resource (Pittock et al., 2015; Endo et al., 2017; Liu et al., 2017). By focusing on the WEF nexus as a three-sector system inter-relationships and sectoral feedbacks can be identified. And, once complexity and interdependency are acknowledged and identified, policies, innovations and governance tools can be developed that seek to reduce the trade-offs that arise from conflicting demands or input competition across the three sectors, such as the use of water for both energy production and irrigation or fisheries, and/or increase the potential for synergy in resource use.

Nexus thinking in this respect is a technical exercise – better data collection, information exchange and systems modelling (interactions between the three sectors) – are key to identifying ways of optimising the system. At the technical implementation level, the challenge then is one of fully modelling sectoral interactions; identifying benefits and co-benefits; and correctly estimating the social costs and benefits of resource use. Nexus tools, for instance, benefit sharing (the transfer of additional value generated in one of the sectors to compensate loss of value generated in the other sectors) can then be developed to facilitate the managerial exercise of nexus thinking; the coordination of resource use and competing interests across the three sectors. Neither exercise is trivial, even with the best of intentions.

Similarly, the accurate estimation of benefits and co-benefits is not a trivial exercise and arguably only feasible if taking a broader perspective than WEF nexus thinking alone (Wichelns, 2017). When goods and services are accurately priced (in that the cost of production fully reflects both private and social costs) the conventional price mechanisms are a powerful tool for resource allocation. However, estimating the social cost of production is complex and there is little agreement even on key social costs such as CO_2 emissions related to climate change. Externalities, both positive and negative, are thus frequently not (accurately) internalised and do not condition the resource allocating role of prices or the market processes that coordinate sectoral supply chain operations.

The price mechanisms in food, energy and water are additionally complicated by policy driven non-neutralities (public policy interventions such as taxation or subsidies change the demand or supply) that distort prices further (Allan et al., 2015). Many countries subsidise food, energy and water, directly or indirectly, to achieve wider social and welfare objectives. While a number of such policies are the result of a recognition that the price mechanism does not fully reflect social costs and benefits, their level is typically unrelated to actual social costs and benefits. Moreover, the tractability of policy effects is complex. For instance, according to some the combination of food subsidies and trade (import) restrictions across the industrialised world leaves food prices artificially higher than in the absence of food-intervention policies (Paarlberg, 2013). Using existing prices to optimise the three-sector WEF systems would in all likelihood affect the allocation of natural resources across these sectors, but would not necessarily lead to greater resource sustainability, climate change resilience or resource productivity. Reporting and accounting rules similarly fail to internalise gains from mutuality and responsible approaches to people and planet (Allan et al., 2015).

Others, however, also highlight important inequities between the three sectors. For instance, the food and energy sectors are both, in large parts, market systems with long, often global, supply chains. These supply chains interact with multiple subsidy and taxation regulations and are dominated by commercially driven stakeholders that themselves only handle a small proportion of the embedded natural resource (Allan et al., 2015).

Finally, an institutional and political economy challenge pervades all aspects of nexus thinking – to implement the technical optimisation and integrated planning across the WEF nexus the literature therefore also stresses the need for institutional and public policy alignment across sectors (Rasul, 2016) and beyond the three sectors (Wichelns, 2017). Such institutional and public policy alignment is, however, a formidable task and involves clear delineation of the costs and benefits that can be generated through nexus thinking, but also clear delineation of the rights to costs and benefits. In particular, the delineation of property rights may assist collaborative governance and incentivise investment in relational equity by enabling interdependency-specific additional value (e.g. additional value generated and maintained through ongoing specialisation and economies of scale).

A property rights approach

In economics commodities and resources are considered bundles of attributes that, in principle, are separable (Barzel, 1997). Property rights are broadly defined as the right to: i) derive benefit, income and welfare from an asset or asset attribute; ii) change the form of an asset or attribute; and, iii) alienation, or transfer of property rights to a third party (Alchian and Demsetz, 1973; Barzel, 1997). For many natural resources these rights are distributed across multiple actors; actors may hold a bundle of rights and ability to exercise rights are limited by technology, and conditioned by social, cultural and institutional practices (Bromley, 1989).

Natural resources as bundles of attributes

A central tenet of property rights economics is that natural resources consists of a bundle of attributes that separately and jointly generate benefit streams. For instance, a river system has both consumptive and non-consumptive attributes, which again are characterised by seasonality, flow, evaporation and flooding attributes of river systems. Within the WEF nexus food production, agriculture consumes water by transforming this into edible produce. By transforming water into edible produce, water is no longer available for other uses, such as energy production. Energy production, such as hydropower generation, makes use of the flow of water to generate electricity. While the flow attribute of river systems becomes affected by such schemes, the water is typically returned to the river system and available to downstream users. Non-consumptive uses also relate to in-river production of food – such as fisheries – and biodiversity. These, in turn, are affected by both irrigation and energy-related consumptive and non-consumptive developments (Nilsson et al., 2005). Irrigation and energy investments also affect flow and flooding attributes of river systems, which in turn relate to the evaporation attribute and the ecology along river systems, for example flora and fauna associated with flood plains.

Water in river systems also has current use and asset attributes. In unregulated river systems property rights chiefly apply to current use rights. A key characteristic of rivers is that they flow, that is water is a fugitive resource. Owners of property rights can choose to use water themselves or trade, although various forms of off-river storage are also possible (Hughes, 2015). In regulated river systems large scale storage of water in-river is possible. However, storing water in dams, for instance, generates additional trade-offs between current consumptive and non-consumptive uses and future such uses. Decisions relating to this trade-off has significant implications for value maximisation and distribution of river systems value.

To the extent that property rights are clearly delineated and enforceable, the use and asset value of water enables arbitrage, or trade, both spatially and temporally. Arbitrage can incentivise water conserving initiatives that free up water for trade, but can also enable property rights holders to benefit from variation in demand conditions. For instance, cereal and grain crop production (broadacre) is more sensitive to variation in the price of water than fruit tree production (horticulture) (Hughes, 2015).

The relative value of natural resource attributes can change separately. For instance, demand for the consumptive attribute of river water is inversely related to rain fall – when the availability of blue (rivers and lakes) and green (in-soil water) increases, the marginal value of river water decreases. Conversely of course, the willingness to pay for water increases substantially when water becomes scarce. Moreover, the demand for water is more price elastic in the long run than in the short run. From growing season to growing season, farmers can alter the crop they produce and thus regulate their demand for water, while industry/households can change technology. Variation in demand conditions on the one hand have given rise to spatial trade, but can also give rise to temporal trade. Water rights holders can trade water during times of high demand, say the transfer of water from broadacre crop production to horticulture crop production during times of water stress, or choose to store water, where feasible, in order to trade when water becomes more scarce, say as a function of normal seasonal variability of weather and agricultural cycles.

Property rights and institutionally contingent value

In property rights theory, the emphasis is on value or welfare generated by attributes. Attribute valuation is a function of the security of property rights, in practice, the ability to exclude others or the legitimate expectation that claims will be respected by others. Property rights theory in economics therefore distinguishes between legal and economic property rights. Legal rights are typically formally recognised rights that are enforced by government and legal institutions. Economic property rights, on the other hand, relate to claiming the benefit stream or welfare generated by bundles of attributes. Economic property rights in the WEF nexus is the benefit stream that is generated by consumptive and non-consumptive uses of water. In market economies, legal rights can enhance economic rights by providing third-party recognition and protection. That is, the legal systems can be used to enforce excludability and ensure compensation where property rights have been violated. For instance, the asset value (economic) of stored water increases when water storage is legally recognised and regulated, leading to a reduction in transaction cost and conflict resolution uncertainty.

However, legal rights are not a necessary condition for economic benefits to exist; they reduce transaction cost and uncertainty in case of conflict resolution and may therefore enhance the economic value of property, but economic benefits exist independent of formal legal recognition. In many emerging and developing countries, legal rights may be diffused, ambiguous or preceded by customs and conventions preceding many legal inventions. Some of these property rights concepts are illustrated in Box 4.1, which focuses on property rights and benefit streams from the bundle of river system attributes.

The extensiveness and completeness of legal property rights differs substantially internationally and even within countries. For instance, agricultural expansion in the United States took place under two different water property rights regimes – the riparian doctrine and the appropriative doctrine (Coman, 1911; Burness and Quirk, 1979). Under the riparian doctrine, properties adjacent to water ways had the legal right to continuous and undiminished flow (Burness and Quirk, 1979). The riparian doctrine is a land-based water allocation system intended to preserve the non-consumptive attributes (flow characteristics) of river systems (Tarlock, 2000). Designed for in-flow uses, such as mills and saws, the riparian doctrine generated considerable first-mover advantage in agricultural practice, with subsequent arrivals, although in practice enjoying similar rights, frequently having to rely on litigation to assert their rights. The cost of litigation frequently resulted in private agreements to avoid the cost and length of court proceedings (Coman, 1911).

The appropriative doctrine, by comparison, established the right to an amount of water, for beneficial use. It is a user-based system designed to enable diversion of flow from in-river use to agriculture (through irrigation), mining or storage (Tarlock, 2000). Rights are typically on a priority basis so that under shortage conditions, lower priority users, for instance newer claims or particular users such as broadacre in relation to horticulture (Hughes, 2015), experience water reductions first (Tarlock, 2000).

The two different legal rights systems in the USA are thus reflective of the river-system attributes they were designed to regulate and the degree of excludability conferred by property rights.[3] They also differ in their treatment of non-legislated value distribution or property rights bundling. For instance, variability in water or value of water can result from incomplete information due to the legislators' lack of detailed knowledge of river systems or local conditions (Ostrom, 2011), short run (seasonal) and long run (climatic) flow variability, measurement/monitoring accuracy and public policy-related water releases intended to maintain the ecological and environmental attributes of river systems. In property rights theory, ownership of any non-contractually, legally or by convention determined or captured *net* value (can be positive or negative) is referred to as residual claimancy.[4] For instance, in the case of the appropriative doctrine, the residual owner of flow variability, for example reduced water flows due to a drought, is the lower priority user; in the riparian doctrine, this remains common property, for example all property rights holders in principle share the residual claimancy. Ownership of water may also be defined in terms of water rights without a priority system, for instance such as in Chile and Mexico (Lefebvre et al., 2012). Residual claimancy in these systems is on a pro rata basis relative to nominal water rights.

Box 4.1 Economic benefits and rights in water, irrigation and energy

Sri Lanka has an irrigation history stretching back some 2500 years, with diversion of water for irrigation and storage purposes (Manchanayake and Bandara, 1999). Water rights (consumptive claims) are formally proportional to land holdings, but economic benefit accrues to the user independent of owner or lease status. Security of claim is, however, sometimes differentiated by seniority (older existing customary users' water allocations are more secure than new users') (Meinzen-Dick and Bakker, 2000). Communities along the rivers are also the claimants of the non-consumptive attribute associated with their use of water, whether this benefit stream is being extracted or not.

Legal rights, associated with the modern nation state of Sri Lanka, are vested with the government and managed by various sectoral government agencies (Manchanayake and Bandara, 1999; Meinzen-Dick and Bakker, 2000). The legitimate expectation that farmers' claims will be respected is based on the recognition of customary use. The development of a hydropower station, as for instance in the Walawe River Basin case (Pittock et al., 2015), meant that claims to both the consumptive and non-consumptive benefits become contested. The economic benefits associated with the non-consumptive attribute was claimed by the Ceylon Electricity Board, but some of the consumptive attributes were also claimed by diverting the natural flow of water and thus reducing the economic benefits claimable by farming communities close to the power station. In recognition of these trade-offs, a benefit sharing scheme was initiated to compensate farmers for loss of income.

In practice, the scheme constituted a payment for transfer of property rights of the consumptive attribute of the river system. On the basis of the cost-benefit analysis, water used for hydropower was found to be more productive and farmers received a monetary compensation that was equal to the foregone income from rice cultivation. However, the cost-benefit analysis did not extend to important social, cultural and economic inter-dependencies related to irrigation and food production practices. The variation in these related benefit streams, initiated by the transfer of property rights to power production, was not costed and accrued in its entirety to the local farming community.

The Chipendeke micro-hydropower scheme in Zimbabwe also functions by diverting water from the river to a micro power plant before returning the water to the river (Pittock et al., 2015). The impact of water diversion is seasonal and localised to nearby farmers – further downstream farmers are not affected. The establishment of the power plant, although extracting economic benefit from the hitherto underutilised non-consumptive attribute, has not resulted in a similar transfer of property rights. The power plant is community owned, and benefits from the non-consumptive attribute, in the form of energy production to support health and educational facilities, extend to all community members who thus also are economic beneficiaries of the non-consumptive attribute. Although the micro-hydropower scheme realised important water-energy interactions, it failed to similarly integrate water-irrigation interactions so that during dry seasons the power plant is shut down for short periods to avoid additional conflict between energy (non-consumptive) and irrigation (consumptive) (Pittock et al., 2015). Managing the tensions between consumptive and non-consumptive uses during the dry seasons has been facilitated by the community ownership of the hydropower plant. In practice, the community continues to claim the benefits from both consumptive and non-consumptive attributes and any variation in the benefits stream generated by either also accrue to the community. Managing the trade-offs (irrigation v energy) has been enabled through continued community negotiations and participatory planning (Pittock et al., 2015).

Being the residual claimant to any increase or decrease in attribute values increases the incentive to invest in property management or maintenance. For instance, lower priority rights holders have a greater incentive to invest in water conservation and storage facilities than higher priority rights holders. Larger water rights holders or water users *may* similarly have a greater incentive than smaller rights holders or users to invest in conservation and storage.

In both cases the actions of other rights holders have an impact on the incentives faced by individual rights holders. In property rights theory, the share of an individual's residual claimancy should correlate with his/her contribution to the average income generated by an asset (Barzel, 1997). For instance, in the case of water conservation the beneficiary of any saved water should correlate with the effort made to conserve this. In the appropriative regime, higher priority property rights holders only have an incentive to conserve water *if* the surplus water can be traded. In the absence of trade water, conservation by the higher priority rights holders leads to additional water for lower priority rights holders, without compensation for effort. In the Walawe example (Box 4.1), residual claimancy accrued to the farming community, not the Ceylon Electricity Board.

In relation to the WEF nexus this principle translates into a correlation between residual claimancy and the availability of water for consumptive and non-consumptive uses during periods of water shortage. During periods of water surplus, the marginal value of water is close to zero, however, during shortages the marginal value of water increases for all stakeholders in the WEF. An individual's residual claimancy should thus reflect the extent to which their behaviour enables additional water availability during shortage periods. Where the delineation of property rights is costly and/or the marginal contribution of individual property rights holder's action to resource availability is difficult to measure or establish, welfare or potential income is left in the public domain. Welfare or income in the public domain is then frequently subject to wealth-consuming capture activity and stakeholders acting with guile. The transaction costs of property rights delineation thus determine the availability of value left in the public domain.

In both a static and dynamic WEF perspective, the delineation of property rights to different attributes provides the basis for arbitrage and trade and can incentivise specialisation and economies of scale. For instance, the separation of consumptive and non-consumptive attributes enables irrigation for agriculture, flow for energy and flow to maintain environmental and ecological services. Economists therefore frequently support regulatory and legislative (institutional) innovations that reduce the transaction costs of property rights delineation, in order to incentivise redistribution of rights to higher value users. Typically, economists support market processes, that is trade, grounded in the willingness to pay for ownership of different stakeholders.

However, as noted earlier, measurement problems relating to establishing the true social costs and benefits of different types of attribute specialisation also mean that prices are not always good indicators of relative social costs. More-over, nexus thinking may itself be an impediment to establishing the true social costs and benefits of attribute utilisation.

Delineation and reallocation of rights

Where the transaction costs of attribute separation are low, relative to potential gains, markets can be developed to facilitate reallocation and use optimisation.

Those that value particular attributes higher can then purchase these in open markets. Where transaction costs of attribute separation are high commodities remain bundled with users making more or better use of some attributes than others. The transaction costs of separation change in response to technology, but also development of third-party and institutional mechanisms that can enforce ownership.

The property rights lens is dynamic. Unbundling, delineation and potentially re-bundling takes place in response to technological and institutional change. As the market value of attributes changes, for instance demand for power for industry and urbanisation, the relative benefits associated with different attributes change too. Provided the expected value of attribute ownership exceeds the transaction cost of delineation (monitoring and enforcement of excludability) there arises an incentive to unbundle property rights. Trade and redistribution of property rights then enables specialisation and economies of scale in attribute utilisation. For instance, the unbundling of consumptive and non-consumptive rights enables specialisation in economic activity associated with food and energy production, respectively. Latterly the unbundling of attributes has also been important for the maintenance of environmental and ecological services of river systems.

Property rights theory has its antecedents in Coase's (1937) analysis of governance of economic activity through markets and firms and economic analysis of externalities (Coase, 1960). In this analysis, the distribution of property rights, in the presence of non-negligible transaction costs, determines the mode and productivity of economic activity. The distribution of property rights that arises in response to particular allocative problems affects the incentive structure of economic activity. This is clearly illustrated in the evolution of the riparian and appropriative property rights regimes, discussed above, that were directed towards non-consumptive and consumptive activities, respectively.

For economists a key ingredient to efficient WEF nexus thinking and more generally to integrated resource management, is the delineation of and trade in property rights, which are market based mechanisms. This however in practice presents two separate challenges. Firstly, delineation is a function of cost and benefits of attribute separation and the alignment of these through residual claimancy. Where prices accurately reflect social costs and benefits, markets can be instrumental in achieving allocative efficiency and enhancing resource productivity. A key policy focus of economists has therefore been to establish and delineate the property rights that can enable trade in scare resources and in this way incentivise changes in use patterns and allocation of resources (Hirshleifer et al., 1969; Burness and Quirk, 1979 Randall, 1981). However, in the presence of informational uncertainty (for instance variation in resource availability and productivity due to climatic short and long-run variability), measurement issues or power imbalances prices are no longer expected to accurately reflect social costs and benefits. With respect to natural resource management this situation arguably remains the more prevalent. Here the allocation of property rights will be instrumental in facilitating increased resource productivity. The recognition of the institutionally contingent nature of property rights security and value here highlight the additional benefits that can be achieved through a relational equity and collaborative governance approach.

Secondly, once in place, property rights regimes and the existing distribution of property rights can be difficult to change. As relative prices change in response to societal preferences and technological innovation, the existing (static) distribution of property rights may result in the over or under consumption of resources' attributes (allocative inefficiency), which in turn can be a source of significant wealth accumulation. For instance, the appropriative rights regime is well suited to private extraction of all water from a river system, resulting in significant environmental damage (Tarlock, 2000). The distribution of property rights, then, is intimately linked with the distribution of wealth and power and any change in demand for the institutions that regulate legal and economic property rights will be endogenous to the existing distribution of wealth and power. Endogeneity in demand for institutions thus gives rise to persistence of inefficient property rights regimes and/or allocation of property rights.

Property rights, relational equity and collaborative governance

The discussion of the WEF nexus literature in the background section and of key aspects of the property rights theory in economics highlight a number of features that affect collaborative governance and investment in relational equity in the WEF nexus.

Firstly, a property rights perspective highlights the productivity enhancing potential of interdependency coordination through market or non-market processes. Natural resource management is characterised by multiple stakeholders whose interests can be competing. Competing demands relate to the use of a resource for different types of economic activity, the functioning of the ecosystem, the spatial and temporal use of resources and, ultimately, the limited availability of resources. Beyond some threshold of users, the availability of resources is insufficient to satisfy the demand of all stakeholders simultaneously and/or at the same time ensure continued production of ecosystems services. This highlights an important dynamic dimension – population growth, technology and climate change all move the number of resource users beyond the threshold where disregarding interdependency becomes costly and inefficient.

Secondly, the emphasis on legal and economic rights, and their alignment, in economic property rights theory highlights the incentive structures that individual and multiple actors respond to. Natural resource management frequently involves a polycentric hierarchy of organisations, competencies and regulations (Ostrom, 2010; Challen, 2000), that separately or interdependently condition the ability to exclude others and the legitimate expectation that a claim will be respected by others. Stakeholders operate at a variety of levels and subject to a variety of decision-making rules and constraints. From higher level coordination and longer-term sharing of water resources between nation states, such as the

Amu Darya/Syr Darya river systems in Central Asia, the Mekong in South East Asia, the Rhine and Danube rivers in Europe, and the Nile and Congo rivers in Africa, to finer level daily decision coordination between farmers, industry and urban households. Decision making, coordination and governance takes place within a variety of regulatory and incentive systems that overlap imperfectly and, at times, are imperfectly implemented (Hughes, 2015). Interdependency in the polycentric management of natural resources can generate incentives for collaborative governance. However, decision making within distinct regulatory and/or institutional frameworks or in the presence of significant power imbalances can also increase incentives to defect from collaborative approaches (Ansell and Gash, 2008).

Thirdly, the residual claimancy concepts in property rights economics highlight the correlation between actions and benefits from actions. River resource management involving a hierarchy of organisations and users results in a series of nested allocation decisions (Hughes, 2015). Decisions at one level in the hierarchy affects not only the parameters of decision making at lower levels in the hierarchy, but also decision making in competing hierarchies. Similarly, resource management may involve a variety of property rights regimes. For instance, Challen (2000) aligns the different hierarchical levels of governance of the Murray Darling Basin in Australia to state property, private property, common property and open access regimes. These different property rights regimes are not simply decentralised subdivisions of property rights, but can have very different rules and conventions for the regulation of water and resource use (Hughes, 2015).

Property rights within the WEF nexus confers significant economic benefits to rights holders. Within this framework collaborative governance and relational equity are means of enhancing resource productivity and the value of property rights. Conversely a property rights perspective highlights the distribution of bundles of rights and thus incentives for benefit-enhancing action. This is particularly the case where property rights are contested, there exists considerable informational uncertainty or measurement issues or power imbalances. For instance, river systems with dam developments experience some 25 times more economic activity than unregulated river systems (Nilsson et al., 2005).

However, although measurement of economic activity is facilitated by the production of marketable outputs, measurement of true social costs, that include wider social, ecological and environmental impacts, is fraught with much uncertainty and typically not accurately costed in market prices. For instance, the example in Box 4.1, from Pittock et al. (2015), reports on the construction of a hydroelectricity reservoir in the Walawe River Basin in Sri Lanka. The costs-benefit analysis (water productivity values) conducted concluded that water used for hydropower was more productive than water used for rice production (by a ratio of 4:1), but did not incorporate significant social benefits derived from irrigation practices, resulting in a misalignment of the residual claimancy. Nevertheless, although estimates of costs are uncertain and contested the awareness and understanding of ecological and environmental impacts are increasingly reflected in governance and regulation. For instance, in Australia, the 2007 Water Act was passed by parliament. This act, at the height of a prolonged drought, effectively transferred water from agricultural use to environmental use by reducing consumptive use by 20 per cent (Hughes, 2015).

Conclusion

This chapter has provided a property rights perspective on natural resource management in the WEF nexus and exemplified key concepts by focusing on the bundle of attributes and some of the residual claimancy associated with river systems. The chapter argues that recognition of the separate and joint benefit streams generated by attributes of natural resources and the concept of residual claimancy can enhance policy development and innovation in resource management.

A property rights perspective highlights the productivity enhancing potential that specialisation and economies of scale based on attribute separation can enable. Trade in and alignment of economic and legal rights provide a means of enhancing the productivity of resources. Where property rights can be cost-effectively delineated and enforced, a property rights perspective highlights the role of markets in facilitating specialisation, economies of scale and spatial and temporal arbitrage. Increasing and competing demands on natural resources in the water-energy-food nexus further facilitate standardisation, frequency of interacting and institutional innovation to further reduce transaction costs.

Where property rights cannot be cost-effectively delineated or enforced, the mapping of residual claimancy can be instrumental in developing inclusive institutions, such as relational equity and collaborative governance approaches to manage resource use. Examples of where ambiguous property rights exist are instances where rights are contested or where property rights have emerged through different, sometimes overlaying, property rights regimes or where there is informational uncertainty and measurement issues or where there are significant power imbalances. Relational equity and collaborative governance, where effective, have the potential to enhance the value of property rights by increasing the legitimate expectation that claims will be respected by others. Moreover, a property rights mapping can here assist cross-sectoral and cross-scale coordination through relational equity and collaborative governance approaches.

A key governance and developmental insight from a property rights perspective is that a mapping of property rights can assist in identifying behavioural opportunities and constraints of the different stakeholders in the WEF nexus. The distinction between economic and legal rights and that of residual claimancy highlights not only who owns what, but also on what basis. Moreover, a property rights perspective can here engage with individuals' and organisations' understanding of "rightful" ownership. In many contexts the establishment of rule of law based regimes or the exertion of the authority of the state may in itself be insufficient to overcome barriers to sustainable management in the

WEF nexus. This will particularly be the case under heightened resource stress or scarcity. Nonetheless, more generally the basis of rights that is enshrined in the rule of law or state authority will in many societies itself be a function, or a reproduction, of property rights contestation. In many emerging and developing countries the state seeks to expand the assertion of economic and political authority *and* (at best) substitute for the absence of "independent" institutions that enables contestation and protection of property rights that have emerged through custom or are even enshrined in law/code. Under such conditions the mapping of property rights – the understanding of who benefits from what and on what basis – is instrumental in protecting the rights of minorities and in developing management and governance structures that have the ability to create consensus around use (in the absence of consensus to protection of WEF).

A mapping of property rights can thus assist in identifying misalignment between economic and legal rights as well as the residual claimancy held by different stakeholders. Such a mapping in itself does not solve resource scarcity or stress, but it does provide necessary information for understanding how the impacts of population growth, economic development and climate change affect resource users in the WEF nexus. Moreover, it does – where political and societal leadership permits – provide necessary information for addressing existing institutional biases and inequities, for instance through complementary (in some cases substitute) coordination mechanisms such as relational equity and collaborative governance approaches.

Moreover, from a process perspective a mapping of property rights can be instrumental in generating a dialogue around design and implementation of changes in resource use and open a venue for including ecological justice perspectives that can include non-human co-existence in the WEF nexus. Here a property rights mapping exercise contributes to a robust strategy for engaging stakeholders and identification of risk minimising strategies in collaborative governance arrangements. Finally, in this process prospective property rights mapping becomes an integral part of the institutional design phase and establishment of realistic timelines for engagement, development and implementation.

Notes

1 We acknowledge here an ongoing debate in the institutional economics literature as to the applicability of the terms property and rights in this context. We use the economic and legal rights throughout and in line with widespread use, but refer readers to Hodgson (2015) for an overview of the debate around those concepts.
2 Cross-scale management involves coordination of institutions across different levels of organisation (say village, local, regional and state) and across space.
3 The two doctrines also reflect the natural environment under which they were first developed, for example rain rich England (Great Britain) or New England (USA) or the arid conditions with multiple uses in the US West, riparian and appropriative, respectively. They also reflect the definition of watersheds, for example narrowly defined as the flowing water or more broadly defined as the areas feeding the flow of

water, riparian and appropriative, respectively. See Tarlock (2000) and Ostrom (2011).

4 The literature often draws a distinction between residual control and residual right to income (or cost). In this chapter, the latter approach is used. See Kim and Mahoney (2005) for a discussion.

References

Alchian, A. and Demsetz, H. (1973). "The property rights paradigm". *The Journal of Economic History*, vol 33, no 1, pp 16–27.

Allan, T., Keylertz, M. and Woertz, E. (2015). "The water-food-energy nexus: An introduction to nexus concepts and some conceptual and operational problems". *International Journal of Water Resources Development*, vol 31, no 3, pp 301–311.

Ansell, C. and Gash, A. (2008). "Collaborative governance in theory and practice". *Journal of Public Administration Research and Theory*, vol 18, no 4, pp 543–571.

Barzel, Y. (1997). *Economic Analysis of Property Rights*. 2nd edn. New York: Cambridge University Press.

Bromley, D. (1989). "Property relations and economic development: The other land reform". *World Development*, vol 17 no 6, pp 867–877.

Burness, H. and Quirk, J. (1979). "Appropriative water rights and the efficient allocation of resources". *The American Economic Review*, vol 69, no 1, pp 25–37.

Challen, R. (2000). *Institutions, Transaction Costs, and Environmental Policy: Institutional reform for water resources*. Cheltenham: Edward Elgar.

Coase, R. (1937). "The nature of the firm". *Economica*, vol 4, no 16, pp 386–405.

Coase, R. (1960). "The problem of social cost". *Journal of Law and Economics*, vol 3, pp 1–44.

Coman, K. (1911). "Some unsettled problems of irrigation". *The American Economic Review*, vol 1 no 1, pp 1–19.

Endo, A., Tsurita, I., Burnett, K. and Orencio, P. (2017). "A review of the current state of research on the water, energy, and food nexus". *Journal of Hydrology: Regional Studies*, vol 11, no 11, pp 20–30.

Hirshleifer, J., de Haven, J. and Milliman, J. (1969). *Water Supply: Economics, technology, and policy*. Chicago, IL: University of Chicago Press.

Hodgson, G. (2015). "Much of the 'economics of property rights' devalues property and legal rights". *Journal of Institutional Economics*, vol 11, no 4, pp 683–709.

Hoff, H. (2011). *Understanding the Nexus: Background paper for the Bonn 2011 Nexus Conference*. Stockholm: Stockholm Environment Institute.

Hughes, N. (2015). *Water Property Rights in Rivers with Large Dams*. PhD thesis, Australian National University, Canberra.

Kim, J. and Mahoney, J. (2005). "Property rights theory, transaction cost theory, and agency theory: An organisational economics approach to strategic management". *Managerial and Decision Economics*, vol 26, no 4, pp 223–242.

Lefebvre, M., Gangadharan, L. and Thoyer, S. (2012). "Do security-differentiated water rights improve the performance of water markets?". *American Journal of Agricultural Economics*, vol 94, no 5, pp 1113–1135.

Liu, J., Yang, C., Cudennec, C., Gain, A., Hoff, H., Lawford, R., Qi, J., de Strasser, L., Yilla, P. and Zheng, C. (2017). "Challenges in operationalising the water-energy-food nexus". *Hydrological Science Journal*, vol 62, no 11, pp 1714–1720.

Manchanayake, P. and Bandara, C.M. Madduma (1999). *Water Resource of Sri Lanka*. Colombo: National Science Foundation.

Meinzen-Dick, R. and Bakker, M. (2000). "Water rights and multiple water uses: A framework and application to Kirindi Oya irrigation system Sri Lanka". *Irrigation and Drainage Systems*, vol 15, no 2, pp 129–148.

Nilsson, C., Reidy, C., Dynesius, M. and Revenga, C. (2005). "Fragmentation and flow regulation of the world's large river systems". *Science*, vol 308, no 5720, pp 405–408.

Ostrom, E. (2010) "Beyond markets and states: Polycentric governance of complex economic systems". *The American Economic Review*, vol 100, no 3, pp 641–672.

Ostrom, E. (2011). "Reflections on 'Some unsettled problems of irrigation'". *The American Economic Review*, vol 101, no 1, pp 49–63.

Paarlberg, R. (2013). *Food Politics: What everyone needs to know*, 2nd edn. New York: Oxford University Press.

Pittock, J., Orr, S., Stevens, L., Aheeyar, M. and Smith, M. (2015). "Tackling trade-offs in the water, energy and food nexus". *Aquatic Procedia*, vol 5, pp 58–68.

Randall, A. (1981). "Property entitlements and pricing policies for a maturing water economy". *Australian Journal of Agricultural Economics*, vol 25, no 3, pp 195–220.

Rasul, G. (2016). "Managing the food, water and energy nexus for achieving the sustainable development goals in South Asia". *Environmental Development*, vol 18, pp 14–25.

Tarlock, D.A. (2000). "Reconnecting property rights to watersheds". *William and Mary Environmental Law and Policy Review*, vol 25, no 1, pp 69–112.

Wichelns, D. (2017). "The water-energy-food nexus: Is the increasing attention warranted, from a research or policy perspective?". *Environmental Science and Policy*, vol 69, pp 113–123.

5 The water-energy-food nexus in agricultural policy

Jonathan C. Cooper

Introduction

This chapter analyses the development and uptake of the water-energy-food (WEF) nexus in the particular context of agricultural policy. The chapter offers a review of literature highlighting examples of nexus thinking in agricultural policy both in the Global North and the Global South as well as at national and international levels. These examples are discussed in detail to demonstrate the effect of integrated approaches to tackling issues of sustainable food production, water management and renewable energy utilisation in agricultural policy. Detailed case studies will demonstrate how nexus thinking has developed in policy-making. The case studies highlight the work of the Department for Environment, Food and Rural Affairs (Defra) in the United Kingdom, the European Union (EU) (across various agencies) and the Food and Agriculture Organisation (FAO) of the United Nations. These three institutions have been selected in order to show examples of governance at national, continental and international levels.

Earlier research aimed to "urbanise" nexus thinking, recognising that increasing urbanisation is a key factor in WEF nexus problems due to changes in land use patterns, population distribution, infrastructure and resource flows (Artioli et al., 2017). In contrast, this chapter examines the WEF nexus from a rural perspective and investigates it in the context of agricultural policy. Although urbanisation is accelerating worldwide, rural areas continue to be the main source of water, energy and food, making a consideration of the WEF nexus in the context of agricultural policy important.

By its very nature, the WEF nexus is a transdisciplinary set of issues (Kurian, 2017) and the inadequacy of existing governance arrangements for tackling the problems posed by the nexus is recognised in the literature (see, for example, Lele et al., 2013). New concepts for the better governance of the nexus represent a growing area of recent scholarly debate (Pahl-Wostl et al., 2018). Ideas of integrative environmental governance (i.e. a range of concepts that link environmental policy with management) have been put forward as an alternative to existing structures and mechanisms (Weitz et al., 2017). One of the major problems of assessing the nexus is methodological: the use of replicable methods is uncommon, methods tend to be confined to disciplinary silos and mostly do not combine quantitative and qualitative approaches (Albrecht et al., 2018). The implications of these methodological issues manifested themselves in the criticism of the validity of nexus-related research findings. Furthermore, not all scholars agree with the importance of nexus thinking. For example, it has been argued that the increasing scholarly and public interest in the WEF nexus is not clearly warranted (Wichelns, 2017).

This chapter begins with a review of literature on nexus thinking in agricultural policy, which identifies examples from national and international governance. This is followed by a section on nexus approaches to agricultural policy, which offers three case studies. The chapter then discusses the challenges facing the integration of nexus thinking in agricultural policy and concludes by offering insights drawn from the case studies.

Nexus thinking in agricultural policy

The agricultural sector faces a broad range of sustainability challenges and a WEF nexus approach is one way of conceptualising these (Pharino, 2017). There is limited literature on examples of nexus thinking in agricultural policy due to the relative novelty of the approach. However, some examples can be found in the literature detailing conditions both in the Global North and the Global South.

In the Global North, examples of nexus thinking can be found in agricultural policy in North America and Europe. In the United States of America, the dual nexus between water and energy has been used as a tool to approach modelling the increased need for irrigation for agricultural production in the context of population increase and climate change (Schwabe et al., 2016). The tripartite WEF nexus has been used as an approach to modelling of an agricultural drought management system for the Great Plains region which is susceptible to water scarcity (Zhang, 2018). A SWOT (strengths, weaknesses, opportunities and threats) analysis of the WEF nexus has also been carried out for land stewardship in the northern Great Plains (Sieverding et al., 2016). Further studies have been carried out in Europe. For example, a study conducted in Sweden showed how spatial analysis could be integrated with WEF modelling in order to quantify the effects of drought on the irrigation requirements of specific crops as a means of providing useful information to policy-makers (Campana et al., 2018). A study conducted in Central and Eastern European countries has used a WEF nexus approach to understand agricultural vulnerability to climate change in a regional political context that influences economic and environmental policy-making in post-communist states (Kantor et al., 2017).

WEF nexus approaches have also been utilised in the Global South. For example, a study conducted in Nepal, a nation that was used as a model for mountainous landlocked countries, has called for an overarching water, energy and food policy in order to address issues, such as land scarcity for food production, poor transportation infrastructure and the integration of hydro-electric power, irrigation and potable water supply (Gurung, 2016). The relationship between climate change and the WEF nexus as key components of agricultural policy have been explored using Tanzania as a case study (Pardoe et al., 2018). The relationship between indicators of agricultural sustainability and water, energy and food poverty has been modelled in a range of Sub-Saharan African countries over a timespan of some decades (Ozturk, 2017).

Furthermore, international studies bridging the North–South divide have drawn upon case studies in Africa, China and the USA to develop a decision support tool for sustainable agriculture using a WEF nexus approach (Tian et al., 2018). This brief literature review demonstrates the range of emerging work on WEF nexus approaches to agricultural policy development both in the Global South and the Global North. The chapter now proceeds to the discussion of case studies of those institutions that are instrumental for the development of agricultural policy on national, continental and international scales.

Nexus approaches to agricultural policy: institutional case studies

This section considers three case studies of policy-making institutions that have, to some extent, attempted to integrate nexus thinking into agricultural policy. Case studies include: Defra, a ministerial department supported by various agencies in the United Kingdom; the EU across various agencies but focused on the Common Agricultural Policy; and the United Nations' FAO.

Department for Environment, Food and Rural Affairs (United Kingdom)

Agricultural policy development in the United Kingdom (UK) is dominated by the Defra, which has been operational in its present form since 2002. Its predecessor institution, the Ministry of Agriculture, Fisheries and Food, was operational for much of the twentieth century. However, agricultural policy is also developed by devolved administrations in Scotland, Wales and Northern Ireland, often with differences in political priorities. There is limited homogeneity in the agricultural sector between nations of the United Kingdom; rather, factors such as terrain, farm size, agricultural practices and products vary, so governance approaches differ. For example, concurrent but quite separate consultation processes on the future of rural/agricultural policy were conducted in each nation of the UK during 2018, following the referendum on the UK's membership in the European Union (EU) held in 2016 (Downing and Coe, 2018). The implications of these differences in political priorities are manifested in the divergent preferences for mechanisms to replace the EU Common Agricultural Policy, and such differences cannot be easily separated from wider political questions of nationalism and unionism.

The policy landscape in the UK has been made more complicated by the fact that energy policy is developed by the separate Department for Business, Energy and Industrial Strategy (and by the Department for Energy and Climate Change until 2016). In spite of these complex governance arrangements, concrete examples of nexus approaches to the development of agricultural policy in the UK have been identified. Further, the impact of the UK's exit from the EU will also be discussed in the context of the WEF nexus.

Previous studies have explored the dual land use conflict between energy generation and food production in the context of the UK agricultural sector (Cooper, 2017). Next, the tripartite WEF nexus in the context of British rural policy-making is examined.

An evidence briefing published in 2016 by the Economic Social and Research Council (ESRC) (one of the UK's major research funding bodies) points out that "there are currently no policies that provide genuinely integrated management of water, energy, food and land" (ESRC, 2016, p. 1). For example, the *UK Bioenergy Strategy* (2012) does not detail the effects of its targets on the water or food sectors; the Water Act (2014) does not refer to the energy or food sectors (ESRC, 2016). The compartmentalisation of land-use policies into mutually exclusive measures for water, energy *or* food is well known in recent and current practice (Sharmina et al., 2015). The interdependency of the nexus on different spatial and temporal scales is of great importance to the future of land-use policy (Sharmina et al., 2015). A study of barriers to decision making on the WEF nexus in the specific context of the UK concluded that transdisciplinary and interdisciplinary approaches to the co-production of knowledge are needed in order to build resilience to shocks (such as climate change), which transcends the sectorality of the current practice (Howarth and Monasterolo, 2016).

However, some evidence of nexus thinking has been identified within Defra in a report by Krzywoszynska (2015). It has been observed that:

> the Department's priorities of the UK leading the world in food and farming, protecting the country from floods and animal and plant diseases, improving the environment, and championing the countryside and improving rural services, all highlight the need for applying nexus perspectives.
>
> (Krzywoszynska, 2015, p. 2)

Thus, there is considerable scope for the wider integration of nexus thinking. A series of examples of incorporating the nexus thinking into Defra's activities has been identified in existing analytical tools and frameworks used by the Department (for example, impact assessments, the ecosystems services approach and the natural capital framework), in the evidence base used by the Department to inform its work and in the operational delivery activities of the Department (Krzywoszynska, 2015). These are complemented by the professional skills and capabilities (that exist within the Department) for utilising nexus approaches. For example, collaborative cross-sectoral working (i.e. between policy teams and with external stakeholders) is encouraged by institutional and cultural drivers within Defra and such practices are characteristic of nexus approaches (Krzywoszynska, 2015). However, nexus thinking could be significantly strengthened by the systematic application of the nexus management concept to inter-relationships between food, energy and water and to considerations of trade-offs in the course of Department's operations (Krzywoszynska, 2015).

Reform of British agricultural policy will be necessitated by the United Kingdom's exit from the EU as a result of Brexit (Helm, 2016, 2017). Models have been developed in order to forecast the impact of Brexit on the WEF nexus, depending upon the nature of that departure, using a fuzzy cognitive mapping approach (Ziv et al., 2018). Although consideration of the future implications of Brexit is beyond the chapter's scope, the end of the Common Agricultural Policy (CAP) in the UK and the formulation of new policy to replace it represent a significant opportunity for the integration of WEF nexus thinking in future British agricultural policy.

The European Union

Various agencies of the EU are responsible for water, energy and food in relation to agricultural policy in the member states. However, the CAP is the principal driving force for agriculture across the EU. Indeed, the CAP was created by the Treaty of Rome, which established the European Economic Community, the precursor of the EU, in 1957.

It has been observed that "in the European Union, given its multilevel governance (MLG) system, the decision competences in the nexus sectors rest on different levels among the European Commission, national governments as well as regional or local authorities" (Venghaus and Hake, 2018, p. 183). This confirms that the complexity of the institutional framework is a major issue for the integration of nexus thinking in EU policy development and implementation differs widely between member states.

The EU Renewable Energy Directive (2009) requires that 20 per cent of energy consumed should be generated by renewable sources and 10 per cent of fuel used for transportation should be renewable biofuels by 2020 – largely in order to limit the growth of greenhouse gas emissions. It has long been recognised that such a policy could cause a dual land use conflict between energy generation and food production, especially in the case of transport biofuels many of which require food crops as a raw material (Summa, 2007). However, the European Commission concluded that this target could be reached without creating "major tensions" between these competing uses of land (Summa, 2007, p. 2).

More recently, the tripartite WEF nexus has been examined on a European level through the quantitative and qualitative analyses of more than 50 policy documents dealing with nexus-relevant sectors, such as agriculture, energy and water. Notable examples included the Common Agricultural Policy, the EU Energy Strategy and the Water Framework Directive (WFD) (Venghaus and Hake, 2018). The results of this study indicate that the term *nexus* itself was used in only one such EU policy document; however, this was in the context of international development beyond the EU (Venghaus and Hake, 2018).

Nevertheless, there are examples of nexus thinking in EU policy even though the term is not used explicitly. For instance, *Roadmap to a Resource Efficient Europe* (European Commission, 2011) is concerned with interdependencies between water, energy and food resources (Venghaus and Hake, 2018). As well as identifying examples of the tripartite nexus in policy, this study also identifies examples of a dual nexus between sectors: water–agriculture, water–energy and agriculture–energy (Venghaus and Hake, 2018).

Although the integration of nexus thinking in policy has proven to be complicated across the EU, complexity increases in organisations with a truly global reach, such as the United Nations.

Food and Agriculture Organisation (the United Nations)

FAO is the principal organisation through which the United Nations (UN) develops international agricultural and rural policy. The WEF nexus was identified by FAO as "a new approach in support of food security and sustainable agriculture" through internal collaboration between its Land and Water Division and its Climate, Energy and Tenure Division (FAO, 2014, p. 1). This represents an example of the interdisciplinary co-production of knowledge, which is integral to nexus thinking itself. This collaborative document identifies the added value that nexus thinking brings to the achievement of institutional aims. It frames the nexus within the broader debate on sustainable development and, crucially, identifies FAO operational areas in which nexus thinking is beneficial (FAO, 2014). These complementary working areas include: evidence, scenario development and response options (FAO, 2014). Evidence includes the various data, such as from earth observation or other indicators, required to assess nexus interaction; scenario development includes the review of strategies, policies and investment decisions for the improved understanding of nexus interrelations; and response options include the planning of an implementation of interventions (such as policies, regulations, investments and incentives) and the evaluation of their impact (FAO, 2014).

The institution itself notes that "underlying the Water-Energy-Food Nexus approach of FAO is a holistic vision of sustainability that recognises and tries to strike balance between the different goals, interests and needs of people and the environment" (FAO, 2014, p. 8).

In addition to demonstrating the significance and value of the WEF nexus within its own operations, FAO has engaged with the broader development of nexus thinking. For example, FAO has proposed a new approach to carrying out WEF nexus assessment – in the particular context of the *Sustainable Energy for All* initiative, a UN global network of stakeholders (Flammini et al., 2014). This assessment approach uses a set of indicators selected based on internationally available datasets and combines quantitative and qualitative assessment methods (Flammini et al., 2014). Furthermore, FAO commissioned the Renewable Energy and Energy Efficiency Partnership to conduct analysis of several agri-food businesses, which specifically addresses the WEF nexus in their operations; case studies of several large multi-national firms were developed (Zahner, 2014).

FAO is not the only international institution that has engaged in the WEF nexus in the context of agricultural policy development. For example, the International Institute for Sustainable Development produced a guidebook on the WEF nexus in agricultural investment, which provides a practical framework for the design and management of land investments that deliver increased water, energy and food security (Bizikova et al., 2014).

Discussion

Through examination of these three case studies that illustrate nexus approaches to agricultural policy in national, continental and international institutions the varying degrees of success in this approach can be compared between these organisations. First, in a national context, although there are no policies which explicitly integrate the management of water, energy and food in the UK, there are concrete examples of nexus thinking in Defra. For example, the integration of nexus thinking into Defra's activities has been identified in existing analytical tools and frameworks used by the Department, in the evidence base used by this Department to inform its work and in the operational delivery activities of the Department. These are complemented by the professional skills and capabilities for utilising nexus approaches, which exist in the Department, such as collaborative cross-sectoral working encouraged by internal institutional and cultural drivers. Defra's nexus-related activities could be classified as an example of relational equity management as this state actor engages with external stakeholders in delivering its core services (Sawhney and Zabin, 2002). Such activities may even go some way towards representing true collaborative governance where non-state stakeholders are engaged in collective decision-making (Ansell and Gash, 2008).

Second, in a continental context, various EU agencies are responsible for water, energy and food in relation to agricultural policy in member states and the complexity of the multilevel governance system is a major issue for the integration of nexus thinking in EU policy development, whilst implementation differs between member states. Although there is very limited use of the term "nexus" in EU policy, there are nevertheless examples of nexus thinking in European policy. There is little evidence to suggest that relational equity management or collaborative governance approaches are used consistently in the EU agricultural policy.

Third, in an international context, FAO identified the WEF nexus as a novel approach in support of its core activities. The nexus approach is used by FAO departments to achieve interdisciplinary co-production of knowledge, which is integral to nexus thinking itself. In addition to defining its own internal FAO WEF nexus approach and demonstrating the significance and value of the nexus within its own operations, FAO has engaged with the broader development of nexus thinking by commissioning new nexus assessment approaches and nexus analyses. It is difficult to frame FAO's approach to the integration of the WEF nexus in agricultural policy in terms of relational equity management or collaborative governance as FAO is not a state actor in the traditional sense but, rather, one agency of an international organisation.

One of the significant enabling factors – common between Defra and FAO – for the successful integration of nexus thinking in agricultural policy at national and international levels is the co-production of knowledge via transdisciplinary and interdisciplinary approaches. Defra encourages such collaborative cross-sectoral working between policy teams and with external stakeholders via internal institutional and cultural drivers. FAO identifies the WEF nexus as a new approach through internal collaboration between its Land and Water Division and its Climate, Energy and Tenure Division. Transdisciplinary and interdisciplinary approaches to the co-production of knowledge, which transcend the sectorality of current practice, have previously been identified as a requirement for decision-making around the nexus (Howarth and Monasterolo, 2016). To some extent at least, Defra and FAO have enabled the integration of nexus thinking in agricultural policy by demonstrating such knowledge production across and between disciplines.

One of the barriers to the successful integration of the nexus approach to agricultural policy on a continental level is the complexity of the multilevel governance system that exists with inter-relationships between pan-European institutions, national governments and regional and local authorities. The implications of integrating nexus thinking at national and international levels remain to be seen as the evidence for the adoption of a nexus approach in Defra and FAO detailed above has come to the fore only in the past few years.

Conclusion

This chapter has presented a review of literature on nexus thinking in agricultural policy identifying examples from governance in the Global North and the Global South. Nexus approaches to agricultural policy have been illustrated by three case studies of national, continental and international institutions: Defra, the EU and FAO. The adopted case study approach is somewhat limited as there is a dearth of relevant information upon which to base analyses of the nexus approach in each institution. This has resulted in inconsistencies in the aspects considered in each case study and therefore restricted comparison between them. The varying degrees of success in the integration of nexus thinking in agricultural policy by these organisations have been discussed in terms of relational equity management and collaborative governance. National and international examples, Defra and FAO, have been found to demonstrate some success in the integration of nexus thinking in their core activities related to agricultural policy-making. The continental example, in the form of the EU, demonstrated limited instances of nexus thinking in European policy whilst the term is not used explicitly; however, the complexity of the multilevel governance system in the EU is a barrier. The co-production of knowledge via transdisciplinary and interdisciplinary approaches has been identified as a significant enabling factor for the successful integration of nexus thinking in agricultural policy at national and international levels.

References

Albrecht, T.R., Crootof, A. and Scott, C.A. (2018). "The water-energy-food nexus: A systematic review of methods for nexus assessment". *Environmental Research Letters*, vol 13, no. 4, 043002. doi:10.1088/1748-9326/aaa9c6.

Ansell, C. and Gash, A. (2008). "Collaborative governance in theory and practice". *Journal of Public Administration Research and Theory*, vol 18, no 4, pp 543–571. doi:10.1093/jopart/mum032.

Artioli, F., Acuto, M. and Mcarthur, J. (2017). "The water-energy-food nexus: An integration agenda and implications for urban governance". *Political Geography*, vol 61, pp 215–223. doi:10.1016/j.polgeo.2017.08.009.

Bizikova, L., Roy, D., Venema, H.D. and McCandless, M. (2014). *The Water-Energy-Food Nexus and Agricultural Investment: A sustainable development guidebook.* Winnipeg: International Institute for Sustainable Development.

Campana, P.E., Zhang, J., Yao, T., Andersson, S., Landelius, T., Melton, F. and Yan, J. (2018). "Managing agricultural drought in Sweden using a novel spatially-explicit model from the perspective of water-food-energy nexus". *Journal of Cleaner Production*, vol 197, part 1, pp 1382–1393. doi:10.1016/j.jclepro.2018.06.096.

Cooper, J.C. (2017). "Rural land use in conflict? Energy and food in the UK". In J. Eastham et al. (eds) *Contemporary Issues in Food Supply Chain Management.* Oxford: Goodfellow.

Downing, E. and Coe, S. (2018). *Brexit: Future UK agriculture policy.* Briefing Paper No. CBP 8218. London: House of Commons Library.

ESRC (2016). *Integrating Water, Energy and Food in Land Management.* Evidence Briefing. Swindon: Economic & Social Research Council.

European Commission (2011). *Roadmap to a Resource Efficient Europe.* COM (2011) 571. Luxembourg: Office for Official Publications of the European Communities.

FAO (2014) *The Water-Energy-Food Nexus: A new approach in support of food security and sustainable agriculture.* Rome: Food and Agriculture Organization of the United Nations.

Flammini, A., Puri, M., Pluschke, L. and Dubois, O. (2014). *Walking the Nexus Talk: Assessing the water-energy-food nexus in the context of the sustainable energy for all initiative.* Environment and Natural Resources Management Working Paper 58. Rome: Food and Agriculture Organization of the United Nations.

Gurung, T.B. (2016). "Enabling water-energy-food nexus: A new approach for sustainable agriculture and food security in mountainous landlocked countries". *Journal of Nepal Agricultural Research Council*, vol 2, pp 46–50.

Helm, D. (2016). *British Agricultural Policy after BREXIT.* Natural Capital Network Paper 5. London: Chartered Institution of Water and Environmental Management.

Helm, D. (2017). "Agriculture after Brexit". *Oxford Review of Economic Policy*, vol 33 (S1), pp S124–S133.

Howarth, C. and Monasterolo, I. (2016). "Understanding barriers to decision making in the UK energy-food-water nexus: The added value of interdisciplinary approaches". *Environmental Science & Policy*, vol 61, pp 53–60.

Kantor, C., McLean, E. and Kantor, M. (2017). "Climate change influence on agriculture and the water-energy-food nexus in Central and Eastern European countries". *Notulae Scientia Biologicae*, vol 9, no 4, pp 449–459.

Krzywoszynska, A. (2015). *Nexus Approaches at Defra*. Defra Fellowship Report. Brighton: The Nexus Network, University of Sussex.

Kurian, M. (2017). "The water-energy-food nexus: Trade-offs, thresholds and transdisciplinary approaches to sustainable development". *Environmental Science & Policy*, vol 68, pp 97–106.

Lele, U., Klousia-Marquis, M. and Goswami, S. (2013). "Good governance for food, water and energy security". *Aquatic Procedia*, vol 1, pp 44–63.

Ozturk, I. (2017). "The dynamic relationship between agricultural sustainability and food-energy-water poverty in a panel of selected Sub-Saharan African countries". *Energy Policy*, vol 107, pp 289–299.

Pahl-Wostl, C., Bhaduri, A. and Bruns, A. (2018.) "Editorial special issue: The nexus of water, energy and food – An environmental governance perspective". *Environmental Science and Policy*, vol 90, pp 161–163.

Pardoe, J., Conway, D., Namaganda, E., Vincent, K., Dougill, A.J. and Kashaigili, J.J. (2018)."Climate change and the water-energy-food nexus: Insights from policy and practice in Tanzania". *Climate Policy*, vol 18, no 7, pp 863–877.

Pharino, C. (2017). "Sustainable challenges in the agrofood sector: The environment food energy-water nexus". In R. Bhat (ed.) *Sustainability Challenges in the Agrofood Sector*. Chichester: Wiley.

Sawhney, M. and Zabin, J. (2002). "Managing and measuring relational equity in the network economy". *Journal of the Academy of Marketing Science*, vol 30, no 4, pp 313–332.

Schwabe, K., Knapp, K. and Luviano, I. (2016). "The water-energy nexus and irrigated agriculture in the United States: Trends and analyses". In J.R. Ziolkowska and J.M. Peterson (eds) *Competition for Water Resources: Experiences and management approaches in the US and Europe*. Oxford: Elsevier.

Sharmina, M., Hoolohan, C., Bows-Larkin, A., Burgess, P., Colwill, J., Gilbert, P., Howard, D., Knox, J. and Anderson, K. (2015). *The Nexus in a Changing Climate: A critique of competing demands for UK land*. Think Piece Series Paper 009. Brighton: The Nexus Network, University of Sussex.

Sieverding, H.L., Clay, D.E., Khan, E., Sivaguru, J., Pattabiraman, M., Koodali, R.T., Ndiva-Mongoh, M. and Stone, J.J. (2016). "A sustainable rural food-energy-water nexus framework for the northern Great Plains". *Agricultural & Environmental Letters*, vol 1, pp 1–4.

Summa, H. (2007). *Energy Crops and the Common Agricultural Policy*. Brussels: European Commission.

Tian, H., Lu, C., Pan, S., Yang, J., Miao, R., Ren, W., Yu, Q., Fu, B., Jin, F-F., Lu, Y., Melillo, J., Ouyang, Z., Palm, C. and Reilly, J. (2018). "Optimizing resource use efficiencies in the food-energy-water nexus for sustainable agriculture: From conceptual model to decision support system". *Current Opinion in Environmental Sustainability*, vol 33, pp 104–113.

Venghaus, S. and Hake, J-F. (2018). "Nexus thinking in current EU policies – The interdependencies among food, energy and water resources". *Environmental Science and Policy*, vol 90, pp 183–192.

Weitz, N., Strambo, C., Kemp-Benedict, E. and Nilsson, M. (2017) "Closing the governance gaps in the water-energy-food nexus: Insights from integrative governance". *Global Environmental Change*, vol 45, pp 165–173.

Wichelns, D. (2017). "The water-energy-food nexus: Is the increasing attention warranted, from either a research or policy perspective?". *Environmental Science & Policy*, vol 69, pp 113–123.

Zahner, A. (2014). *How Agrifood Firms are Building New Business Cases in the Water Energy-Food Nexus*. Vienna / Rome: Renewable Energy & Energy Efficiency Partnership / Food and Agriculture Organization of the United Nations.

Zhang, J. (2018). "The water-food-energy nexus optimization approach to combat agricultural drought: A case study in the United States". *Applied Energy*, vol 227, pp 449–464.

Ziv, G., Watson, E., Young, D., Howard, D.C., Larcom, S.T. and Tanentzap, A.J. (2018). "The potential impact of Brexit on the energy, water and food nexus in the UK: A fuzzy cognitive mapping approach". *Applied Energy*, vol 210, pp 487–498.

Part II
The nexus in practice

6 Water-energy-food nexus and human security in northwestern Kenya

Jeremiah Ogonda Asaka

Introduction

Resources on water-energy-food (WEF) nexus research can be traced back to the 1980s (United Nations University, 2019). Its most critical contribution being in nuancing our understanding of the causes and impacts of resource extraction and/or utilisation particularly in a globalising world and in providing modelling tools that enable us to capture and analyse the linkages and interdependencies between different resources as is the case with the WEF nexus. Since the idea of the WEF nexus was first introduced, its conceptualisation has dynamically evolved with new studies providing novel insight(s) and/or perspective(s) on existing phenomena such as the resource curse.

This chapter is based on an acknowledgement of the dynamism in WEF nexus research and sits at the intersection of research on the WEF nexus, the impact of climate on it and, in turn, the WEF nexus's impact on security. In the context of this chapter the term "security" refers to "human security" which is understood as freedom from fear, freedom from want and freedom to live with dignity (Annan, 2005). The chapter discusses WEF nexus governance in relation to human security sharing the understanding of collaborative governance and relational equity management with that adopted by the editors of this collection and outlined by Sawhney and Zabin (2002) and Ansell and Gash (2008).

This chapter's geographical focus is on northwestern Kenya, which forms part of the Karamoja cluster – a transboundary conflict-prone region located between the borders of Kenya, Uganda and South Sudan (Simonse, 2011). In this region human security is not only very much dependent on the availability of, and access to, resources, such as water, energy, food and pastureland, but also on the prevailing climatic conditions. The chapter discusses the WEF nexus in the case of northwestern Kenya and, within it, Turkana County. Both cases highlight the critical importance of nexus based thinking in designing and implementing policies for the WEF sectors. The cases also draw attention to the inter-relationships between threats to the WEF sectors and associated governance challenges, and the governance of human security. Finally, they bring to fore the impediments to effective WEF nexus governance and human security stemming from a State-centric and unidimensional – only relating to violent conflict – conceptualisation of security.

The chapter draws on field data, including interviews and participant observation, collected in 2013 and 2016, and on review of the literature. The selection of key interviewees and case studies was purposeful. Interview transcripts were qualitatively analysed based on themes identified through the literature review and emerging from the analysis of primary data.

Following the introduction, the chapter discusses the concept of human security and the inter-relations between human security and challenges to the governance of the WEF nexus. Using the case of northwestern Kenya, the impact of land use changes, climate variability and climate change, and the discovery of new water and energy resources on local communities is described. In addition, the discovery of oil in Turkana County – within the larger area of northwestern Kenya – and its impact on local communities are outlined. This is followed by a critical discussion of these cases through the lens of collaborative governance, enhanced by effective relational equity management. The chapter concludes by considering implications for the effective governance of the WEF nexus as well as for human security in northwestern Kenya.

Conceptualising the WEF nexus in the context of human security

Defining human security

Security can be understood from a variety of perspectives (Williams and McDonald, 2018). There is a long-standing debate on what security means and how it should be achieved (see e.g. Owen, 2004; Newman, 2010; Gjørv, 2012; Williams and McDonald, 2018). Usually at the centre of this debate there are three key concerns: security for whom, security from what and security by whom. Sharing a people-centred conceptualisation of security, this chapter adopts an understanding of security underpinned by the following premises: (1) for security to be relatable to the human experience it has to be centred on people and not the State; (2) security threats are not limited to violence and war; and (3) the responsibility for ensuring security should not be exclusively the privilege of the State, but a collaborative effort involving multiple, State and non-State, actors.

These are the main principles of what is currently termed "human security". The first succinct conceptualisation and coherent articulation of human security is found in the United Nations Development Programme (UNDP) Human Development Report 1994. Human security was then understood in terms of freedom from fear and freedom from want and dates back to the founding days of the United Nations (UN) in 1945 (UNDP, 1994). In 2005, Kofi Annan, then Secretary General of the UN, defined human security as freedom from fear, freedom from want *and* freedom to live with dignity (Annan, 2005). Human security is therefore not simply a concern regarding the protection of human life from threats to its core but also regarding the empowerment of people so that they can contribute to their own protection. Although this is not a universally accepted definition of security, it is widely accepted and used by both scholars and practitioners worldwide. This chapter adopts this definition as the basis of its understanding of security.

It is worth emphasising that human security shifts the referent object of security from State to people understood either as individuals or communities (MacFarlane, 2004), acknowledging that a State-centric conceptualisation fails to capture the breadth and variety of threats to human life. The conceptualisation of human security in the 1990s grouped human security threats into seven dimensions of human security, including food security, economic security, health security, environmental security, personal security, community security and political security (UNDP, 1994). Table 6.1 provides a brief overview of what each dimension entails. These dimensions remain useful for the in-depth analysis of human security.

Table 6.1 Overview of human security dimensions

Security Dimension	Details
Food security	Food security refers to "a situation that exists when all people, at all times, have physical, social and economic access to sufficient, safe and nutritious food that meets their dietary needs and food preferences for an active and healthy life" (FAO, 2001, p. 49). In most developing countries, such as Kenya, "food insecurity and poverty are twin concerns, as lack of food security causes poverty, and any efforts directed towards eradicating poverty positively affect food security" (Oluoko-Odingo 2011, p. 2).
Economic security	Conventionally, economic security relates to access to stable and dignified employment and income. According to the UNDP (1994, p. 25): "economic security requires assured basic income – usually from productive and remunerative work, or in the last resort from some publicly financed safety net". It should however be noted that the traditional narrow focus of economic security means that a considerable proportion of the world's population engaged in productive but non-remunerative work is not accounted for in economic security analyses. In view of this, economic security, particularly in economies that are not well-integrated into the international monetary economy (as, for example, some communities in northwestern Kenya), should be understood as livelihood security.
Health security	Health security is concerned with disease as a threat to human life. UNDP (1994, p. 27) notes that: "in the developing countries, the major causes of death are infectious and parasitic diseases while in industrial countries the major killers are diseases of the circulatory system".
Environmental security	The environment can be a source of both human security and human insecurity (Homer-Dixon, 1999; Carius et al., 2004; UNEP, 2004; Ali, 2007; UNEP, 2009; Floyd and Mathew, 2013; Adger et al., 2014). It provides ecological services, which are critical for the survival of all forms of life including human life. Meanwhile, air pollution, land degradation, deforestation, biodiversity loss, and natural disasters such as drought and hurricanes are all aspects of the environment that contribute to human insecurity.

Security Dimension	Details
Personal security	According to the UNDP (1994), personal security means protection of human life from the threat of physical violence. In poor and rich countries "human life is increasingly threatened by sudden, unpredictable violence and ... the threats take several forms namely: threats from the State (physical torture); threats from other States (war); threats from other groups of people (ethnic tension); threats from individuals or gangs against other individuals or gangs (crime, street violence); threats directed at children based on their vulnerability and dependence (child abuse); and, threats to self (suicide, drug use)" (UNDP, 1994, p. 30).
Community security	Community security is premised on the fact that community – a group of people who share a common cultural identity and/or ancestry – can be a source of both security and insecurity. For example, "the extended family system offers protection to its weaker members and many tribal societies work on the principle that heads of households are entitled to enough land to support their family" (UNDP, 1994, p. 31). Conversely, inter-ethnic mistrust, tension and rivalry often lead to deadly violent conflict as is commonly the case in the Karamoja cluster, northwestern Kenya (Simonse, 2011). Moreover, communities have suffered insecurity – such as slavery and State led violation of the rights of indigenous people – by the mere fact of their common identity.
Political security	Human security is premised on respect for human rights: "one of the most important aspects of human security is that people should live in a society that honours their basic human rights" (UNDP, 1994, p. 32). Therefore, political security can be understood as freedom from politcal witchhunt, political detention, political marginalisation, torture and extra-judicial killing among other forms of human rights violations. It also means freedom of speech, right to information and freedom to participate unhindered in the political process of one's country.

Source: Compiled by the author.

The WEF nexus in the context of human security

Human security should not be confused with or misconstrued as activities promoting human development. Due to the conceptualisation originally offered by the UNDP, human security is closely related to human development; while human development is concerned with widening people's choices, human security is concerned with people being able to exercise the choices available to them "safely and freely" (UNDP, 1994, p. 23). In that context, there is a close interrelation between WEF nexus considerations and human security. Considering the seven dimensions of security, food security is directly linked to and affected by challenges to the WEF nexus. This is also the case with environmental security. Meanwhile, economic security, by impacting on an individual's livelihood, could be the root cause of WEF nexus challenges. Finally, personal (in)security, community (in)security and political (in)security could preclude the adoption or impede the application of a collaborative governance approach, enhanced by effective relational equity management, in addressing WEF nexus challenges.

In deciding on the nodes of the resource nexus to use in analysing resource interrelations, synergies and trade-offs, it is critical for the selected nexus nodes to capture all key aspects of the context evaluated, enhancing the adopted nexus's analytical utility and nuancing the understanding we gain from its application. For instance, Andrews-Speed et al. (2015) made the case for a five-node nexus comprising land, energy, water, food and minerals for the analysis of global resource challenges and the governance challenges and opportunities they present. Whereas a five-node nexus might appear more comprehensive than a three- or four-node one, its contextual realism in relation to a specific area and/or set of circumstances might limit its utility.

This edited collection is premised on the three-node WEF nexus. In this chapter, the WEF nexus has been adopted for the analysis of resource challenges and their effective governance in the context of northwestern Kenya. In addition, land use governance has been acknowledged and considered as a supplementary dimension impacting on the effective governance of the nexus in the region.

The case of northwestern Kenya

The northwestern region of Kenya falls under the country's arid and semi-arid lands (ASALs). Administratively, the region falls under seven counties, namely Samburu, West Pokot, Turkana, Laikipia, Isiolo, Marsabit and Baringo. Geographically, this chapter considers northwestern Kenya as the region that is located: (1) completely inside the Turkana County and West Pokot County boundaries; (2) partially inside Baringo County's northern tip; and (3) partially inside Samburu County, along its western border.

Northwestern Kenya is home to at least three major pastoralist communities, namely the Samburu, the Pokot and the Turkana, with pastoralism being the main economic activity in the region and the main source of livelihood and/or lifeline for most people living in it. Pastoralism in its nomadic form prevails, although agro-pastoralism is also common. Whereas nomadic pastoralists move with their livestock periodically in search of pasture and water, agro-pastoralists are generally settled, practice crop farming and do not move with their livestock. Instead, they herd and water their livestock during the day and return them home in the evening. Livestock mobility in both cases is very much linked to seasonal climatic variations, which influence the inconsistent spatial distribution of forage and water across the vast region (Galvin, 2009; Asaka and Smucker, 2016). For instance, rainfall in Samburu County and drought in West Pokot County may cause Pokot pastoralists to move their livestock to Samburu

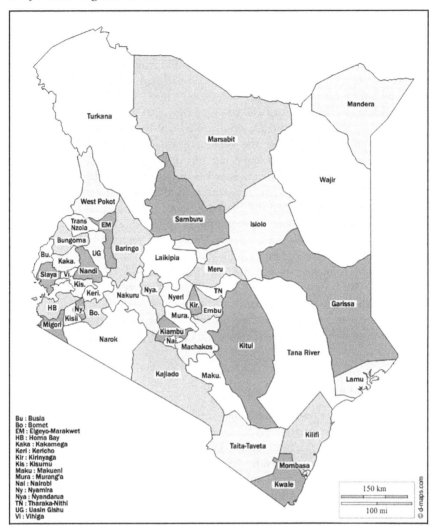

Figure 6.1 Map of Kenya
Source: https://d-maps.com/carte.php?num_car=35033&lang=en.

County in search of pasture and water and vice versa. For the pastoralist communities of northwestern Kenya, the availability of water and pastureland is
key to survival. Livestock mobility occasioned by the search for these resources
often brings communities together. However, in northwestern Kenya, competition for resources, instead of cooperation often leads to violent conflict between
the communities involved (Asaka and Smucker, 2016).

Inter-ethnic violent conflict is a common phenomenon in the region, generated by a variety of factors best viewed as feeding each other. These
include land use change, climate variability and climate change, and resource

competition, as well as cattle rustling, proliferation of small arms, *moran* (warrior) culture and political incitement among other things (Mkutu, 2002, 2007; Schilling et al., 2012; Opiyo et al., 2012; Njiru, 2012; Daher et al., 2018). The impact of land use change, of climate variability and climate change, and of the discovery of new water and energy resources will be discussed in the following sub-sections within the context of the effective governance of the WEF nexus.

The impact of land use change

With pastoralism as the main source of livelihood in the region and, hence, with its critical importance of water and pastureland for the local communities, land use change has had a significant, negative, impact in the area. In the recent past, land use change has manifested itself through the emergence and spread of private and community conservancies. Wildlife conservation as a land use type practised through these conservancies has been swiftly developing and competes with livestock raising through pastoralism for access to finite land and water (Asaka, 2018). For example, in the Samburu area pastureland for live-stock is rapidly being converted to land for wildlife conservation with serious implications for the local communities, as the following excerpts affirm:

The areas where these [wildlife] conservancies and [tourist] lodges are located used to be community grazing land. But now the community is not allowed to graze their livestock on the land any more. Meaning they have to look for grazing land elsewhere. For example, if you go to the expansive Sera[1] conservancy, about 120 square kilometres has been fenced off for rhino conservation. So (in) that area, no grazing (is allowed). The impact of such a structure in this area is big. Because, for one, these structures are located in prime areas where water is accessible and pasture available. Even the location of [tourist] lodges is always at a spring, river ... Prime areas. Then the community is left with less desirable places that barely support their livelihood.

(Interviewee 23, 26 July 2016)

Previously, we used to live and graze our livestock freely with the exception of [Samburu] national reserve that has always been restricted. But now you have restrictions even on land that we accessed freely before the con-servancies were established. And such restriction is on large pieces of land, in some cases running into thousands of hectares. [...] my concern is with the pace and scale of change. It would have been ok if change was gradual. But here is (the) case where my access to [prime] grazing land is being restricted. The alternative livelihood [tourism] I am being told to adopt is not thriving. And corruption is also creeping in. There is nothing I am gaining. That is where it becomes challenging.

(Interviewee 1, 22 June 2016)

As these excerpts show, the land use change has led to increasingly diminishing access to previously available water and pastureland, impacting negatively on the livelihood of local communities. Furthermore, considering the low returns from tourism relative to pastoralism, the proposed alternative source of livelihood appears non-viable. The situation is further compounded by an apparent lack of trust between local communities and those designing and implementing the policy. This is owing to perceived corruption, as evidenced by the study's participants. In essence, the new land use type negatively affects the pre-existing land use type without counterbalancing benefits leading those affected to either resist such a change or seek better alternatives. In the case of northwestern Kenya, both strategies are evident (see e.g. Cruise and van der Zee, 2017; Munyeki, 2017; Ngirachu, 2017).

The impact of climate variability and climate change

Climatic variability has already been negatively affecting pastoral communities in parts of Kenya through increased unpredictability and intensity of rainfall and drought (Galvin, 2009). Specifically in northwestern Kenya, with communities highly dependent on pastoralism, climate variability has been negatively impacting on human security, threatening food and, in particular, water security (Schilling et al., 2015) and forcing pastoralists to move into new areas thereby increasing the likelihood of conflict.

Conflict between pastoralist groups in northwestern Kenya increases significantly in the periods following prolonged drought as pastoralists seek to restock (Schilling et al., 2012). In their study of motives for cattle raiding among the Turkana and Pokot, Schilling et al. (2012) found that hunger and drought were key motives among the Turkana, while payment of dowry and accumulation of wealth were the most important motives among the Pokot. In addition, the likelihood of violent conflict between pastoralist groups and private landowners in the region is directly proportional to the severity and length of a drought. Private landowners occupy areas that are more favourably located in terms of pasture availability and water accessibility relative to the areas inhabited by pastoralists. In times of prolonged drought and in the absence of resource sharing arrangements between private landowners and pastoralists, the pastoralists drive their livestock into private lands in search of water and pasture, increasing the likelihood of conflict.

Climate change acts as a threat multiplier as it further compounds the governance challenges of the food and water sectors by adding to the complexity of the already multifaceted causal mechanisms of human insecurity and the emergence of conflict (Opiyo et al., 2012). It undermines livelihoods, compromises culture and individual identity, increases migration that people would rather have avoided, and undermines the ability of States to provide the conditions necessary for human security (Adger et al., 2014). For example, in Samburu, a complex interplay of factors such as climate variability – exacerbated by climate change, resource competition and land-use change – have contributed to threats to people's access to food and water. In turn these threats, together with political incitement, have in the recent past led to periodic and deadly violent conflicts (see Cruise and van der Zee, 2017; Munyeki, 2017; Ngirachu, 2017).

The impact of new discoveries of water and energy resources

Emerging energy resources, such as the Lake Turkana Wind project in Marsabit County and the recently discovered oil in Turkana County, and water resources – notably, an underground water reservoir in Turkana County – add to the already complex interplay between the WEF nexus and human security in the region (Fong, 2015; Johannes et al., 2015). Oil and water can lead to cooperation, but both also have potential for conflict (Carius et al., 2004; Schilling et al., 2015). In the case of northwestern Kenya, as noted by Daher et al. (2018, p. 62):

> it remains unclear how the entry of these new resources will shape the human security landscape in northwestern Kenya and the Karamoja cluster, and across the greater horn of Africa region. Energy and water are already emerging as frontiers for potential conflict, primarily at the sub-national level (e.g. the case of Turkana oil exploration project), and cooperation, primarily at the international level (e.g. the energy sharing pact between Kenya and Ethiopia).
>
> (Fong, 2015)

The Turkana County oil discovery

Turkana is one of the 47 counties of Kenya, within northwestern Kenya which forms the Kenyan portion of the Karamoja cluster – a transboundary conflict-prone region located between the borders of Kenya, Uganda and South Sudan (formerly Sudan) (Simonse, 2011). The county is primarily home to the Turkana people – a marginalised Kenyan nomadic pastoralist ethnic group. Notably, the Ilemi Triangle, a disputed region claimed by three States namely Kenya, South Sudan and Ethiopia, is within Turkana County (Mburu, 2002; Amutabi, 2010). Mburu (2002, p. 17) describes the Ilemi Triangle as the "home for ethno-linguistic communities; the Turkana, Didinga, Toposa, Inyangatom, and Dassanech, who are members of the larger ethno cultural groups of Ethiopia, Kenya, Uganda and Sudan, but traditionally migrate to graze in the triangle". Kenya has a de facto control over the Ilemi Triangle. Importantly, resource related violent conflict and threats to food and water accessibility are defining characteristics of the human life experience in the County.

Turkana falls under parts of Kenya that have historically been marginalised with regards to public service provision. The remoteness of the place from the capital, its harsh climatic conditions, tough terrain and historical factors among others have been blamed for the region's marginalisation at least up until 2010 when Kenya adopted a devolved government system, which created Turkana County.

Similarly to the rest of northwestern Kenya, Turkana has long grappled with challenges regarding food and water accessibility as well as inter-ethnic conflict and disease, negatively affecting human security in the County. Turkana's insecurity is mostly driven by lack of resources, but also stems from socio-cultural and political factors (Mkutu and Wandera, 2013). There are at least four contributing sources of conflict: environmental stressors, border disputes in the Ilemi Triangle, damming of the main tributaries of Lake Turkana, and discovery of oil (Johannes, Zulu and Kalipeni, 2015). All present particular challenges for the governance of the WEF nexus and, by extension, threats to human security.

Tullow Oil has been prospecting for oil in Kenya since 2010, and, in March 2012, discovered oil in Turkana County (Tullow Oil, 2012). Since the oil discovery, a number of studies have been conducted on the potential implications of the oil find. For instance, Mkutu (2014) argued that if the oil find is not handled well it may worsen existing inter-communal conflicts and potentially trigger a new one, especially due to forced displacement of communities without compensation. In a related study, Johannes et al. (2015, p. 162) concluded that: "The resource curse is not inevitable. However, the early lack of transparency is a source of mistrust, affirms local fears, and is a potent sign that the oil project in Turkana may have gotten off on the wrong foot." Furthermore, they advise that the Kenyan government should resolve existing conflicts and ensure sustainable security through the establishment of robust conflict management and resolution institutions before venturing into the extraction of oil (Johannes et al., 2015). Schilling and others also posited that unmet community expectations present a key pathway through which the discovery of oil may bring more misery than good to the area (Schilling et al., 2015).

In June 2018, Kenya became the first East African country to join the ranks of oil producers and exporters (Kiplang'at, 2018). In July 2018, however, Tullow Oil suspended its operations in Turkana following weeks of protests from the local Turkana people.

This was not the first time Tullow Oil had to suspend its operations due to protests. In 2013, operations were briefly halted and Tullow Oil staff were withdrawn from the site following disputes over land rights with the Turkana people (see Mkutu, 2014). On the latest occasion, in July 2018, the protests came only days after a landmark oil revenue sharing agreement (Omondi, 2018) had been concluded between Turkana County and the national government. This agreement was not considered fair by a few of the local communities and some of their elected leaders, bringing to the fore the critical importance of stakeholder involvement and effective relational equity management (Etyang, 2018). The now disputed oil revenue sharing agreement allocates 75% of oil revenue to the national government, 20% to the Turkana County government, and 5% to the local community. Notably, the local community had demanded a 10% oil revenue allocation, but their County government settled for 5% following a meeting with the President at the Statehouse in Nairobi. Hence, the perceived inequitable distribution of the oil revenue is one of the causes of the impasse (Herbling and Burkhardt, 2018).

In addition, the perceived favouritism towards foreigners – manifested through the provision by the national government of round-the-clock armed security whilst locals are negatively affected by violence and illegal activities – is another cause of the impasse. According to some Kenyan media reports, protests started when cattle rustlers raided the region, killing people and taking off with large herds of cattle (Lutta, 2018). Aware of the round-the-clock armed security provided to Tullow Oil's infrastructure and workers, the locals blamed the national government for consistently failing to ensure their protection while it is quick to do so for the recently discovered oil and the infrastructure associated with it.

The discovery of oil in Turkana County and the impact of its management on the local community have highlighted the fact that the government applies a single-sector approach to resource management and/or governance and views land, water and food as peripheral to energy (oil) in this particular case. Furthermore, although there is a degree of collaborative governance of the energy (oil) resource realised through a public-private partnership, it evidently does not adequately involve all stakeholders. In particular, whereas the two public partners (County Government of Turkana and National Government of Kenya) and their private partner (Tullow Oil) are satisfied with the revenue sharing agreement, other stakeholders – namely the local community – remain deeply dissatisfied. The public-private partnership brought the synergistic benefits of co-production for the nation, the County and, by extension one would expect, the local communities (Mouraviev and Kakabadse, 2016). However, in its current form and with the process followed for its design and agreement, it appears to have failed to acknowledge, consider and address the expectations and needs of the local community. In addition, the process of exploitation and management of the relatively newly discovered oil, failed not only to involve all stakeholders but also to effectively manage their relational equity by building trust and engaging them. Furthermore, it did not seek to harmonise the multiple and competing priorities of the WEF sectors through enhancing the relational equity of all actors and by doing so undermined any attempt to exercise collaborative governance.

Collaborative governance of the WEF nexus in northwestern Kenya

Effective governance of the WEF nexus and, by extension, of human security in northwestern Kenya remains a challenge. This is primarily due to three key factors: (1) the variety of (in)security drivers in the region and the complexity of their interrelations; (2) the lack of nexus thinking in addressing WEF governance challenges and, hence, some of the underlying causes of human insecurity; and, (3) the unidimensional understanding of security adopted by the government of Kenya and its State-centric approach in addressing security concerns.

There are numerous challenges to the governance of the WEF sector and of human security in northwestern Kenya. These include, but are not limited to, resource scarcity (e.g. water and pastureland) due to numerous causes including land use change (e.g. rapid conversion of livestock grazing land to land for wildlife conservation; see Asaka, 2018), climate variability and resource abundance (e.g. the case of Turkana oil); all impacting on one or more of the WEF nexus dimensions. Furthermore, climate change acts as a threat multiplier and considering the climate sensitive nature of pastoralism, the dominant source of livelihood in the region, presents an additional challenge. The multitude of threats and the complexity of their interrelations necessitates an integrated and multi-stakeholder approach that will enable their holistic consideration to inform the design and implementation of policy.

The prevailing single-sector, rather than WEF nexus focused approach, does not permit the holistic consideration of synergies, trade-offs and inter-connections. In addition, the prevailing unidimensional conceptualisation of human security – that does not acknowledge the link between WEF nexus challenges and human security in the region – renders current policy and governance mechanisms ineffectual, if not in some cases damaging as shown in earlier sections.

Foregrounding of violent conflict by the national government at the expense of effective governance of the WEF nexus and appropriate resolution of WEF nexus challenges, means that its approach is skewed in favour of militarisation. The latter fails to address those challenges thereby compounding the security problem of the region. In this context, the national government's approach is largely reactionary and often primarily involves the use of armed force to address violent conflict. In other words, the Kenyan government's approach to security issues predisposes it to prescribe military solutions independently of the root cause of the security threat. From a WEF nexus perspective, this approach cannot achieve much because it focuses more on addressing symptoms (individual instances of violent conflict) instead of their root causes by failing to consider, in an integrated and holistic manner, WEF nexus challenges and to acknowledge their inter-relations with and impact on human security.

This approach has resulted, in certain instances, in proactive government policies aimed at addressing underlying issues having an adverse effect and compounding rather than resolving WEF nexus challenges and, by extension, human security ones. For example, between the late 1960s and the early 1980s, the government's sedentarisation programme sought to settle nomadic communities in the region by strategically sinking boreholes across it in the hope of having these communities settle around such water points (see, for example, Little, 1985; Krätli and Swift, 1999). The programme produced largely disastrous results including the intensification of overgrazing, particularly around the water points, that in turn negatively impacted on the availability and accessibility of water and food for these communities as well as their economic, personal and health security (see Table 6.1). Similarly, the drive towards converting livestock grazing land to wildlife conservation land is seen as "green grabbing" (Greiner, 2012), and will likely further complicate the human security situation in the region by presenting new WEF nexus challenges. This is especially the case considering how unsustainable the conservation model that has been chosen for implementation in the region is (Asaka, 2018).

Finally, in the prevailing understanding of security, the State remains the sole actor responsible for providing it and this compounds the impact of a unidimensional conceptualisation of security as security from violent conflict. Local communities and non-governmental organisations have a critical role to play in addressing WEF nexus challenges and, by extension, challenges to human security. Nonetheless, the dominant narrow understanding of security, privileges the State thereby rendering other actors irrelevant. This impedes a collaborative governance approach in addressing those concerns. It further renders immaterial any consideration regarding relational equity management – the latter understood in this edited collection as the government's efforts to identify the relationships of all actors and manage those it considers critical whilst defining – through the legal and regulatory frameworks – the boundaries within which these relationships are shaped and materialise.

Conclusion

This chapter used the dual analytical lens of collaborative governance and relational equity as conceptualised by Sawhney and Zabin (2002) and Ansell and Gash (2008) and provided a discussion of the interlinkages between effective WEF nexus governance and human security using the case of northwestern Kenya, highlighting the impact of ineffective WEF nexus governance and its critical implications for human security. It further sought to bring to the fore the critical role of collaborative governance and relational equity management in effective WEF nexus governance.

The chapter has shown that a State-centric and unidimensional conceptualisation of security is a hindrance to collaborative governance, impeding the involvement of multiple stakeholders and failing to acknowledge the critical significance of WEF nexus governance and its impact on human security. Furthermore, by studying Turkana County's conditions, within the larger northwestern Kenya context, the chapter emphasised the benefits of a relational equity approach to collaborative governance. It also highlighted the detrimental impact of disregarding key stakeholders and their expectations, needs and objectives.

There are a number of implications for WEF nexus governance and, in particular, relational equity-informed collaborative governance in the specific context of Kenya, with implications for the governance of human security in the region.

Firstly, considering the WEF sectors in isolation fails to address the complexity of their interrelations. The design and implementantion of policies for the WEF sector should be based on a WEF nexus thinking which is directly linked with adopting a collaborative governance approach enhanced by effective relational equity management. Such approach will permit the analysis of each of the WEF sectors not in isolation, but in relation to the others, highlighting synergies, competing demands and trade-offs. Probing the links between the individual WEF nexus elements and their inter-linkages will also feed into the broader picture of resource related security concerns. A resource nexus-informed analysis makes this possible.

Secondly, considering the centrality of climate variability and, therefore, climate change in northwestern Kenya, it is critical to consider their impact and implications in any WEF nexus analysis. Climate variability and climate change should inform policy design and implementation for the WEF sector. Addressing climate change – a complex transboundary phenomenon – requires a collaborative approach involving multiple stakeholders from both the public and private sectors, from multiple levels of government (local, regional, national) and across borders, at international level.

Thirdly, collaborative governance is underpinned by the involvement of State and non-State actors (Ansell and Gash, 2008). With this in mind, the current State-centric and unidimensional understanding of security is a barrier to collaborative governance in northwestern Kenya. A central feature of human security is that it can be best achieved through a multi-stakeholder approach and by considering a multitude of dimensions and the root causes rather than the symptoms of violent conflict. Adopting an approach underpinned by a human security perspective will permit the involvement of other actors, including NGOs and the private sector, enabling collaborative governance and enhancing it through effective relational equity management.

Lastly, collaborative governance is not only underpinned by the involvement of State and non-State actors, but it is characterised by their engagement in a consensus based decision-making process. Critical in enabling and facilitating this process is effective relational equity management, ensuring that all stakeholders have been involved in a collaborative and consensus based decision-making process. The government has a critical role in acknowledging and seeking to engage all stakeholders as well as providing, through regulatory and legal frameworks, the platform for this engagement and the relationships between stakeholders.

A key limitation of this study and its implications for the governance of the WEF nexus is its narrow contextualisation within the confines of northwestern Kenya. Future research should consider the relevance and applicability of the identified implications for policy design and implementation for the WEF nexus and, by extension, human security in areas with similar socio-economic, political and natural conditions as well as areas where these are significantly different from those found in the region discussed here.

Note

1 The official size of the Sera conservancy according to the Sera conservancy 2015–2019 management plan is as follows: the total area is 340,450 hectares out of which 51,740 hectares are core conservation area (where no livestock grazing is allowed) and an additional 10,700 hectares are fenced off specifically for rhino conservation. This means that in total 62,440 hectares of prime land that was previously available for livestock grazing is no longer available for this purpose.

References

Adger, W.N., Pulhin, J., Barnet, J., Dabelko, G.D., Hovelrud, G.K., Levy, M., ... Vogel, C. (2014). "Human security". In C.B. Field, V.R. Baros, D.J. Dokken, K.J. Mach, M.D. Mastrandrea, T.E. Bilir, ... L.L. White (eds) *Climate Change 2014: Impacts, adaptation, and vulnerability. Part A: Global and sectoral aspects. Contribution of Working Group II to the Fifth Assessment Report of the Intergovernmental Panel on Climate Change*. New York: Cambridge University Press.

Ali, S.H. (ed.) (2007). *Peace Parks: Conservation and conflict prevention*. Cambridge, Massachusetts: MIT Press.

Alkire, S. (2003). *A Conceptual Framework for Human Security*. Oxford: Center for Research on Inequality, Human Security and Ethnicity.

Amutabi, M.N. (2010). "Land and conflict in the Ilemi triangle of East Africa". *Kenya Studies Review*, vol 1, no 2, pp 20–36.

Andrews-Speed, P., Bleischwitz, R., Boersma, T., Johnson, C., Kemp, G., and VanDeveer, S. (2015). *Want, Waste or War? The global resource nexus and the struggle for land, energy, food, water and minerals*. New York: Routledge.

Annan, K. (2005). "'In larger freedom': Decision time at the UN". *Foreign Affairs*, vol 84, no 3, pp 63–74.

Ansell, C., and Gash, A. (2008). "Collaborative governance in theory and practice". *Journal of Public Administration Research and Theory*, vol 18, no 4, pp 543–571.

Asaka, J.O. (2018). *Transformations in Conservation Governance and Implications for Human Security: The case of Kenya's northern rangelands*. PhD thesis, University of Massachusetts, Boston.

Asaka, J.O., and Smucker, T.A. (2016). "Assessing the role of mobile phone communication in drought-related mobility patterns of Samburu pastoralists". *Journal of Arid Environments*, vol 128, pp 12–16.

Carius, A., Dabelko, G.D., and Wolf, A.T. (2004). *Water, Conflict and Cooperation*. Washington, DC: Woodrow Wilson Center for International Scholars.

Cilliers, J. (2004). "Human security in Africa: A conceptual framework for review". Africaportal and Institute for Security Studies. [Online]. 1 January. [Accessed 13 March 2019]. Available from: www.africaportal.org/publications/human-security-in-africa-a-conceptual-framework-for-review/.

Commission on Human Security. (2003). *Human Security Now*. New York: United Nations.

Cruise, A., and van der Zee, B. (2017). "Armed herders invade Kenya's most important wildlife conservancy". *The Guardian*. [Online]. 2 February. [Accessed 20 January 2019]. Available from: www.theguardian.com/environment/2017/feb/02/armed-herders-elephant-kenya-wildlife-laikipia.

Daher, B., Lee, S., Mohtar, R., Asaka, J.O., and VanDeveer, S. (2018). "Security, climate change and the nexus". In R. Bleischwitz, H. Hoff, C. Spataru, E. van der Voet and S. VanDeveer (eds) *Routledge Handbook of the Resource Nexus*. New York: Routledge.

Duffield, M., and Wadell, N. (2006). "Securing humans in a dangerous world". *International Politics*, vol 43, pp 1–23.

Etyang, H. (2018). "Turkana locals reject 5% share of oil revenue, cite lack of consultation". *The Star*. [Online]. 21 May. [Accessed on 20 January 2019] Available from: www.kionjo.com/news/client/mobile/newsarticle/Turkana-locals-reject-five-per-cent-share-of-oil-revenue–cite-lack-of/d08f4d37-9af9-4188-a8ee-940ba231caa6.

Floyd, R., and Mathew, R.A. (eds). (2013). *Environmental Security: Approaches and issues*. New York: Routledge.

FAO (Food and Agriculture Organisation). (2001). *The State of Food Insecurity in the World 2001: Food insecurity: When people live with hunger and fear of starvation*. Rome: FAO.

Fong, C. (2015). *Water, Land and Oil: Drivers of major upheaval in the lower Omo Valley and Turkana*. Oakland, CA: International Rivers.

Galvin, K.A. (2009). "Transitions: Pastoralists living with change". *Annual Review of Anthropology*, vol 38, pp 185–198.

Gasper, D. (2007). *Human Rights, Human Needs, Human Development and Human Security: Relationships between four international "human" discourses*. The Hague: Institute of Social Studies.

Gjørv, G.H. (2012). "Security by any other name: Negative security, positive security, and multi-actor security approach". *Review of International Studies*, vol 38, no 4, pp 835–859.

Greiner, C. (2012). "Unexpected consequences: Wildlife conservation and territorial conflict in northern Kenya". *Human Ecology*, vol 40, no 3, pp 415–425.

Herbling, D. and Burkhardt, P. (2018). "Tullow's Kenya oil operations threatened as impasse endures". *Bloomberg Markets*. [Online]. 17 July. [Accessed on 20 January 2019] Available from: www.bloomberg.com/news/articles/2018-07-17/tullow-oil-may-halt-turkana-operations-in-kenya-over-impasse.

Homer-Dixon, T.F. (1999). *Environment, Scarcity and Violence*. Princeton, NJ: Princeton University Press.

Human Security Center. (2005). *Human Security Report 2005: War and peace in the 21st century*. New York: Oxford University Press.

Johannes, E.M., Zulu, L.C., and Kalipeni, E. (2015). "Oil discovery in Turkana County, Kenya: A source of conflict or development?". *African Geographical Review*, vol 34, no 2, pp 142–164.

King, G., and Murray, C.J.L. (2001). "Rethinking human security". *Political Science Quarterly*, vol 116, no 4, pp 585–610.

Kiplang'at, J. (2018). "Kenya beats odds to become first East African nation to export oil". *Daily Nation*. [Online]. 4 June. [Accessed on 20 January 2019]. Available from: www.nation.co.ke/news/Kenya-s-journey-as-an-oil-exporter-starts/1056-4593378-j9fim8z/index.html.

Krätli, S. and Swift, J. (1999). "Understanding and managing pastoral conflict in Kenya: A literature review". Institute of Development Studies: University of Sussex. [Accessed on 13 March 2019]. Available from: http://citeseerx.ist.psu.edu/viewdoc/download?doi=10.1.1.505.7930&rep=rep1&type=pdf.

Little, P.D. (1985). "Social differentiation and pastoralist sedentarization in northern Kenya". *Africa: The Journal of the International African Institute*, vol 55, no 3, pp 243–261.

Lutta, S. (2018). "Villagers break into oil base in protest against insecurity". *Daily Nation*. [Online] 1 July. [Accessed on 20 January 2019] Available from: www.nation.co.ke/news/Villagers-break-into-oil-base-in-protest-against-insecurity/1056-4640348-373ij1/index.html.

MacFarlane, S.N. (2004). "What is human security? A useful concept that risks losing its political salience". *Security Dialogue*, vol 35, no 3, pp 368–369.

Mburu, N. (2002). "Delimitation of the elastic Ilemi triangle: Pastoral conflicts and official indifference in the Horn of Africa". *African Studies Quarterly*, vol 7, no 1, pp 15–37.

Mkutu, K. (2002). "Pastoralism and conflict in the Horn of Africa". Africa Peace Forum/ Saferworld/University of Bradford.

Mkutu, K.A. (2007). "Small arms and light weapons among pastoral groups in the Kenya–Uganda border area". *African Affairs*, vol 106, no 422, pp 47–70.

Mkutu, K.A. (2014). "'Ungoverned space' and the oil find in Turkana, Kenya". *The Round Table: The Commonwealth Journal of International Affairs*, vol 103, no 5, pp 497–515.

Mkutu, K.A. (2015). "Changes and challenges of Kenya Police Reserve: The case of Turkana County". *African Studies Review*, vol 58, no 1, pp 199–222.

Mkutu, K. and Wandera, G. (2013). "Policing the periphery: Opportunities and challenges for Kenya Police Reserves". Small Arms Survey, Graduate Institute of International and Development Studies. Geneva. [Accessed on 13 March 2019]. Available from: www.smallarmssurvey.org/fileadmin/docs/F-Working-papers/SAS-WP15-Kenya-Policing-the-Periphery.pdf.

Mouraviev, N. and Kakabadse, N. (2016). "Conceptualising public-private partnerships: A critical appraisal of approaches to meanings and forms". *Society and Business Review*, vol 11, no 2, pp 155–173.

Munyeki, J. (2017). "Security forces shoot 500 cows in Laikipia as herders protest". *The Standard*. [Online] 30 March. [Accessed on 20 January 2019]. Available from: www.standardmedia.co.ke/article/2001234496/security-forces-shoot-500-cows-in-laikipia-as-herders-protest.

Newman, E. (2010). "Critical human security studies". *Review of International Studies*, vol 36, pp 77–94.

Ngirachu, J. (2017). "Britain's foreign secretary Boris Johnson welcomes KDF deployment to Laikipia". *Daily Nation*. [Online]. 27 March. [Accessed on 20 January 2019] Available from: www.nation.co.ke/news/Britain-Boris-Johnson-military-KDF-deploy-Laikipia/1056-3853870-147ytcc/index.html.

Njiru, B.N. (2012). "Climate change, resource competition and conflict amongst pastoral communties of northern Kenya". In J. Scheffran, M. Brzoska, G.H. Brauch and J. Schilling (eds) *Climate Change, Human Security and Violent Conflict*. Berlin: Springer.

Oluoko-Odingo, A. (2011). "Vulnerability and adaptation to food insecurity in Kenya". *Annals of the Association of American Geographers*, vol 101, no 1, pp 1–20.

Omondi, G. (2018). "Revenue deal sets stage for Turkana oil exports". *Business Daily*. [Online] 23 May. [Accessed on 20 January 2019]. Available from: www.businessdailyafrica.com/news/Revenue-deal-sets-stage-for-Turkana-oil-/539546-4577114-xlhqjmz/index.html.

Opiyo, F.E.O., Wasonga, O.V., Schilling, J. and Mureithi, S.M. (2012). "Resource based conflicts in drought prone northwestern Kenya: The drivers and mitigation mechanisms". *Wudpecker Journal of Agricultural Research*, vol 1, no 11, pp 442–453.

Owen, T. (2004). "Human security – conflict, critique and consensus: Colloquium remarks and a proposal for a threshold based definition". *Security Dialogue*, vol 35, no 3, pp 373–387.

Sawhney, M. and Zabin, J. (2002). "Managing and measuring relational equity in the network economy". *Journal of the Academy of Market Science*, vol 30, no 4, pp 313–332.

Schilling, J., Locham, R., Weinzierl, T., Vivekananda, J. and Scheffran, J. (2015). "The nexus of oil, conflict, and climate change vulnerability of pastoral communities in northwest Kenya". *Earth System Dynamics*, vol 6, pp 703–717.

Schilling, J., Opiyo, F.E.O. and Scheffran, J. (2012). "Raiding pastoral livelihoods: Motives and effects of violent conflict in north-western Kenya". *Pastoralism: Research, Policy and Practice*, vol 2, no 25, p 53.

Simonse, S. (2011). *Human Security in the Borderlands of Sudan, Uganda and Kenya: Key advocacy issues from the perspective of a grassroots peace building programme for warrior youths.* Utrecht: IKV PAX CHRISTI.

Tullow Oil. (2012). "Ngamia-1 oil discovery in Kenya rift basin. Tullow Oil". Press Release. [Online] 26 March. [Accessed on 20 January 2019]. Available from: www.tullowoil.com/media/press-releases/ngamia-1-oil-discovery-in-kenya-rift-basin.

UNDP (United Nations Development Programme). (1994). *Human Development Report 1994.* New York: Oxford University Press.

UNEP (United Nations Environment Programme). (2004). *Understanding Environment, Conflict and Cooperation.* Nairobi, Kenya: UNEP.

UNEP (United Nations Environment Programme). (2009). *From Environmental Conflict to Environmental Peacebuilding: The role of natural resources and the environment.* Nairobi, Kenya: UNEP.

United Nations General Assembly. (2012). *66/290.* Follow-up to paragraph 143 on human security of the 2005 world summit outcome. United Nations.

United Nations University. (2019). "The nexus approach to environmental resource management. United Nations University". Institute of Integrated Management of Material Fluxes and of Resources. [Accessed on 20 January 2019]. Available from: https://flores.unu.edu/en/research/nexus.

Williams, P.D. and McDonald, M. (eds). (2018). *Security Studies: An introduction.* 3rd edn. New York: Routledge.

7 Relational equity management in water-energy-food nexus governance

The case of the Aral Sea Basin restoration programmes

Aliya Tankibayeva and Aigul Adibayeva

Introduction

The Aral Sea is a saline lake in Central Asia on the border of the two independent states of Kazakhstan and Uzbekistan. Part of the lake is on Kazakhstan's territory, whilst another part belongs to Uzbekistan. Mainly supplied by the Amu Darya and Syr Darya rivers, its drainage basin covers the territories of a few countries such as Tajikistan, Turkmenistan and Uzbekistan, and smaller areas of Kyrgyzstan, Kazakhstan, Afghanistan and a very small part of Iran (see Figure 7.1 for details).

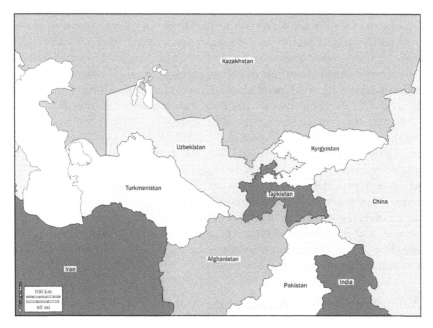

Figure 7.1 Map of Central Asia indicating five states – Kazakhstan, Kyrgyzstan, Tajikistan, Turkmenistan and Uzbekistan – and the Aral Sea between Kazakhstan and Uzbekistan

Source: https://d-maps.com/index.php?lang=en.

Resulting from irrigation strategies during the Soviet time, the Aral Sea, once the fourth largest lake in the world, shrank by more than two-thirds in volume and surface area in less than 50 years. Between 1986 and 1987, desiccation continued and led to the split of the Aral Sea into the North Aral Sea and the South Aral Sea. In approximately 2009 to 2010, the South Aral Sea split further into eastern and western water reservoirs and a lake in-between the two. In 2009, the southeastern lake disappeared, occasionally receiving water due to ground water and meltwater inflows, as well as other natural and anthropogenic causes. Overall, from 1961 to 2008, the Aral Sea shrank by more than 70 per cent: its surface size decreased from 66,100 sq. km to 10,100 sq. km (Kosarev and Kostianoy, 2010). Following the dramatic shrinkage of the sea area, the water salinisation increased to a concentration that drove away aquatic plants and animals. Salinisation of soil resulted in desertification of the sea basin, salt storms and loss of biodiversity. In addition to the ecological effects, the desiccation caused significant deterioration of the socio-economic situation in the Aral Sea region. Six million hectares of land became unsuitable for agriculture (Bosch et al., 2007). Commercial fishery completely stopped in 1980, dropping to zero compared to 43,430 tons of fish in 1960 (Bosch et al., 2007). Adverse effects have been observed on the population's health and living conditions. These multiple negative impacts have led to migration from the affected areas.

After the disintegration of the Soviet Union, the Central Asian republics (Kazakhstan, Uzbekistan, Kyrgyzstan, Tajikistan and Turkmenistan) became independent states. The approach to water management that was adopted by the Soviet Union could not accommodate the emerging interests and demands of the newly formed countries. Acute concerns were raised regarding environmental sustainability and how to effectively meet the demands for water, energy and food (WEF). This chapter outlines the evolution of the WEF nexus approach to the management of the WEF sectors in the Aral Sea Basin region from the relational equity perspective. The following section defines relational equity in the context of the Aral Sea. Then the chapter offers an appraisal of the available research regarding the WEF nexus in the Aral Sea Basin region. The next section provides an assessment of developments in the application of the nexus approach to WEF governance in the region. This is followed by an analysis of cases where the relational equity perspective was instrumental in designing and implementing effective nexus management interventions. The concluding section reflects on trajectories for further development of the WEF nexus management in the Aral Sea Basin.

Relational equity in the context of the Aral Sea's WEF nexus

In this chapter, relational equity is conceptualised as an integrated set of actions by multiple stakeholder groups, where actions are devised and implemented through collaborative engagement of various groups with respect to their needs and desired outcomes. Relational equity is seen as an approach to address complex issues aiming at the inclusive, effective and efficient delivery of solutions. This approach ensures coherence of actions and delivery of the outcomes by means of shared understanding, mutual contribution and long-term commitment.

Relational equity is inherent to the nexus. A nexus can be described as "a process to link ideas and actions of different stakeholders under different sectors and levels for achieving sustainable development" (Endo et al., 2017, p. 22). The WEF nexus can be seen as a qualitative extension and upgrading of Integrated Water Resource Management (IWRM). Highlighted in 2002 by the Global Water Partnership, the Institute of Water Resources Planning (IWRP) recognised the advantage of the coordinated management of water, land and associate resources. IWRP explicitly stated that achieving sustainable water management is conditional to all-stakeholder participation, good governance, science-aided solutions, interstate cooperation on transboundary issues, and overall intention to move from sector-by-sector to more intersectoral and cross-sectoral approaches (GWP, 2004; Lenton and Muller, 2009).

The concepts of IWRM have been well received worldwide including in the Aral Sea region (Cai et al., 2003; Karther et al., 2015). However, over the more than three decades since its conception, the IWRM implementation in the Aral Sea region showed certain critical limitations: there was a tendency to retain technical over socio-ecological focus; implementation remained largely within the water sector; and public participation was insufficient (McDonnel, 2008). When issues are complex and interdependent, integrative management is needed for deriving sustainable solutions (Carley and Christie, 2000). To effectively apply integrative management, it is critical to adopt an approach to managing high-intensity interactions of multiple stakeholders and consequently ensure continuous feedback and adjustment in actions and policies in line with these inputs and needs of the stakeholders (Carley and Christie, 2000).

Countries in the Aral Sea Basin region had largely inherited the water, energy and food infrastructure built in the Soviet Union. In particular, management of the water and energy sectors during the Soviet time was transboundary by design; it was centrally planned and monitored. Kyrgyzstan and Tajikistan, the upstream countries, have at their disposal territories with significant water resources. Short of other sources of energy, the two countries increase water storage in reservoirs to meet their energy needs by means of hydropower production. In contrast, the Republics of Uzbekistan, Turkmenistan and Kazakhstan have much smaller volumes of renewable inland water resources. Having sufficient energy from oil and gas, these three countries require, however, that the bulk of water from transboundary rivers be supplied in summer to meet irrigation needs and avoid uncontrolled winter flooding (Pohl et al., 2017). Before the disintegration of the Soviet Union in 1991, a centrally managed system that reconciled water, energy and food uses to meet the needs of all five republics was implemented (Karther et al., 2015, 2017). The system, however, was viable only in the context of a centrally planned economy (Libert et al., 2008; Rakhmatullaev, Abdullaev and Kazbekov, 2017).

Researchers identified three types of effort undertaken in the beginning of the 2000s within the national agendas of countries in the Aral Sea Basin region focusing: (1) on water; (2) on water and energy; and (3) on water, energy and agriculture (Kubo et al., 2009). Despite the efforts to enforce IWRM, Kubo et al. (2009) further noted that all three sets were framed mainly from the economic rationale. In the 2000s, the cooperation between countries in the region focused mostly on technical matters and on those issues where countries perceived some national security threats (Sojamo, 2008). In contrast to this narrow focus, the nexus approach could facilitate a wider and more inclusive polylogue in order to ensure and enhance the interplay of technical, institutional, cross-sectoral and legal aspects toward a comprehensive, as well as shared, understanding of all stakeholders' needs regarding the present and future of the Aral Sea region.

The WEF nexus in the transboundary governance of the Aral Sea Basin

This section assesses the evolution of the WEF governance in the Aral Sea Basin from the nexus perspective paying special attention to the International Fund for Saving the Aral Sea (IFAS) and its long-term transboundary work. The IFAS establishment in 1993 was the result of earlier calls of the Central Asian leaders (of Kazakhstan, Kyrgyzstan, Tajikistan, Turkmenistan and Uzbekistan) and water management agencies to minimise the ecological atrocities and assist in the rehabilitation of the Aral region. The IFAS was designed, and has received recognition from international actors, as a transboundary institute that facilitates regional cooperation with the international community over the Aral Sea issues.

Headed by the chairing state's president, the structure of the IFAS includes the Inspection Committee, the Board, the Executive Committee (where representatives of the five Central Asian nations sit), the Interstate Commission on Water Coordination, the Interstate Commission on Sustainable Development, the water basin commissions on Amu Darya and Syr Darya and the scientific hydrological units.

The IFAS' legal framework reflects core international conventions in the environmental and transboundary water management fields. These include the 1992 Rio Convention on Biological Diversity and Climate Change, the 1992 Helsinki Convention on the Protection and Use of Transboundary Watercourses and International Lakes, the 1994 United Nations Convention to Combat Desertification and others. In 2008, the IFAS received the status of the UN General Assembly observer, which was followed by the resolution "On Cooperation of the UN and IFAS" in April 2018.

The work of the IFAS is underpinned by the concept of relational equity. The IFAS has various roles: being a beneficiary of states' and donors' contributions, identifying priority areas for action, inviting projects from national, international, private and public entities. Some projects are financed directly from the allocations to the IFAS, whereas the IFAS may seek funding for others and serves as either an operator, facilitator, legal enabler or a monitoring agency on them. The IFAS repeatedly states that its principal role is to serve as a platform for integrating diverse stakeholders in order to solve the complex issues in the Aral Sea Basin, facilitate dialogue and ensure normative, institutional and financial support for stakeholders' approved actions. In this capacity, the IFAS is not a governmental body, nor a full-fledged operator of the programmes. Moreover, being responsible for facilitating dialogue at the highest national and regional levels, the IFAS also has access to institutional stakeholders across multiple sectors. Nonetheless, the IFAS does not have any binding mandates other than those stipulated in the agreements with each partner.

By its Charter, in addition to any donations, the IFAS is entitled to receive obligatory financial contributions from each member country. Initially, member states agreed to contribute up to 1 per cent of state expenses to the IFAS funds annually. By 2009, it became clear that contributions were not made regularly and countries claimed that fulfilling contributions in the full amount was unrealistic. As a result, in 2009 for downstream countries (Kazakhstan, Uzbekistan and Turkmenistan) contributions were lowered to 0.3 per cent of state expenses and for upstream countries (Kyrgyzstan and Tajikistan) to 0.1 per cent (Sehring and Diebold, 2012). This suggests that for many years the IFAS has been underfunded.

At the same time, a possible reason for lowering contributions relates to the activities in which the IFAS established itself as a regional institution. The IFAS performs normative and legislative functions that create regulatory and institutional bases for various actions. With the facilitation of the IFAS, 15 regional and local conventions were signed as the output of official meetings and summits of the Central Asian leaders. Some of them were conducted in the UN framework, such as the UN Conference on Sustainable Development of Countries in the Aral Sea Basin in 1995, followed by the Nukus Declaration. The IFAS has been able to operationalise frameworks for coordinated actions of multiple stakeholders. However, this multiplicity of actions, at various levels, contributed to certain ambiguity regarding the IFAS' legal status and how its financing is arranged. The IFAS' scope of work and its objectives are periodically reviewed by the Council (i.e. the heads of the member states) in consultation with the international donor community. According to the statutory documents, the IFAS is accountable for its results to its Board and Council. The participation of multiple stakeholders is authorised by the states, as well as assignment of the accountabilities for the results. Accountability of the actors, including accountability of the IFAS to other actors, is decided within each particular arrangement. Overall, the conclusion is that the strength of the accountability mechanism is different from project to project, thus making the effectiveness of the IFAS somewhat unpredictable.

The analysis suggests that the IFAS work is dependent on the availability and capacity of the national institutions involved in the implementation of certain projects. The Central Asian countries look for governing structures that may holistically address water, agriculture and energy issues (Abdullaev and

Rakhmatullaev, 2016). However, the existing national institutional and legal arrangements often presented certain difficulties for the implementation of actions on a regional scale (Sehring and Diebold, 2012).

Framework for actions: Aral Sea Basin Programmes

The IFAS has been the main facilitator of three consecutive Aral Sea Basin Programmes (ASBP-1, 2 and 3). Each ASBP should be viewed as a broad framework of actions comprising various programmes and projects of diverse scale and duration.

ASBP-1

ASBP-1 was adopted by the heads of the IFAS member countries in 1994. The programme included two stages – preparatory with a budget of about USD 30 million for three to five years; and implementation that was planned for another 10 to 15 years. The second stage started in 1997 and numerous projects and activities were initiated aiming at the restoration and the mitigation of the consequences of the Aral Sea desiccation. During ASBP-1, attention was paid mainly to the prevention of further desiccation, the mitigation of the environmental consequences, and the modernisation of the water, energy and irrigation infrastructure. The projects launched by the ASBP-1 had varied trajectories of implementation, some of them were extended, and others were delayed, merged with other projects or continued into the ASBP-2.

ASBP-2

There was no official end of the ASBP-1. However, in 2003 the Heads of the IFAS member states adopted a new framework for actions – ASBP-2. Prior to this, in 2002 in the city of Dushanbe, Tajikistan, the Heads of the IFAS founding countries instructed the IFAS to develop a "Programme of concrete actions to improve the ecological and socio-economic situation in the Aral Sea basin for 2003–2010", which became ASBP-2. The ASBP-2 had 14 priorities including: more effective and efficient use of water; upgrading water and agricultural infrastructure; designing a technologically sound monitoring system; preventing desertification and salinisation of waters, soils and sand dust. Priority five was a conceptually new dimension focusing on the improvement of the livelihoods in the localities, such as the implementation of public health programmes in the region, job creation and the provision of potable water. Development of environmental education, enhancing the role of non-governmental organisations and effective public participation in addressing the Aral Sea problems were outlined as essential success factors in relation to this priority and for the programme in general.

The donor involvement in the development of the ASBP-2 was smaller compared to ASBP-1. About 98 per cent of ASBP-2 activities were funded by contributions of the member states, which amounted to more than 1 billion USD from 2002 to 2010. Most actions in ASBP-2 were undertaken at the national level.

It should be noted, that rapid economic transformation affected the implementation of the ASBP-2. First, increased oil prices and therefore more economic and job opportunities in the energy sector, led to more strategic attention being paid to the energy sector by member countries. Second, water issues had become a priority beyond the Aral Sea Basin. They gained attention in the wider context of sustainable development that made it into each country's national strategic priorities. Each country initiated the exploration of the concept of Integrated Water Resource Management (IWRM). Overall, the ASBP-2 period was challenging for making substantial progress in the Aral Sea Basin region. The main difficulties were seen in adjusting the legal and institutional bases for effective water management, especially focusing on effective stakeholder involvement. The next section analyses the directions taken in ASPB-3 for resolving those challenges.

ASBP-3

The third programme, for the period 2011 to 2015, had as its ultimate intended outcome the improvement of the living conditions of people in the Aral Sea Basin region and progress towards the region's sustainable development. The following four priority areas were set: IWRM with due consideration of the interests of all states in the region; environmental protection; socio-economic development; and strengthening of the institutional and legal frameworks. Compared to the 14 priority areas of ASBP-2, the priorities of the ASBP-3 were more comprehensive as well as more complex and multifaceted. This was the result of the more integrative design of the ASBP-3 constitutive programmes and projects.

Among the lessons learned from the ASBP-2 implementation, the IFAS highlighted the difficulties of cooperating at the international level and the insufficient engagement of international donors and development institutions. To improve the cooperation frameworks, ASBP-3 classified the projects as: those to be implemented by countries and financed from their national budgets; projects that are regional in scope; projects that address the ASBP-3 general goals and their several dimensions; and projects that address one of the ASBP-3 dimensions. The identification of the scope and sources of financing intended to ensure better financing and clarity for stakeholder engagement. In line with the four priority areas, the IFAS asked countries to prepare and submit project proposals.

Three of the four priority areas remained the same as in ASBP-2. The difference was in specifying improvement in institutional and legal mechanisms as a priority area, whereas environmental monitoring was integrated with the priority of aiming for environmental protection. Furthermore, the activities were focused on knowledge acquisition about the IWRM principles and on the development of the institutional and legal bases for implementing IWRM in the Aral Sea Basin region. The analysis of the ASBP-3 projects suggests that although the three priority areas remained the same, the approach had changed; project design became both user- and uses-focused. Focus on the users meant an attempt to engage end users in planning and implementing projects. Focus on uses meant that programmes were focused on having greater service orientation so that programme outcomes can be shared and used for a variety of purposes. The possibility of multi-purpose uses (e.g. use of data for more than one purpose) offers more opportunities to ensure a project's financial self-sustainability and greater socio-economic impact. This shift in approach to project design revealed the need for a cross-sectoral approach to development efforts in the Aral Sea Basin and the enhancement of the capabilities of all stakeholders.

ASBP-4 and the Central Asian Nexus Dialogue project: intended actions

In May 2016, the Executive Committee of the IFAS, with the assistance of the German Society for International Cooperation (GIZ) through its programme "Transboundary Water Management in Central Asia", initiated the first regional meeting of the working group for designing the ASBP-4. In addition to the country representatives to the IFAS, the Regional Environmental Center for Central Asia (CAREC) and the World Bank took part in planning. It is expected that the ASBP-4 will be implemented in conjunction with wider initiatives, such as the Central Asian Dialogue project (CAREC-EU, 2016), the updated Regional Environmental Action Plan for Central Asia (REAP, ICSD, 2001–2012), the Climate Adaptation and Mitigation Programme for Aral Sea Basin (CAMP4ASB, IDA, World Bank, IFAS, CAREC, 2016–2021) and others.

The ASBP-4 will continue to focus on four broad goals including the integrated use of water resources, environmental protection, socio-economic development, and improvement of institutional and legal mechanisms. However, the ASBP-4 essentially intends to apply the WEF nexus approach. Specifically, the IFAS will be the main recipient of the programme entitled *CA Nexus* (Phase I). This is a European Union (EU)-funded programme entitled "Central Asian Dialogue project: Fostering water, energy, and food security nexus dialogue and multi-sector investment". The project is part of the global NEXUS initiative funded by the EU and aims to improve water management worldwide. In December 2016, CAREC and the International Union for Conservation of Nature and Natural Resources (IUCN) were approved for implementing the CA Nexus activities.

The CA Nexus project explicitly stated its relational focus – its main objectives and activities are designed to identify relevant stakeholders and strengthen their institutional capacity for collaborative and multi-sectoral actions. Stakeholders are intended to include broad categories of actors at the basin/local, national, regional and international levels. In the analysis report of November 2017 by CAREC, two conceptual differences in terms of the role allocations to different stakeholders were proposed: (1) water users were identified as stakeholders to carry out pilot activities; and (2) state authorities responsible for energy, water resources and agriculture were seen as prior partners, following from the assignment to state authorities of responsibilities for economic development, environmental protection and for attracting investment. At present, the Action Plan for ASBP-4 is under development.

Relational equity in the Aral Sea Basin programmes

Stakeholder management approaches in ASBP-1, 2, 3 and 4

The analysis of the three completed ASBPs and intended ASBP-4 provides useful insights into their approaches to stakeholder management. This section analyses changes in stakeholder management during the ASBPs' implementation.

With the changes of the ASBPs' goals from solely environmental to those of wider socio-economic impact, stakeholder management turned from less user-focused to more participative. In ASBP-1 donors' engagement was high, which helped to ensure massive investment into complex infrastructural projects. However, the positive impact of the implemented project could have been much greater if the local stakeholders had taken part in the design of the project.

ASBP-2 tacitly acknowledged the positive role of a relational equity approach. However, as the nations were unwilling to engage in regional cooperation at that time, the projects were carried out at the national level. Potential donors had not been involved in the design of ASBP-2, which resulted in very limited funding available for projects with regional impact. Relational equity in the form of collaborative, multi-purpose and multi-user solutions materialised at the national, rather than the regional, level.

ASPB-3 intended to establish (a) a productive dialogue with the international development and water initiatives and (b) a cross-sectoral dialogue, whilst encouraging stakeholder engagement at each level within the sector. In particular, the IWRM implementation was more effective and sustainable in projects where all stakeholders understood the mutually beneficial nature of the IWRM approach and were ready to adjust their water uses accordingly. Overall, lessons from ASBP-3 showed that the achievement of the desired socio-economic improvements was more feasible and the programme outcomes were more sustainable when a relational equity approach was applied to (a) solutions at interstate, regional level; (b) solutions requiring collaboration with donors and development institutions; (c) cross-sectoral solutions; (d) relations among actors within a sector; and (e) relations across all four domains.

In February 2019, the CA Nexus project partnered with the IFAS to help develop a relational equity approach for ASBP-4 which is at its planning stage. The CA Nexus presented a proposal aimed at stakeholder engagement, where actors at the local, national, regional and international levels were identified. In contrast to the ASBP programmes, there are two differences in stakeholder engagement as proposed by the CA Nexus. First, at the local level, the water users' associations are expected to implement the pilot activities, which will be followed by analysing this pilot stage. Second, in addition to agencies purely responsible for economic development, governmental bodies responsible for water, agriculture and energy were identified as main project partners. The relational equity is therefore viewed as a means to mainstream the nexus approach to the policy level, which is evidenced by the partnership between the IFAS and the CA Nexus, although the precise modalities of stakeholder engagement are yet to be identified.

The Kok-Aral Dam: relational equity and project outcomes

This section analyses aspects of relational equity management activities carried out during the construction of the Kok-Aral Dam. The project has achieved the restoration of water levels in part of the Northern Aral Sea, and produced a number of positive social and economic effects.

Prior to the Kok-Aral Dam project, in 1992, the restoration of the Northern Aral Sea had been initiated by the local communities. It had received donor support in 2001 and had been completed in 2005 during the ASBP-2. The main activity was the construction of the Kok-Aral Dam, which keeps waters in the Northern part of the Aral Sea. The sandy dam was constructed in 1992 by local communities, but it was not strong enough to sustain increased water levels and was ruined in 1993. Local construction companies and executive bodies found funds to recreate the dam, also sandy. In 1998 it was strengthened with concrete slabs, but nonetheless was destroyed by a storm. In 2001, the Kazakhstani government approached the World Bank for technical assistance and a loan for the dam's reconstruction. As a result, in 2006, earlier than scientists expected, an increase in the water level was recorded. Consequently, water salinisation decreased and some fish species revived. Positive effects on the local climate and the health of local communities were also observed.

The success of the project was due to engaged local enterprises such as fisheries, ecological organisations and scientists. Based on the local NGO *Aral Tenizi*, a strong network of fishermen and fishery enterprises was formed, and it negotiated with governing bodies on a range of issues regarding the development of commercial fishery in the local area. Overall, the outcomes of reconstruction have been very impressive. In 2003, the sea's surface increased by 870 sq. km, that is, the total area covered by water increased from 2,414 to 3,288 sq. km; and the volume of water in the sea increased by 11.5 cubic km (from 15.6 to 27.1 cubic km). From 2014 to 2016, fish catch increased by 65 per cent up to eight thousand tons annually. Eight fish processing plants are currently in operation, out of which three comply with the Eurocodes (i.e. the EU standards) and can sell their products abroad (Energyprom.kz, 2017).

In addition, the development of other economic activities, such as folk crafts, small livestock farming and small wool processing, was triggered by the revival of fishery. The main lessons toward further work on improving the situation in the Aral Sea Basin region suggest that the alignment of environmental and socio-economic objectives, as well as the alignment of local, national and regional objectives, are necessary. The peculiarity of this case is that the relational equity approach was actually driven by varied local stakeholders who were interested in finding a solution, and then supported by larger institutional actors, rather than the other way around, which would have been typical for many large-scale projects.

Relational equity for cross-sectoral governance

Drawing on the lessons learned during the ASBP-1, the effective mechanisms of aligning the local, national and regional objectives are yet to be developed. ASBP-2 announced modernising water management structures in the Aral Sea Basin. Consequently, ASBP-3 announced application of an IWRM approach in water management structures in the Aral Sea Basin region. The IWRM considers a river basin to be a core management unit – waters of a river are indivisible and serve multiple uses, thus creating interdependencies and sometimes competition for water allocation across sectoral uses. A basin-based approach to water management ensures better coordinated allocation, increased efficiency in water usages and faster response to changes in one or more sectors. Regarding water management, the relational equity approach becomes an immediate, natural choice in managing river basins given that the equitable allocation of water across uses is by definition an integral property of IWRM. This subsection delineates lessons learned from practical aspects of the IWRM implementation in the Aral Sea Basin.

Two basin-level organisations within the IFAS have existed since its creation, and even earlier – the Basin Water Organisation (BWO) Amu Darya with headquarters in Urgench, Uzbekistan, and the BWO Syr Darya with headquarters in Tashkent, Uzbekistan. BWOs act in concert with the interstate agreements, and are responsible for the allocation of water, the maintenance of the water and energy infrastructure within their areas of jurisdiction, and other activities, such as environmental protection of areas, the maintenance of relations with the stakeholders and so on. Both BWOs are structured into subunits based at the level of basin management – the first level is that of BWO, which consists of sublevels managing large water complexes (infrastructural but also morphological). The second level is responsible for controlling smaller hydraulic points and small associated infrastructure – small dams, pumps, gauging stations and so on (Zonn et al., 2009). This structure aims to satisfy the demands of basin users (Horinkova and Abdullaev, 2003). It is worth emphasising that with the addition of participatory structures, such as water user groups, river basin councils and water user associations, both water allocation services and water uses have improved. According to Dukhovny's (2018) stakeholder analysis of BWOs, their communication is mainly with IFAS and national ministries to which the BWOs are accountable within national borders. This limits the BWOs' effectiveness in cases beyond their jurisdiction, for example in emergency or unintended discharge/use of water in some other parts of the rivers.

In contrast to the interstate BWOs Amu Darya and Syr Darya, the situation with the IWRM implementation at the national level is much more complicated. Rakhmatullaev et al. (2017) analysed different pathways of member countries to optimise water management structures and legislation linking localities and national water management structures. Within the IWRM and in other initiatives, establishment of various forms of water users' associations was undertaken in a range of countries. Water users' associations and groups were seen as cross-sectoral local bodies performing a water governance function in a locality. Their viability was challenging due to lack of skills and operational capacities, as well as owing to the gaps in the legislative and regulatory frameworks, particularly at the local level.

In 2008–2009, the Japan International Cooperation Agency (JICA) conducted surveys in Uzbekistan, Kyrgyzstan and Tajikistan to analyse the preparedness of the water management structures in the Syr Darya river upper basin for the adoption of IRWM. The survey, as well as later studies (e.g. Rakhmatullaev et al., 2017), concluded that the member states' legislation had provisions to permit the establishment of integrated water management structures. However, the regulatory bases directly supporting the operation of these structures at the local level of basin management were insufficient or missing.

The experience with the IWRM implementation in the Aral Sea Basin provides evidence that relational equity essentially improves cross-sectoral basin water management. Nonetheless, legal and regulatory bases have to be developed in order to make cross-sectoral governance effective.

Relational equity for socio-economic development

The analysis of Aral programmes shows that existing water, food and energy interdependencies in the Aral Sea Basin do not positively affect livelihoods in the local areas. In this chapter, livelihoods are defined as ways and routines people use to secure their subsistence, that is, ways to have socio-economic means sufficient for satisfying their needs throughout their life span. The improvements achieved in the conditions of livelihoods in the Aral Sea Basin region, vary significantly across countries and even within localities within countries. Among all programmes, the ASBP-3 attempted adopting a more integrative approach to mitigating the socio-economic consequences of the Aral Sea desiccation. Yet, the majority of efforts did not aim to tackle the water-energy-food-livelihood interdependency. The main reason is the historically inherited economic structure in the areas of the Aral Sea Basin. This structure is based on a single product or activity. The focus on cotton can be observed in the agricultural sector of Uzbekistan and Turkmenistan, meaning that the livelihood of a large number of people depends solely on this industry. In some localities, livelihoods are solely dependent on fishery (Aralsk, Kazakhstan), whereas in others solely on energy production (Kyrgyzstan and Tajikistan). The new challenge for the relational equity approach is to link the water-energy-food nexus to livelihood and to mobilise stakeholders to focus on the issues that have yet to be addressed.

Some efforts to approach the WEFL nexus have been made. In ASBP-2 and 3, in addition to direct investment in infrastructure, such as building water pipelines and equipping schools and hospitals, certain efforts were made to support, transform and diversify economic models in the area. The purpose was to enhance the economic participation of people and create more environmentally and economically sustainable livelihoods. For example, a two-year initiative started by GIZ in 2009 and then with IFAS, CAREC and the Asian Development Bank (ADB) as partners, aimed to increase the economic well-being of people living in the Aral Sea Basin area and achieve environmental sustainability. In particular, the project entitled Enhancing Economic and Environmental Welfare (EEWA) assisted farms and fisheries to enable their technical and economic capabilities to ensure their operational sustainability thus facilitating more sustainable economic models in the region.

A renewed attempt to ensure sustainable livelihoods in the Aral Sea Basin areas can also be observed in the agenda of international development organisations and national governments. The expected outcomes of the intended ASBP-4 include ensuring regional peace and conflict prevention, human security, as well as adaptation to climate change. Between 2012 and 2015, the UN Human Security Trust Fund, a multi-stakeholder foundation, completed a project in Uzbekistan on Sustaining Livelihoods Affected by the Aral Sea Disaster. The project aimed at enhancing economic security for various populations residing in the affected area and building capacity of institutional actors for multi-sectoral actions. Overall, the UN General Assembly resolution 66/290 (2012) highlights human security as a comprehensive approach to identifying cross-cutting challenges to human survival, livelihood and dignity of people, and subsequently a framework for actions addressing those challenges. Furthermore, the human security approach in the UN documents is operationalised based on relational equity elements, such as integrated action of multiple stakeholders, partnership, and localisation of actions to ensure that actions relate to needs. In November 2018, the UN Secretary General reaffirmed that the Fund will continue to seek support of various stakeholders to help countries of the Aral Sea Basin to improve the livelihood of the people residing in it.

Conclusion

The Aral Sea problems serve as a vivid illustration of how the relational equity concept could be useful in finding the appropriate solutions for the WEF nexus. Table 7.1 shows progression in the application of relational equity to the nexus governance over many years, during the implementation of the three programmes (ASPB-1, 2, 3).

Relational equity management offers considerable opportunities for improving the nexus governance in the Aral Sea Basin. When actions are devised and implemented by collaboratively engaging multiple stakeholders and with respect to their needs and desired outcomes, relational equity management can set a

Table 7.1 The Aral Sea basin: Application of the relational equity approach to the WEF nexus governance

	ASPB-1	ASPB-2	ASPB-3
Programme's principal outcomes	• Ecological situation stabilised in the Aral Sea Basin. • Northern Aral Sea waters replenished resulting in revived fishery and improved economic conditions of the local population.	• Maintained and improved the results achieved during ASBP-1. These include stabilisation of the ecological situation, new or redesigned solutions for supply of drinking water, mitigation of health and economic effects on the livelihoods in the localities. • The international water law was introduced to the national decision-making.	• Maintained the outcomes of ASBP-1 and 2. • Offered more integrated solutions to improve efficiency of water uses, irrigation, and productivity and efficiency of land uses • Modernised hydrometer logistical services, achieved greater standardisation of data forms, created shared regional data platform and fostered the data exchange practices • Assessed existing economic models in the Aral Sea Basin and made suggestions for enhancing the economic opportunities for localities with respect to environmental sustainability.
How the relational equity approach was used	• Mainly driven and operationalised by the local stakeholders	• Relational equity is one of the constituent components of IWRM. • There has been a shift in ASBP-2 programme goals from solely environmental restoration to addressing the socio-economic needs of local populations.	• Relational equity is one of the constituent components of the IWRM. • Solutions were offered that had multi-use orientation. • ASPB-3 piloted basin water management structures.

	ASPB-1	ASPB-2	ASPB-3
Lessons learned	• Application of relational equity is possible at any stage of programme design and implementation. • The relational equity approach enhances the usefulness and sustainability of projects'/programmes' outcomes.	• Principal stakeholders are to be reached and invited to engage in dialogue before the start of a project/programme.	• Relational equity management is to develop more detailed tools and means for bringing together stakeholders in order to address interdependencies between WEF nexus and livelihood.

Source: Compiled by the authors.

framework that would permit the better and faster achievement of the nexus governance goals. The experience of the Aral Sea Basin programmes and related governance efforts suggests that the task for the relational equity management theory is to create an interdisciplinary knowledge structure which will be useful for both academics developing nexus theories and for practitioners adopting the approach in an effort to enhance WEF nexus governance.

Appendices

Table 7.2 The Aral Sea Basin Programme 1 (ASBP-1): summary of activities

Programme goals
1. Stabilisation of the environmental situation in the Aral Sea Basin.
2. Restoration of the affected environmental conditions of the Aral Sea region.
3. Improved water and land management in the basin, creation of appropriate management structures.
• Stage 1: 1994–1997, USD 30 million.
• Stage 2: since 1998 (no official end date), implementation, USD 500–750 million.

Programme activities and funding	Funders and operators	Users/beneficiaries
Regional strategy for water management	World Bank, United Nations Development Program (UNDP), United States Agency for International Development (USAID), Water Resource Management and Agricultural Production in Central Asia (WARMAP), International Fund for Saving the Aral Sea (IFAS) Board, experts	Policy-making institutes, governments, water governance structures

Programme goals
1. Stabilisation of the environmental situation in the Aral Sea Basin.
2. Restoration of the affected environmental conditions of the Aral Sea region.
3. Improved water and land management in the basin, creation of appropriate management structures.
- Stage 1: 1994–1997, USD 30 million.
- Stage 2: since 1998 (no official end date), implementation, USD 500–750 million.

Programme activities and funding	Funders and operators	Users/beneficiaries
Ensuring the stability of dams and reservoirs	Trust Fund of the Government of Switzerland, Central Asian states	Central Asian economies, dams, irrigational fields, local communities
Hydro-meteorological-services (assessment report)	Switzerland, Central Asian states, UK	Governments, hydro-meteorological services
Environmental information system	TACIS-WARMAP experts	IFAS, governments, water and agriculture governance structures
Water quality management (assessment reports, proposals for institutional and legal frameworks)	UK, Netherlands	Governments, water governance structures, water users
Drainage Sector Development Strategy for Uzbekistan	Experts of the Ministry of Agriculture and Water Resources of Uzbekistan	Government, water governance bodies, drainage facilities
Restoration of wetlands (USD 3.9 million)	National and international experts, Global Environment Facility (GEF)	Regional economy, people residing in wetland areas in Uzbekistan and Tajikistan
Restoration of the Northern Aral Sea (USD 65 million)	Government of Kazakhstan, World Bank	Dam facilities, local economy, fishery, livelihood (Kazakhstan)
Environmental studies in the Aral Sea Basin	International donors	Multiple users, policy-making institutes, governance structures, academic structures
Syr Darya River Flow Regulation and Delta Development Project, a component of the umbrella Project on Regulation of the Syr Darya River Flow and Preservation of the Northern Aral Sea	Italy	Dam facilities, local economy, fishery, livelihood (Kazakhstan)

Programme goals
  1. Stabilisation of the environmental situation in the Aral Sea Basin.
  2. Restoration of the affected environmental conditions of the Aral Sea region.
  3. Improved water and land management in the basin, creation of appropriate management structures.
  • Stage 1: 1994–1997, USD 30 million.
  • Stage 2: since 1998 (no official end date), implementation, USD 500–750 million.

Programme activities and funding	Funders and operators	Users/beneficiaries
Clean water supply, sanitation and health – Uzbekistan (USD 120 million) Clean water supply, sanitation and health – Turkmenistan (USD 30.3 million) Clean water supply, sanitation and health – Kazakhstan (USD 7.7 million)	World Bank, Germany, The Kuwait Fund, Canada (Canadian International Development Agency), USA, France, Netherlands, UNDP, GEF	Local population residing in the basin area, local economies
Integrated water and land management project in the upper watershed		National and local water governance and land governance structures, water users
Operational management of water resources		Water users, water management structures
Capacity development		National and local water governance and land governance structures, water users
Water and Environment Management Project (WEMP) (USD 21.5 million)		Regional environment and regional economy, water and environmental governance structures, water and environment facilities, public awareness campaigns

Source: Compiled by the authors.

Table 7.3 The Aral Sea Basin Programme 2 (ASBP-2): summary of activities

Programme goal
 Improvement of the environmental and socio-economic situation in the Aral Sea Basin.
 Four directions:
 (1) water management; (2) socio-economic development; (3) ecology; and (4) ecological monitoring.
 Time: 2003–2010
 Funding: USD 2 million

Programme activities	Funders and operators	Users/beneficiaries
Kazakhstan 2002–2007 Ecological and social projects in Kyzylorda region: building sanitation system for drinking water, modernisation of local water infrastructure, forestation	Kazakhstan's contribution to the IFAS, various donors	Local environment and the economy, local population, national and local water governance structures, water management facilities
Kyrgyzstan 2002–2007 Rehabilitation of tailings and irrigation systems, prevention of natural hazards, construction and modernisation of rural water supply and sanitation, public health care system, repair and maintenance of water infrastructure	Kyrgyzstan's contribution to the IFAS, various donors	Local environment and the economy, local population, national and local water governance structures, water management facilities
Tajikistan 2002–2007 Dushanbe International Forum on Freshwater Dushanbe International Conference on Regional Cooperation in the basin's transboundary rivers; expeditions, meetings of donors and preparation of the project The Civic Initiatives Support Centre (ARAL-CISC). Various energy projects, water supply and sanitation systems, road reconstruction, construction tunnels, housing, secondary schools, hospitals, new irrigated land.	Tajikistan's contribution to the IFAS, various donors	IFAS, governments, policy-making bodies, water, energy and agriculture governance structures, academic organisations

Programme goal
Improvement of the environmental and socio-economic situation in the Aral Sea Basin.
Four directions:
(1) water management; (2) socio-economic development; (3) ecology; and (4) ecological monitoring.
Time: 2003–2010
Funding: USD 2 million

Programme activities	Funders and operators	Users/beneficiaries
Turkmenistan 2002–2007 Reconstruction of the interstate collectors – "Ozerny" and "Daryalik" in the Dashoguz velayat; commissioning of two hydrometric posts in the Lebab velayat, continued construction of two hydrometric posts on the Ozerny and Daryalik collectors in Dashoguz velayat, reconstruction of flood-control dams on the Amu Darya River and a collector-drainage network in the Biratinsky district; potable water and energy supply to affected localities	Turkmenistan's contribution to the IFAS, various donors	Local energy governance structures, energy production facilities, local economy, national economy, people residing in the basin area
Uzbekistan 2002–2007 Reconstruction of dams in Djyltyrbar gulf and Mezhdurechensk reservoir; testing and introduction of new water-efficient irrigation methods, forestation, informational campaigns, drinking water supply to affected areas, nutrition supply programmes, medical assistance and establishment of diagnostic facilities in affected localities	Uzbekistan's contribution to IFAS, various donors	Local economy, people residing in basin area, water, agriculture and municipal governance structures, water facilities, irrigation fields
Central Asia Regional Water Information Base (CAREWIB) 2003–2010 Information sharing across the basin countries	Funded by the Government of Switzerland and its agencies; specialists of Scientific-Information Center (SIC), Interstate Commission for Water Coordination (ICWC), IFAS, Global Resource Information Database located in Arendal (Norway) (GRID-Arendal), United Nations Economic Commission for Europe (UNECE), water organisations	Different levels of access to governments, water and agriculture governance, water, energy, agriculture facilities, researchers, students, public

Programme goal
   Improvement of the environmental and socio-economic situation in the Aral Sea
   Basin.
   Four directions:
   (1) water management; (2) socio-economic development; (3) ecology; and (4) ecological
   monitoring.
   Time: 2003–2010
   Funding: USD 2 million

Programme activities	Funders and operators	Users/beneficiaries
Improved information exchange on water resources in EECCA (Eastern Europe, Caucasus and Central Asia, bloc of countries) countries based on the Central Asian Regional Water Information Base (Phase II), 2008 to present Information sharing across water management organisations across basin countries	Funded by the UN Economic Commission for Europe and the Government of the Russian Federation	Water management organisations
Integrated Water Resources Management in Ferghana Valley (IWRM-Fergana)	Swiss Agency for Development and Cooperation (SDC), International Water Management Institute (IWMI), organisations of Tajikistan, Kyrgyzstan and Uzbekistan	Farmers, irrigation management structures, water management structures, water user associations
Ferghana Valley Canal Automation Project	SDC, the Interstate Commission for Water Co-ordination (ICWC) of IFAS, SIGMA, under the supervision of the Syr Darya Basin Water Organization (BWO)	Irrigation facilities, water users, irrigation management, BWO Syr Darya
Regional Research Network "Water in Central Asia" (CAWa) (2008–2011, and 2012–2014)	German Federal Foreign Office, the scientific-technical component of the Water Initiative for Central Asia ("Berlin Process") implemented by SIC ICWC IFAS	Policy-making institutes, water, energy, agriculture governance structures, academic and scientific structures, students, the public
Rural Enterprise Support Project (Phase II)	Swiss Government Parallel Grant Financing for Sub-components 2b and 2c	Rural governance structures, rural entrepreneurs, local economy, national economy

Source: Compiled by authors.

Table 7.4 The Aral Sea Basin Programme 3 (ASBP-3): summary of activities

Programme goals
  1. Achieve integrated use of water resources.
  2. Environmental protection.
  3. Social and economic development.
  4. Improvement of institutional and legal mechanisms.
  • Stage 1 preparatory: 2009–2012
  • Stage 2: Third Action Programme to assist the countries of the Aral Sea Basin, 2011–2015

Programme activities	Funders and operators	Users/beneficiaries
IFAS signed memorandum of cooperation with United Nations Regional Centre for Preventive Diplomacy for Central Asia (UNRCCA), UNECE, United Nations Economic and Social Commission for Asia and the Pacific (UNESCAP), Organization for Security and Cooperation in Europe (OSCE), World Bank, German Society for International Cooperation (GIZ) and the United States Agency for International Development (USAID), 2010		IFAS, its constituent bodies
Preparatory survey on integrated water resources management in the Syr Darya River Upper Basin, 2008–2009	JICA, governments of Kyrgyzstan, Uzbekistan, Tajikistan	Hydrometeorological services and other water management structures, stakeholders interested in knowing the preparedness of the water management structures in the Syr Darya river upper basin for adoption of IRWM
The Executive Committee of IFAS held over 100 seminars, meetings, consultations, meetings with senior staff of the UN, OSCE, European Parliament and representatives of the donor community, 2009–2012		The outcome of these activities was introduction of the international legislative framework regarding water management, international water law, environmental protection practices and conventions.
IFAS and the UN Food and Agriculture Organization (FAO) held a seminar on "Mutually Acceptable Mechanism on Integrated Use of Water Resources in Central Asia through Applying Scenario Approach", 2012		Various users and beneficiaries of sectoral synergies

Programme goals
1. Achieve integrated use of water resources.
2. Environmental protection.
3. Social and economic development.
4. Improvement of institutional and legal mechanisms.
- Stage 1 preparatory: 2009–2012
- Stage 2: Third Action Programme to assist the countries of the Aral Sea Basin, 2011–2015

Programme activities	Funders and operators	Users/beneficiaries
Two evaluative projects were implemented: 1. "Comprehensive analysis of the economic assessment of the integrated use and protection of water resources of the Aral Sea basin", 2010–2012 2. "Analysis of the vulnerability of economic infrastructures to the aftermath of climate change: Kazakhstan, Kyrgyzstan and Turkmenistan", 2010–2012	USAID, IFAS	Various users from multiple sectors
Project "Implementation of IWRM in the Aral Sea Basin: practical steps at the national level. Delta Wetlands Monitoring Section Syr Darya", 2010–2013	OSCE, IFAS	IWRM implementers, policymakers
Project "Central Asia Hydrometeorology Modernization", 2011–2021	World Bank, IFAS	Owners, operators and other internal users of hydrometeorology services in Kyrgyzstan and Tajikistan, external users of information and services could benefit from information sharing and common standard for the hydrometeorological data in Kazakhstan, Kyrgyz Republic, Tajikistan and Uzbekistan.

Source: Compiled by the authors.

References

Abdullaev, I. and Rakhmatullaev, S. (2016). "Setting up the agenda for water reforms in Central Asia: Does the nexus approach help?" *Environmental Earth Sciences*, vol 75, no 10. doi:10.1007/s12665-016-5409-8.

Beglov, I.F. (2011). "Central Asia Regional Water Information Base – CAREWIB". In C. Madramootoo and V. Dukhovny (eds) *Water and Food Security in Central Asia*. NATO Science for Peace and Security Series C: Environmental Security. Dordrecht: Springer.

Bosch, K., Erdinger, L., Ingel, F., Khussainova, S., Utegenova, E., Bresgen, N. and Eckl, P. (2007). "Evaluation of the toxicological properties of ground- and surface-water samples from the Aral Sea Basin". *The Science of the Total Environment*, vol 374, no 1, pp 43–50.

Cai, X., McKinney, D.C. and Rosengrant, M.W. (2003). "Sustainability analysis for irrigation water management in the Aral Sea region". *Agricultural Systems*, vol 76, no 3, pp 1043–1066.

Cai, X., Rosengrant, M., McKinney, D. and Ringler, C. (2001). "Holistic Water Resources-Economic Modeling". World Water and Environmental Resources Congress. [Online]. Available at: https://ascelibrary.org/doi/10.1061/40569%282001%2971.

Carley, M. and Christie, I. (2000). *Managing Sustainable Development*, 2nd edn. London: Routledge.

Dukhovny, V.A. (ed.) (2018). *The Future of the Amu Darya Basin in the Context of Climate Change*. Tashkent: SIC ICWC Central Asia.

Elliff, C. and Kikuchi, R. (2015). "The ecosystem service approach and its application as a tool for integrated coastal management". *Natureza & Conservação*, vol 13, no 2, pp 105–111.

Endo, A., Tsurita, I., Burnett, K. and Orencio, P. (2017). "A review of the current state of research on the water, energy, and food nexus". *Journal of Hydrology: Regional Studies*, vol 11, pp 20–30.

Energyprom.kz (2017). "Fisher blooming in Kazakhstan". EnergyProm. [Online]. Available at: www.energyprom.kz/ru/a/reviews/v-kazahstane-rybnyj-bum-obemy-svezhej-ry by-vyrosli-na-19-za-god-konservirovannoj-na-6.

GWP (Global Water Partnership). (2004). *Catalyzing Change: A handbook for developing integrated water resources management (IWRM) and water efficiency strategies*. Sweden: Global Water Partnership (GWP). Technical Committee. [Online]. Available at: www.gwp.org/globalassets/global/toolbox/publications/catalyzing-change-handboo k/01-catalyzing-change.-handbook-for-developing-iwrm-and-water-efficiency-strategies -2004-english.pdf.

GWP (Global Water Partnership). (2018). "About IWRM". [Online]. Available at: www. gwp.org/en/gwp-SAS/ABOUT-GWP-SAS/WHY/About-IWRM/.

GWP (Global Water Partnership). (2019). "History". [Online]. Available at: https:// www.gwp.org/en/About/who/History/.

Horinkova, V. and Abdullaev, I. (2003). "Institutional aspects of water management in Central Asia: Water users associations". *Water International*, vol 28 no 2, pp 237–245.

Hornidge, A.K., Oberkircher, L., Tischbein, B., Schorcht, G., Bhaduri, A. and Manschadi, A. M. (2011). "Reconceptualising water management in Khorezm, Uzbekistan". *Natural Resources Forum*, vol 35, no 4, pp 251–268.

Hornidge, A.K., Oberkircher, L., Tischbein, B., Schorcht, G., Bhaduri, A., Awan, U. and Manschadi, A.M. (2016). "Reconceptualising Water Management in Khorezm,

Uzbekistan". In D. Borchardt, J.J. Bogardi and R.B. Ibisch (eds) *Integrated Water Resources Management: Concept, research and implementation.* Dordrecht: Springer.

Karther, D., Abdullaev, I., Boldgiv, B., Borchardt, D., Chalov, S., Jarsjo, J., Nittrouer, J.A. (2017). "Water in Central Asia: An integrated assessment for science-based management". *Environmental Earth Sciences*, vol 79, p 690. doi:10.1007/s12665-017-6994-x.

Karther, D., Chalov, S. and Borchardt, D. (2015). "Water resources and their management in central Asia in the early twenty first century: Status, challenges and future prospects". *Environmental Earth Sciences*, vol 73 no 2, pp 487–499.

Kosarev, A. and Kostianoy, A.G. (2010). "Introduction". In A.G. Kostianoy and A. Kosarev, *The Aral Sea Environment*. Berlin: Springer.

Kubo, H., Tateno, K., Watanabe, A. and Kato, Y. (2009). "Human and environmental symbiosis in Central Asia: Through the water management of the Aral Sea Basin crisis". *Transition Studies Review*, vol 16, no 2, pp 467–478.

Lenton, R. and Muller, M. (2009). *Integrated Water Resources Management in Practice: Better water management for development.* London: Routledge.

Libert, B., Orolbaev, E. and Steklov, Y. (2008). "Water and energy crisis in Central Asia". *China Eurasia Forum*, vol 6, no 3, pp 9–20.

Martius, Ch., Lamers, J., Wehrheim, P., Schoeller-Schletter, A., Eshchanov, R., Tupitsa, A., Khamzina, A., Akramkhanov, A. and Vlek, P. (2004). "Developing sustainable land and water management for the Aral Sea Basin through an interdisciplinary research. Water in agriculture". *Australian Centre for International Agricultural Research (ACIAR)*, Proceedings No 116, Canberra, pp 45–60.

McDonnel, R.A. (2008). "Challenges for Integrated Water Resources Management: How do we provide the knowledge to support truly integrated thinking?". *International Journal of Water Resources Development*, vol 24, no 1, pp 131–143. doi:10.1080/07900620701723240.

Pohl, B., Kramer, A., Hull, W., Blumstein, S., Abullaev, I., Kazbekov, J., Reznikova, T., Strikeleva, E., Interwies, E. and Gorlitz, S. (2017). *Rethinking Water in Central Asia.* Bern: Swiss Agency for Development and Cooperation (SDC).

Rakhmatullaev, S., Abdullaev, I. and Kazbekov, J. (2017). "Water-energy-food-environmental nexus in Central Asia: From transition to transformation". In S.S. Zhiltsov, I. S. Zonn, A.G. Kostianoy and A.V. Semenov (eds) *Water Resources in Central Asia: International context.* The Handbook of Environmental Chemistry, vol 85. Cham, Switzerland: Springer.

Roll, G. (2003). *Aral Sea.* Lake Basin Management Initiative Regional Workshop for Europe, Central Asia and the Americas, St. Michael's College in Vermont, USA, June 2003, pp 18–23.

Sehring, J. and Diebold, A. (2012). *From the Glaciers to the Aral Sea: Water unites.* Berlin: Trescher Verlag.

Schlüter, M. and Herrfahrdt-Pähle, E. (2011). "Exploring resilience and transformability of a river basin in the face of socioeconomic and ecological crisis: An example from the Amudarya River Basin, Central Asia". *Ecology and Society*, vol 16, no 1, pp 32–50.

Sojamo, S. (2008). "Illustrating co-existing conflict and cooperation in the Aral Sea Basin with TWINS approach". In M. Rahaman and O. Varis, *Central Asian Waters.* Helsinki: Helsinki University of Technology.

Worbes, M., Botman, E., Khamzina, A., Tupitsa, A., Martius, A. and Lamers, J. (2006). "Scope and constraints for tree planting in the irrigated landscapes of the Aral Sea Basin: Case studies in Khorezm Region, Uzbekistan". *ZEF-Discussion Papers on Development Policy, No. 112*, Center for Development Research, Bonn, December

2006, pp 1–49. [Online]. Available at: www.researchgate.net/publication/23516500_ Scope_and_constraints_for_tree_planting_in_the_irrigated_landscapes_of_the_Aral_ Sea_Basin_case_studies_in_Khorezm_Region_Uzbekistan.

World Bank. (2004). *Aral Sea – Water and Environmental Management Project.* Washington, DC: World Bank Group. [Online]. Available at: http://documents.worldba nk.org/curated/en/314201474588456706/Aral-Sea-Water-And-Environmental-Managem ent-Project.

Zonn, I.S., Glantz, M., Kosarev, A.N. and Kostianoy, A.G. (2009). *The Aral Sea Encyclopedia.* Berlin: Springer.

8 Using oilfield produced water in agricultural crop irrigation

An opportunity for integrative water management for food and energy production?

Tanja Srebotnjak

Introduction

California is among the world's biggest agricultural producers (State of California, Department of Finance, 2018; California Department of Food and Agriculture, 2017). To support its agriculture, California makes use of one of the largest interconnected water systems ever built. It serves 30 million people and delivers irrigation water to nearly 5.7 million acres of farmland (Hundley, 2001). The system was designed to mitigate one of California's biggest constraints to growth: highly limited and unevenly distributed freshwater resources. Yet, California is facing several significant challenges related to water, including increasing drought and flood risk, deteriorating water quality and potential ecological collapse of the important Sacramento-San Joaquin River Delta due to weaknesses in California's current water governance system (Public Policy Institute of California, 2011). The state also lacks critically needed water resource data, especially on groundwater. The exceptional drought that afflicted much of the United States' West and Southwest between 2013 and 2016 brought renewed attention to the need to reform the current system and move it onto a sustainable path. If California is to provide adequate water for its growing population and economy, it needs to act now and prepare for increased water insecurity.

Within the context of water availability and distribution, the food-energy-water nexus plays a critical role in California's Central Valley. The Central Valley is home to significant agricultural and crude oil production, a combination that can create tensions concerning water resource allocations among users and the protection of water quality. Oil producers may compete with farmers for water for well drilling, production and maintenance operations, while simultaneously generating large quantities of so-called oilfield produced water (OPW) that needs to be handled safely. Farmers are also concerned about threats to soil and groundwater quality from oil-production related spills, well integrity issues and malfunctions. State and local governments as well as administrative and regulatory agencies seek to manage water resources in accordance with their constituents and operational/legislative mandates.

This confluence of stakeholders and historical and geographical circumstances make food and energy production in California's Central Valley a suitable case study for examining the WEF nexus from the perspectives of collaborative governance and relational equity. Specifically, this chapter investigates the potential for using OPW in agricultural crop irrigation taking into account California's historically shaped regulation of water and wastewater and the current state of knowledge regarding the safety of OPW reuse in agriculture. Rather than outright condemning the practice of OPW application in agricultural crop irrigation, the chapter describes the current state of stakeholder relationships and governance approaches that could lead to harnessing the opportunities of OPW reuse, while addressing its safety concerns.

The remainder of the chapter is organised as follows. The next section provides a brief overview of water use in agriculture and energy production in the Central Valley. This section is followed by an overview of California's legal and regulatory framework on water, especially wastewater, followed by an examination of the potential risks of using OPW in crop irrigation. The chapter then examines the potential synergies of OPW reuse through a WEF lens; identifies the stakeholders and their respective viewpoints; and considers how their relationships and current dialogues are shaping OPW governance. The chapter concludes by summarising the preceding discussion and providing some recommendations that may facilitate OPW use within a WEF framework in the Central Valley focusing on relational equity and collaborative governance of water in the context of oil and food production.

The contribution of water to agriculture and energy production in the Central Valley

California's food and oil and gas sectors are both sizeable industries that contribute billions annually in state revenue and are linked to several hundred thousand direct and indirect jobs. In 2015, California's agriculture sales were $47 billion, while the direct economic output of oil and gas production was valued at $111 billion (California Department of Food and Agriculture, 2017; Los Angeles County Economic Development Corporation, 2017). Both sectors are inextricably linked to water. Agriculture claims more than 61 per cent of the 38 billion gallons of water consumed every day in California, nearly all of it for crop irrigation (U.S. Geological Service, 2018). Oil and gas production also requires substantial amounts of water during exploration, extraction, maintenance and refining processes. Although oil production in California has been in roughly steady decline since its peak in the 1980s, the industry still used approximately 210.6 million gallons of water per day in 2012, a 32 per cent increase compared with 1999 (Tiedeman et al., 2016). The increase is partially attributable to the maturation of many of California's oil fields, which now require secondary and tertiary oil recovery technologies, such as steam flooding, that are more water intensive than primary extraction methods. Hydraulic fracturing, while on the rise in other parts of the country, has seen less rapid growth in California and is less water intensive than in other parts of the country. However, water use per unconventionally stimulated well and per unit of energy produced is typically higher when compared with conventional production (Tiedeman et al., 2016).

Considering the co-location of energy and food producers in the chronically water stressed Central Valley, it is not surprising that the oil industry faces scrutiny regarding its water use and treatment. With respect to wastewater, OPW production in California has increased from a water-to-oil ratio (WOR) of 7 in 1999 to one nearly 16 in 2012 (Thompson, 2015). Considering the 201 million barrels of crude oil produced in 2015, this translates to approximately 3.2 billion barrels (equivalent to 134 billion gallons or 411 thousand acre-feet) of OPW. Approximately 65 per cent of the wastewater is injected under pressure into so-called Class II injection wells under a programme overseen by the federal Environmental Protection Agency (EPA),[1] some of which are used for enhanced oil recovery. The remainder is disposed of in surface evaporation ponds and smaller volumes are sent to sewage systems or to other beneficial uses such as agricultural and landscape irrigation, road application for dust mitigation and groundwater recharge.

As the state grapples with recurring droughts, the oil industry continues to use freshwater and produce huge amounts of wastewater. During the record-breaking 2011–2016 drought, Governor Jerry Brown instituted mandatory conservation measures and farmers received far less water than their contractually agreed allotments via the State Water Project, the system of aqueducts and canals that distributes water from the Sacramento and San Joaquin rivers to the farms in the Central Valley. This forced farmers to fallow acreage and caused revenue losses in the billions (Thompson, 2015). To partially make up for the shortage of water deliveries, farmers increased groundwater pumping, which has increased groundwater aquifer compaction, subsidence and salination in parts of the Central Valley which impact groundwater recharge. Climate change is expected to further exacerbate water shortages in the Central Valley and hence potential competition for water between food and energy production. One study estimates that most of California's 58 counties will likely face moderate to severe water stress by 2050 (Reig et al., 2013). It may thus appear that food and energy production are on a collision course over their respective water needs.

California water law and governance

To understand the water-energy-food (WEF) nexus in California, one has to look at how the state allocates, administers and adjudicates its limited water resources at the state level and with its partners at the federal and local levels. California's water law and policy are closely tied to the state's historical development, climatic factors and the uneven distribution of water.

Key federal and state institutions involved in water policy and governance

Historically, water policy and governance in California evolved from private control (1850s–1880s) to public control at the local and state levels (1880s–1910s), from there to control being concentrated at the state and federal levels (1910s–1950s) and finally to a tense and volatile cooperation between state and federal government and environmental and other groups favouring stricter environmental protections (1960s–present) (Olson-Raymer, 2014).

At the federal level, Congress and the EPA are the main actors involved in developing and enforcing federal clean water and safe drinking water laws. The EPA also supports municipalities with municipal wastewater treatment and participates in efforts to reduce pollution and enhance protections for watersheds and other sources of drinking water. In California, the State Water Resources Control Board ("State Water Board") was created by the State Legislature in 1967 to:

> preserve, enhance, and restore the quality of California's water resources and drinking water for the protection of the environment, public health, and all beneficial uses, and to ensure proper water resource allocation and efficient use, for the benefit of present and future generations.
>
> (California Water Boards, State Water Resources Control Board, 2018a, p. 1)

The State Water Board has jurisdiction over both water allocation and water quality protection, thus enabling it to comprehensively manage the state's water resources. The State Water Board is divided into nine regional Water Quality Control Boards (RWQCB). The EPA, the State Water Board and its regional boards work together to implement and enforce a system of federal, state and regional (Basin level) water laws and regulations. For example, the RWQCBs develop, implement and amend Basin Plans to reflect differing climatic, topographical, geological and hydrological conditions with approval by the State Water Board and the EPA. This vertical division insinuates a strong governing system, when in reality, water law and policy in California are the result of fights among an overwhelming array of different stakeholders over a limited supply that is further complicated by historical imbalances in the distribution of political power and financial resources, lack of preparedness for emerging threats such as climate change and misalignment of political jurisdictions and hydrological boundaries.

California's water rights system

At the foundation of California water policy are water rights, which grant the holder the right to *use* water, but not to *own* it. Water law also stipulates that the water must be put to *reasonable* and *beneficial use*, as defined in the California Water Code (California Water Boards, State Water Resources Control

Board, 2018b, p. 3). Water rights originally included municipal and industrial uses, irrigation, hydroelectric generation and livestock watering, but have recently been expanded to include recreational use, fish and wildlife protection and enhancement and aesthetic enjoyment (California Water Boards, State Water Resources Control Board, 2018c). California recognises four main types of water rights: *riparian*,[2] *appropriative*,[3] *overlying*[4] and *prescriptive*.[5] These types of water right, respectively, assign water use rights as a correlative share, on a "first in time, first in use" basis, as a correlative share of underlying groundwater and on the basis of continued, unchallenged use for at least five years (particularly in the case of public access to shorelines, lakes and rivers).

When legal disputes arose between riparian and appropriative water right holders, the California Supreme Court ruled in *Lux v. Haggin* (69 Cal. 255; 10 P. 674) that riparian rights have priority over appropriative rights, but for some time the ruling went mostly unenforced. This prompted the passage of the Water Commission Act of 1914, which established today's permit process managed by the State Water Board and established a hierarchy of "senior" and "junior" water rights holders. Pre-1914 water right holders ("senior") are largely shielded from reviews of and changes to their rights by the State Water Board, whereas rights granted post-1914 have been subject to increased scrutiny and detail. During times of water shortages, the most recent right holders ("junior") are the first required to reduce or discontinue their use. Priority in these cases is based on the date that the full permit application was filed with the State Water Board (California Water Boards, State Water Resources Control Board, 2018c).

Groundwater rights remained largely unregulated with the exception of the aforementioned overlying rights and adjudicated groundwater basins.[6] For decades, this uneven (and scientifically unsound) treatment of different types of freshwater has been criticised by environmentalists, local governments, water agencies and others since groundwater is an intrinsic and significant part of the state's hydrology. At last, and spurred by the recent exceptional drought, the 2015 Sustainable Groundwater Management Act (SGMA) laid out a comprehensive framework for managing local groundwater more sustainably (cf. section 4). Among its key provisions is the requirement for water districts to end over-drafting and bring basins into balanced levels of pumping and recharge (California Department of Water Resources, 2018).

As the state's water resources are increasingly oversubscribed and dwindling due to climate change, pollution and inefficient use, the State Water Board's task to grant and administer water permits for private or commercial uses creates tension with its mandate to conserve and manage water resources in the public trust. Specifically, under the public trust doctrine,[7] water resources are to be monitored and protected as the property of all citizens of the state, not for specific groups, interests or entities. This principle includes the protection of waters for commerce, navigation and fisheries, but also for their recreational and ecological values (California Water Boards, State Water Resources Control Board, 2018c).

Water rights in the context of the water, energy and food nexus

The food and energy sectors must also meet California's condition of putting water to uses that are reasonable and beneficial to the state and citizens of the state. As food and energy are both critical necessities of human life, water used for farming and energy production can be judged *beneficial*. Thus, the question is whether the *amounts* of water used are *reasonable*. Water in California is approximately allocated 50 per cent, 40 per cent and 10 per cent to environmental, agricultural and urban uses (Public Policy Institute of California, n.d.). Of the 40 per cent of water going to agriculture, more than 90 per cent is used to irrigate approximately nine million acres of farmland. Over the past decade, crop mix has shifted from lower revenue annual crops such as watermelons and tomatoes to higher value perennial crops such as almonds, grapes and citrus fruit (27 per cent share in California in 1998 to 32 per cent in 2010; in the Central Valley from 33 per cent to 40 per cent). Improvements in seed and crop quality (e.g. crop productivity and pest resistance) and agricultural technology (e.g. farm automation, irrigation system efficiency) have led to increases in farm output, while water use simultaneously decreased by about 15 per cent. Thus, in overall and economic terms, agriculture is becoming more efficient in its water use per dollar of output produced. Yet, the sector as a whole contributes only \$47 billion (2 per cent) to the state's \$2.6 trillion GDP, a decline from 5 per cent in the 1960s (Public Policy Institute of California, n.d.; State of California, Department of Finance, 2018; California Department of Food and Agriculture, 2017). In comparison, the oil and gas industry used approximately 1.2 per cent of the state's non-agricultural freshwater in 2012, while generating \$111 billion in revenue (Tiedeman et al., 2016). Thus, in terms of economic value generated per unit of freshwater expended, the industry creates more economic value per gallon of water than agriculture. The latter also sends more revenue and tax dollars to local and state governments than agriculture. Yet, with respect to supporting livelihoods, agriculture sustains far more jobs than the oil and gas industry; employing more than 400,000 workers compared with the fossil energy sector's approximately 143,000 direct jobs (Martin et al., 2016; Los Angeles County Economic Development Corporation, 2017)

The two sectors also differ in their dependence on historical water rights: the dominant role of agriculture in California's water appropriation is closely tied to the historical distribution of water rights: many long-established farms and ranches hold senior water rights and wield substantial political power.[8] The oil and gas industry in contrast purchases much of its water from water districts and other suppliers, whilst also reusing wastewater in enhanced oil recovery operations. Overall, the state has five times more water committed to rights holders than there is available in all rivers and streams combined and any reform will require support from powerful agricultural producers. Thus, a more comprehensive and integrated water management framework will not only be good practice for agriculture and the energy sector, but for the state as a whole as it prepares for future growth and the impacts of climate change.

Water quality law and regulations

Growing crops and producing energy not only requires large volumes of water, but also water of sufficient quality. Water quality in California is monitored and managed under both federal and state law. The federal Clean Water Act (CWA) of 1972 and its amendments established national water quality goals and set both water quality and technology-based standards as well as a permitting and licensing system for discharging pollutants to waters of the United States (California Water Boards, State Water Resources Control Board, 2008). The primary regulatory programme of the CWA is the National Pollutant Discharge Elimination System (NPDES). It regulates point source discharges into waters of the United States through a permit system, including specific controls for toxic discharges, and establishes the appropriate monitoring and reporting system for the regulated effluent source. However, agricultural "return flows", such as *"discharges of dredged or fill material associated with normal farming, ranching, or silviculture activities such as ploughing, cultivating, minor drainage, and harvesting for the production of food, fibre, and forest products or upland soil and water conservation practices"* (U.S. Environmental Protection Agency, 2018a, Exemptions), are largely exempt from NPDES.

If the water quality standards and other tools of the CWA fail to achieve water quality appropriate for the designated uses, Total Maximum Daily Loads (TMDLs) serve as a backstop to protect surface water quality. TMDLs, which cover both point and nonpoint sources of water pollution, are increasingly used in California to achieve water quality objectives. In turn, states have authority to require federal projects that are anticipated to impact water quality, such as U.S. Army Corps of Engineers drainage and dredging projects, to obtain a water quality certification as per section 404 of the CWA that the water quality impacts resulting from the project comply with the applicable provisions of the CWA (specifically sections 301, 302, 303, 306, and 307).

At the state level, California's main legal instrument for water quality is the Porter-Cologne Water Quality Control Act of 1969. It gives the main responsibility for the state's water quality to the State Water Board and provides it with authority over surface water, groundwater, wetlands and both point and nonpoint sources of pollution. The law ties California law to the CWA, specifically the NPDES system, for point source pollution prevention and regulation.

The nine semi-autonomous Regional Water Quality Control Boards administer the day-to-day implementation of the Porter-Cologne Act and manage water quality at the basin level with the help of Water Quality Control Plans. These plans allow for both forward-looking planning as well as implementation of current water quality objectives and the determination and protection of beneficial water uses. The plans are reviewed every three years and must be approved by EPA.

Quality regulations for the oil and gas industry

In addition to the CWA and the Porter-Cologne Act, important water quality control mechanisms for oil and gas producers in California are the State Water

Board's Waste Discharge Requirements (WDRs) and EPA effluent regulations. The WDRs regulate point discharges that are exempt from the CWA and the Porter-Cologne Act. However (and relevant for OPW reuse), exemptions may be granted for sewage and wastewater to land application, underground injection, Regional Water Board clean-up actions, gas condensate, soil amendments, drilling waste, discharges associated with the reuse or other recycling of wastes or salvaged materials and waste treatment in fully enclosed units (California Regional Water Boards, 2018).

At the federal level, EPA began regulating oilfield wastewater effluents in 1979 with the Oil and Gas Extraction Effluent Guidelines and Standards (40 CFR Part 435) (U.S. Environmental Protection Agency, 1979). The regulations apply to oilfield activities including exploration, drilling, production, well treatment and completion on land, offshore, in coastal areas, stripper wells and facilities operating to use wastewater for agriculture and wildlife. Extraction methods covered by the regulations include both conventional and unconventional extraction methods (coalbed methane is exempt) and apply to the following waste streams: produced water (OPW, which is typically the largest source of wastewater), produced sand, drilling fluids and cuttings, well treatment, workover and completion fluids. The 1979 regulations initially required no discharge of any pollutants, which promoted the injection of OPW into Class II underground injection wells. Many of these wells pump OPW into aquifers deemed too salty or containing hydrocarbons that render them unsuitable for other uses. However, California's Division for Oil, Gas and Geothermal Resources (DOGGR), the state's oil and gas industry regulator, has inappropriately allowed more than 6,000 Class II wells to inject into protected aquifers, thus endangering a potential future source of water and the environment. DOGGR's Class II injection well programme is currently under review and will likely see changes in management and oversight to reduce the risk of injection into protected aquifers (California Department of Conservation, 2018, p. 22077).

EPA's Oil and Gas Extraction Effluent Guidelines and Standards require OPW wastewater used for agricultural and wildlife propagation to not exceed a daily maximum concentration for oil and grease of 35 mg/L (such application is only allowed West of the 98th Meridian). It also must be of "good enough quality" to be usable for the intended purposes such as livestock watering or crop application (U.S. Environmental Protection Agency, 1979). However, OPW is otherwise exempt from most federal environmental laws and regulations, because it is not classified as hazardous waste and thus not covered by federal environmental statutes such as the Resource Conservation and Recovery Act (RCRA) and the Clean Water Act (CWA).

Water quality regulations for farmers and ranchers

The California Irrigated Lands Regulatory Program was set up in 2003 to protect surface water from agricultural pollution and requires owners of irrigated property and ranchers to test their agricultural runoff and to develop nutrient management plans for their land. Groundwater protection regulations were added to the Program in 2012 (California Water Boards, Central Valley-R5, 2018). The state's nine regional Water Quality Control Boards (RWQCB) have substantial authority on how to manage water quality within their jurisdictions. Their responsibilities include regulating pollutant discharges that pose a risk to surface and groundwater quality.

The Irrigated Lands Regulatory Program specifically addresses wastes discharged from irrigated agricultural lands, including sediments, pesticides and nitrates. Prior to 2003 agriculture operated largely unregulated under a waiver. Since then, the RWQCBs started replacing the waiver with regional and commodity-based Waste Discharge Requirements (WDRs), which are issued under Agricultural Orders. Fines can be imposed on farmers and other regulated entities (any landowner managing irrigated property) for failing to register with their respective RWQCB and comply with the WDRs or obtain conditional waivers for them. Compliance regulations vary by RWQCB, in part to respond to different regional needs and contexts. Despite these regulatory programmes, excessive nutrient loads from agricultural runoff impact on many watersheds and basins in California.

State and federal regulation of wastewater

The use of reclaimed wastewater for beneficial uses dates back at least to the nineteenth century. Federal agencies have traditionally left regulatory authority to the states, the exception being the federal NPDES permit system. In addition, the EPA has identified Priority Pollutants[9] in regulations dealing with municipal and industrial wastewater motivated by their risks to human health and the environment (U.S. Environmental Protection Agency, 1984). For the most part, the focus has been on managing pathogen survival and the risk of infectious diseases. Regulations target wastewater treatment level (primary, secondary, tertiary), access to and contact with treated wastewater at the site of application (e.g. setback distances, fencing, signage) and crop types allowed to receive treated wastewater and waiting periods between application and crop processing. Together, these approaches have been considered effective in minimising the risks associated with using reclaimed wastewater for irrigation in agriculture (The National Academies of Sciences, Engineering and Medicine, 1996).

At the state level, California, in particular, has a long history of promoting the application of reclaimed wastewater in agriculture and other sectors. The California Water Code, Section 13520, specifies Reclamation Criteria as *"levels of constituents of reclaimed water, which will result in reclaimed water being safe from the standpoint of public health, for the uses to be made"* (The National Academies of Sciences, Engineering and Medicine, 1996, p. 145). Moreover, in Wection 13521, it tasks the State Department of Public Health (CDPH) to *"establish statewide reclamation criteria for each type of use of reclaimed water where such use involves the protection of public health"* (The National Academies of Sciences, Engineering and Medicine 1996, p. 142). While the regulations have evolved over time, they still focus on the following basic elements of risk management and process control (The National Academies of Sciences, Engineering and Medicine 1996):

- The level of wastewater treatment required (primary treatment, secondary treatment, oxidised, filtered, coagulated, disinfected etc.);
- The permissible upper limits for selected water quality parameters to ensure wastewater treatment reliability and acceptable end-use levels of chlorine residual and turbidity (i.e., cloudiness of the water);
- Treatment reliability provisions;
- Site management practices that prevent workers and residents from being exposed to applied water and contaminated soils at the application site (providing for adequate setback distance, limiting public and worker access, posting warning signs, cross-connection prevention, hydraulic loading rate etc.); and
- Water management practices that minimise contamination of crops (specifying method of irrigation and/or types of crop permitted, requiring waiting period for crop harvesting or animal grazing, maximum water application rate etc.).

A comparison of selected trace elements and organic chemical pollutants in treated wastewater effluent under the California Water Code (sections 13520 and 13521), with effluents meeting the National Drinking Water standards, shows that the codes result in effluent which is as good as and better than that complying with the federal National Drinking Water Standard (NDWS) in the tested cases, thereby potentially making the California Water Code specifications a model for the rest of the country (The National Academies of Sciences, Engineering and Medicine 1996).

Oilfield produced water

As California's water resources continue to dwindle, some water districts, farmers and oil companies point to a potential synergy between growing food and producing energy that centres on the reuse of oilfield produced water (OPW) to irrigate agricultural crops. OPW, which is a mixture of formation brines and materials used in the oil production process, is the largest single waste stream in oil production. Specifically, for every barrel of crude oil, California oil producers bring an average of 15 barrels of OPW to the surface, for an estimated total of 21 billion barrels per year (Chittick and Srebotnjak, 2017). OPW has been used for surface applications, for example irrigation of crops, de-icing roads or promoting wildlife propagation, for 30 years. However, in California, its reuse in agriculture has so far been limited to only a small number of water districts[10] in the Central Valley, that is, the Cawelo Water District, the North Kern Water District, the Jasmin Mutual Water District and the Kern-Tulare Water District near the City of Bakersfield in Kern County.

One of the reasons for the limited application of OPW is that it is very high in salinity – total dissolved solids (TDS) content can be as high as 460,000 parts per million (ppm) (Otton and Mercier, 2018). Additionally, it may contain heavy metals, naturally occurring radioactive isotopes and hazardous chemicals that are used during well drilling, oil production and maintenance operations in varying concentrations with little monitoring and testing data, making untreated OPW a risky commodity (Benko and Drewes, 2008). However, as the state's demand for water continues to grow whilst supplies are shrinking or becoming less reliable, more farmers and water districts are looking at OPW to supplement their freshwater resources. The annually generated OPW could provide a reasonably steady and sizeable supply of water, although actual volumes may vary depending on production changes and market conditions.

Health concerns related to oilfield produced water

Before recommending the reuse of OPW in agriculture, the safety concerns voiced by scientists and environmental, consumer and community health advocacy groups should be addressed. There is limited information on the chemical composition of OPW, in particular for OPW from wells that have been hydraulically fractured using mixtures of toxic and hazardous chemicals, sand and water. One study determined that more than 632 chemicals are used in the USA for oil and gas production (Colborn et al., 2011). For 353 of them, for which Chemical Abstract System (CAS) numbers were identified, more than 75 per cent are known to affect the skin, eyes and other sensory organs, as well as the respiratory and gastrointestinal systems and the liver. Moreover, more than half impact the brain and nervous system and a quarter are classified as carcinogenic and/or mutagenic (Colborn et al., 2011). Another study found that wastewater from 95 per cent of hydraulically fractured wells in California, in addition to heavy metals and high TDS, contained measurable and, in some cases, elevated concentrations of benzene, toluene, ethylbenzene and xylenes (BTEX) and polycyclic aromatic hydrocarbon (PAH) compounds (Chittick and Srebotnjak, 2017). BTEX and PAH have a wide range of adverse health effects, including respiratory and sensory organ impairment, neurological, reproductive and haematological effects, as well as being carcinogenic. There are few scientific studies focusing specifically on the bioaccumulation of OPW-type contaminants by soils and crops. It is therefore difficult to understand and predict what, if any, acute and/or long-term effects the use of OPW in irrigation might have on soil and crop health, the effects of their consumption on humans and animals and the safety of agricultural workers and residents living near OPW application sites.

The literature on agricultural reuse of municipal wastewater and sewage sludge found mostly negligible threats to consumer health. This is because toxic organic and inorganic trace elements were found not to have transferred from soil to plant tissues or that their translocation to edible parts of the crop under normal agricultural conditions did not typically reach levels high enough to harm consumers (The National Academies of Sciences, Engineering and Medicine, 1996). Copper and zinc, two of the more common trace elements in sludge, are translocated to vegetative parts of the plant. However, they are not deemed to be of concern because their accumulation in the plant causes rapid growth stunting (phytotoxicity), limiting the entry of contaminated plants into the food chain. Scientists also believe that the soil-plant barrier is another mechanism reducing the translocation and accumulation of toxic compounds in plants' edible portions. Several metals, such as chromium-III, mercury and lead, are also highly insoluble or are strongly adsorbed to soil or plant roots, which means that they are generally not translocated into the edible plant parts regardless of the quantities present in the soil. Exceptions to the soil-plant barrier are selenium, molybdenum and cadmium. It is also difficult to estimate the potential toxicity of heavy metals in OPW from their measured total soluble concentrations. Owsianiak et al. (2013, 2015), for example, found that the bioaccumulation patterns and resulting eco-toxicity depend on the metals' accessibility and bioavailability in the soil, which in turn are influenced by environmental chemistry factors such as soil pH, organic matter content and the pore water concentration of other metals.

Current oilfield produced water practices in the central valley

The Central Valley Regional Water Quality Control Board (Central Valley RWQCB) reports that the four Central Valley water districts in the Bakersfield area that accept OPW receive approximately 50,000 acre-feet of OPW ($1.6x10^{10}$ gallons) per year from four oil companies, including Chevron, to supplement irrigation of about 95,000 acres of crops for human consumption. The two biggest users among the four water districts, the Cawelo and North Kern Water Districts, together use approximately 20,000–30,000 acre-feet ($0.65x10^{10}$–$0.98x10^{10}$ gallons) of OPW per year. The Central Valley RWQCB further asserts that water produced from wells that have been hydraulically fractured is not applied to crops grown for human consumption, that it has never authorised such practice, and that OPW undergoes pre-treatment to remove sediments, skim off hydrocarbons and other constituents before being sent to storage ponds, where it is blended with freshwater (California Water Boards, Central Valley RWQCB, 2018). Moreover, the Central Valley RWQCB requires that the oil companies test the produced water for certain chemicals to "*ensure that there will not be any negative impacts associated with the use of their produced water*" (California Water Boards, Central Valley RWQCB, 2018, p. 1).

Irrigation with OPW is regulated by Waste Discharge Requirements (WDRs) issued by the Central Valley RWQCB that provide for a conditional use of the mixed water for irrigation, establish maximum discharge limits for providers of OPW and require monitoring. But the state is also encouraging water reuse and recycling, which includes OPW, provided that the water is suitable for the intended use (California Water Boards, Central Valley RWQCB, 2018). In addition to the WDRs, the Central Valley RWQCB works to accomplish this through Water Quality Control Plans. In one example, the Tulare Lake Basin Water Quality Control Plan from 2004 states that "*blending of wastewater with surface or groundwater to promote beneficial reuse of wastewater may be allowed where the Regional Water Board determines such reuse is consistent with other regulatory policies set forth or referenced herein*" (California Water Boards, Central Valley RWQCB, 2018, p. 2).

The state and federal water quality regulations (cf. sections 3.2 and 3.3) only provide for limited management of OPW reuse. The Central Valley RWQCB has therefore recently expanded its monitoring parameter list to include those required for testing by the Groundwater Monitoring Model Criteria adopted through Senate Bill 4 (SB4),[11] California's main law on oil and gas well stimulation (California Water Boards, Central Valley RWQCB, 2018). The RWQCB is in the process of further updating its monitoring requirements to include "*all chemicals being used by oil producers during their drilling, maintenance, and production activities from wells that supply produced water for irrigation and those chemicals are included in the monitoring requirements for the produced water*" (California Water Boards, Central Valley RWQCB, 2018, p. 2).

There are few studies specifically on the uptake of OPW constituents in soil and plants but more is known about the bioaccumulation of contaminants from other sources of pollution such as smelters and mines as well as the application of sewage sludge on agricultural lands. Several dozen studies have linked such pollution to detrimental effects on soil and plant health. Fliessbach et al. (1994) and Khan et al. (2000), for example, show the negative effects on soil productivity resulting from heavy metal contamination. Furthermore, a study in Tongzhou District (Beijing, China) in 2007 examined waste water-irrigated soils used to grow radish, maize, spinach, green cabbage, cauliflower, turnip and lettuce. It found significant correlations between heavy metal concentration in soils and the edible parts of plants for cadmium, copper, lead and zinc (Khan et al., 2008). In addition, environmental, community and public health groups have voiced concerns about the potential risks to agricultural workers, livestock and the environment. One study reports that cows exposed to oil and gas related chemicals and pollution via the air, water and soil showed multiple health symptoms. These included rashes, respiratory and growth problems and reproductive failure (Bamberger and Oswald, 2014). There are as yet no studies on agricultural worker exposure to OPW, but the evaporation of OPW in open ponds has sickened people in their vicinity (Clean Water Action, 2014)

There are old records on the testing of blended OPW water used in irrigation, including testing for priority pollutants and petroleum constituents. These note that testing found that a few samples of OPW water distributed for irrigation – that is, after pre-treatment and blending with surface water and/or groundwater – exceeded the drinking water standards for arsenic (0–62 µg/L), nitrate (0–14 µg/L) and boron (0–1.1mg/L) (California Water Boards, Central Valley RWQCB, 2018). These records further invigorated the vocal opposition to OPW reuse by environmental and health advocacy groups and led to growing public concern.

The water-energy-food nexus of oilfield produced water reuse for crop irrigation

The reuse of OPW in crop irrigation is an opportunity for harnessing synergies in the water demands of the food and energy sectors in the Central Valley, if it can be done safely. This context provides a useful testing ground for WEF approaches to reduce freshwater use and increase productivity in both the food and energy sectors. It is particularly relevant with regards to the need for effective collaborative governance and strengthened shared interests (and hence relationship equity) among the different stakeholders in relation to the joint management of water as a scarce resource. The main stakeholders are: the oil and gas industry, which is seeking to dispose of its main waste stream; the farmers and agricultural operators and local water districts who want safe and reliable water supplies for farms and communities; farming communities who desire safe working conditions; environmental and public health advocacy groups, who are concerned about environmental damages and consumer safety; and the Central Valley RWQCB as the agency tasked by the state legislature with protecting the waters of California and preserving all present and future beneficial uses of those waters (California Water Boards, Los Angeles-R4, 2018).

Considering the geographical overlap between farming and oil and gas production in the Central Valley and the existence of state and local policies supportive of wastewater reuse, the key obstacle to a successful integration of OPW into local water uses is the alignment of stakeholder interests around the issue. Such alignment boils down to the question of whether it can be demonstrated that OPW reuse in agriculture can be practised safely. An objective and exhaustive proof would provide oil producers with an option to manage a substantial waste stream, farmers with a supplementary source of irrigation water, and communities, consumers and environmental groups with assurance that the practice is safe for people's health and the environment.

There are two major hurdles, however, towards this alignment. The first is lack of accepted scientific data and the second is insufficient strength of and trust in the inter-stakeholder relationships as well as limited institutional capacity on the part of the Central Valley RWQCB to collaborate effectively with all stakeholders.

Thus, in a first step and before rejecting OPW reuse outright as too risky, the issue deserves a thorough and objective review according to scientifically appropriate methods. This is the focus of recent action by the Central Valley RWQCB. In 2016 activists delivered a petition with more than 350,000 signatures to California Governor Brown calling for an immediate stop of OPW reuse in the state's agriculture (Center for Biological Diversity, 2016). In light of this pressure and the negative media coverage, in 2016, the Board convened a Food Safety Expert Panel (FSEP) to advise it in OPW-related crop safety matters (California Water Boards, Central Valley RWQCB, 2018). The Central Valley RWQCB took this step although crop safety falls primarily under the jurisdiction of the California Department of Public Health; a reflection of the interdependent relationship between food growers and oil and gas producers and water in the Central Valley.

The membership of FSEP includes public health and food safety experts in addition to representatives from oil companies, agricultural associations and members of state and federal environmental, natural resources, and agriculture agencies (California Water Boards, Central Valley RWQCB, 2018). Meetings of the FSEP are generally open to the public and include time for discussion and public comment. The Central Valley RWQCB has also contracted a science advisor to review the available data and carry out a study of crop residues of OPW constituents. The FSEP has held nine public meetings between January 2016 and July 2018 with the primary goal to investigate potential threats to food safety from OPW. The anticipated output is one or more white paper(s) assessing the state of knowledge, identifying remaining data gaps and recommendations regarding the further regulation of OPW reuse in agriculture. The panel is encouraged but not required to reach unanimous consensus in its findings and recommendations (California Water Boards, Central Valley RWQCB, 2018).

These efforts show that the Central Valley RWQCB is trying to listen to the concerns and needs of the main stakeholders and attempting to find a mutually acceptable solution on the basis of science and data. However, the second obstacle – that is, lack of trust among the stakeholders and fraught historical relationships – is somewhat constraining the chances of success of this effort. Historically oil and gas producers and environmental and public health advocacy organisations have been at opposite ends of the table concerning the need to regulate industry practices. The fossil fuel industry has had a relatively free rein in California. Moreover, it carries considerable economic and political influence in the Central Valley, especially in Kern County, where the industry is a key contributor to jobs and local government revenue. Bakersfield high school, for example, located in the county's government seat, is the home of "The Drillers". The complicated relationship between local communities and the oil industry has not improved with the surge in fracking in the USA and the renewed attention the practice has brought to the industry.

While it is mostly environmental and health advocacy groups that are organising opposition to the industry in general and OPW reuse for irrigation in particular, there are also farmers who view the practices of the oil industry negatively or at least with some level of suspicion. This group includes smaller and organic farmers, some of whom openly support the environmental groups. At least one farmer sued oil companies, in 2017, for allegedly contaminating groundwater supplies through underground oilfield wastewater injection. Earlier, in 2014, 145 farmers, 171 vintners and local business owners called on Governor Brown to place a moratorium on water-intensive fracking and illegal dumping of wastewater in unlined pits in order to protect diminishing water supplies (CBS, 2017; Food and Water Watch, 2014)

As a result, there is a lack of collaborative relationships between the oil industry on the one side and some farmers and environmental and health advocacy groups on the other. However, the relationship between farmers, and especially "big ag", and environmental and health groups is also rocky. The latter challenge farmers for dangerous farm working conditions, unsustainable water resource use that causes ground subsidence (on average 25cm per year in the Central Valley) and the poisoning of drinking water with arsenic, whilst the farmers argue that growing food should be a higher priority than protecting some endangered species (The Mercury News, 2018; The Guardian, 2018).

These tensions raise the stakes for the Central Valley's RWQCB FSEP. Some concerns regarding potential conflicts of interest and transparency have already surfaced when the Central Valley RWQCB invited experts to join the panel without seeking full input from external stakeholders such as agricultural community groups and environmental and public health organisations. The FSEP is reviewing the available data on OPW use in crop irrigation and has contracted its own field studies. It is therefore critical for the FSEP to balance the calls from advocacy groups to be expansive and thorough with the demands of the oil industry, which provides funding for the studies, to follow the previously agreed scope of work and complete it in a timely manner and without mission creep. The Central Valley Water Board maintains an FSEP web page with information and meeting updates and interested parties can sign up to its mailing list (California Water Boards, Central Valley RWQCB, 2018). It has also repeatedly indicated that it will take immediate action if the studies and additional information reveal that the current practice is imposing unacceptable risks to consumers, but it has yet to define what unacceptable means. Based on the data presented at its public meetings, the FSEP stated that statistical tests of the sampled crops for more than 100 oil and gas production-related chemicals, metals and other components have not signalled any problems. If problems were to be found, however, the Central Valley RWQCB could respond in a number of ways. It could – temporarily or permanently – stop OPW use for crop irrigation for producers associated with elevated testing results or for all OPW deliveries. However, since it is state policy to encourage wastewater recycling and reuse, the Central Valley RWQCB is likely to work with oil producers, local water districts, the FSEP and/or others to develop plans and regulations to address the issues that have been identified and seek practical remedies. This would likely include amending the Waste Discharge Requirements (WDRs), which conditionally allow OPW to be used for irrigation and specifying monitoring and testing requirements. It is likely that oil producers would bear the costs of such a monitoring programme. The Central Valley RWQCB might also extend the work programme of the FSEP to develop new work plans to fill data gaps. For example, studies could explore the potential risks from oil and gas chemicals and compounds that have no state or federal health standards, or have insufficient scientific knowledge of their human health effects.

While the FSEP is carrying out its work, the Water Board is letting OPW use for irrigation continue – a stand that is not unilaterally welcomed by the advocacy groups and some farmers. Moreover, at its July 2018 meeting, the Central

Valley RWQCB updated attendees on new and expanding OPW. It had received applications from two oil companies (E&B Natural Resources and Sherwood Hills LLC) for a new project with OPW discharges of 9,400 acre-feet per year being designated for up to 4,500 acres of cropland (citrus, nuts, grapes, silage or grain crops). In addition, Hathaway LLC, CA Resources Production Corporation, the Kern-Tulare Water District and the Jasmin Ranches Mutual Water Company proposed to expand their existing OPW use.

While the existence of the FSEP and the willingness of the main stakeholders to participate in its efforts is a welcome sign for collaboration under the leadership of the Central Valley RWQCB, it remains to be seen to what extent relational equity can grow in the process. Oil producers have taken notice of the effects negative public campaigning can have on their operations, while advocacy groups recognise the role of the oil industry in the local economy and many farmers are not strictly opposed to OPW use but would prefer having a seal of regulatory safety and approval. As a result, and in the absence of new findings raising significant concerns, it is likely that OPW will continue to be used in agriculture. It is also likely that the Water Board will implement some form of monitoring schedule and perhaps step up oversight and enforcement compared with the past 30 years of the practice's existence.

Conclusions and recommendations

This chapter discussed the case study of reusing oilfield produced water (OPW) from energy production for irrigation in agriculture within the context of the synergies and tensions in the WEF nexus. It explained the legal and regulatory history, the present state of water allocation, use and quality control, the risks associated with OPW reuse within the current system and the current collaborative governance approach taken by the Central Valley RWQCB in the context of the tenuous relationships among the main stakeholders.

OPW reuse presents an opportunity for the food and energy sectors to collaborate in addressing their water needs. However, the case study shows that such collaboration, while seemingly logical, does require relationship building underpinned by regulatory frameworks in order to use the practice safely. Specifically, in the case of OPW, the early primary actors 30 years ago were the oil and gas industry, as well as water districts and farmers, while other stakeholders such as organisations representing environmental, public health and consumer interests were absent. Only as OPW reuse entered the public limelight in the context of the controversial practice of hydraulic fracturing and was the subject of campaigns by environmental and health advocacy groups, did the regulatory lead, the Central Valley RWQCB, respond. It created an expert panel, the FSEP, to collect more information and conduct scientific studies regarding the consumer and environmental safety of the practice. Even with the relatively open and public-facing work of the FSEP, concerns remain regarding conflicts of interest and trust in the panel's findings. A potential weakness in the current set-up is that the work conducted by FSEP and the contracted science advisor depends on (i) the oil industry for funding; and (ii) the industry and farmers for access to land and facilities for testing.

While the FSEP provides a venue for the different stakeholders to engage with one another, the combination of conflict over water rights, sectoral isolated decision-making and various levels of historical and present animosity among the stakeholders has so far impeded true collaboration. Moreover, it has hindered the harnessing of potential synergies in managing scarce water resources for energy and food production within parameters that protect public health and the environment. If, however, the FSEP can succeed in carrying out its work in a transparent, scientifically sound and trustworthy manner, then the recommendations of the panel could lead the way to tapping the full potential of OPW and hence mitigate California's thirst for water. For this to happen, the following recommendations are made:

1   The Central Valley Regional Water Quality Control Board should review the charter and processes involved in identifying experts for its Food Safety Expert Panel in order to make them transparent and more inclusive. It should also ensure that all panel members have no conflicts of interest and, if they do, that they declare them publicly. The Water Board should also expand the Panel to include representatives from local communities living near fields receiving OPW irrigation water, the regional agricultural worker associations and consumer health and safety advocates.

2   The Central Valley RWQCB, with the support of the FSEP and relevant state agencies (e.g., the California EPA, the California Department of Food and Agriculture, the California Department of Public Health) should ensure that the studies carried out and/or reviewed by the FSEP represent the full spectrum of health, agricultural and environmental concerns. It should also commission further studies to fill remaining data gaps. In this context, the Central Valley RWQCB should consider expanding the envisioned output/ scope of the FSEP. Alternatively, it should consider initiating a follow-up process with relevant partner agencies to address the safety of OPW reuse for (1) consumers, (2) agricultural workers, (3) communities living near application sites of OPW irrigation water, (4) soil and plant health and (5) safety of animals fed crops irrigated with OPW.

3   To support point 2, the Central Valley RWQCB should identify sources of public funding and sign agreements with oil and farm operators to ensure the independent continuation of the scientific studies and secure necessary access to land and facilities.

4   During the period that data and information is being collected, OPW used for irrigation should remain at historical levels and not increase. This implies putting the proposed new and expansion projects on hold. OPW should be tested regularly by third-party laboratories for the range of constituents identified by the FSEP; at several points along the production, delivery and use chain, but – as a minimum – at the point of delivery to the farmer. Moreover, the Central Valley RWQCB should track fields and

crops receiving OPW as well as the volumes delivered/used in a publicly accessible database.

5   The FSEP should develop its recommendations only when the collected data and scientific assessment of OPW reuse are comprehensive and detailed enough to allow for evidence- and science-based decision-making.

6   The Central Valley RWQCB should update its WDRs in accordance with the FSEP's recommendations and implement them in a timely manner. Continued monitoring data should be made publicly available and easily accessible.

7   The Central Valley RWQCB should consider maintaining a process by which concerns submitted to it, by any stakeholder, can be transparently reviewed and responded to.

These recommendations provide for continued use of OPW in agriculture, while ensuring it is safe for the environment, workers and consumers. While OPW reuse concerns a practice currently applied on a small scale in a specific region in California, it already connects to millions of consumers across the United States and globally. Thus, the present process has implications for society at large and successful navigation of the safety assessment of OPW can result in both substantial water savings in California and a practice that is environmentally sound and trusted. While it is too early to conclude on whether the process will succeed, the case study has positive and cautious lessons for other WEF nexus issues. First, it shows that as water becomes more scarce, food and energy producing sectors can and do look for ways to cooperate and use the resource more efficiently, but to be successful they have to invest in building trust and relational equity. The lead regulatory partner in this process needs to ensure that the concerns of all stakeholders are heard and addressed equitably, while maintaining high levels of integrity, transparency and accountability. Second, OPW is the oil and gas sector's largest waste stream and its limited reuse highlights that there exist as yet no fully exploited water sources for reuse and hence efficiency gains. If such sources come with potential environmental, health and safety concerns, it is critical for the food and energy sectors to not shroud their partnership in secrecy but to involve all affected stakeholders in an open and transparent dialogue that is based in scientific fact.

Notes

1   Class II underground injection wells are wells used to inject fluids associated with oil and natural gas production such as OPW. They can serve the final disposal of such fluids or be used for enhanced oil recovery such as steam and water flooding. While the EPA oversees and enforces the programme, the agency may give "primacy" to states to administer their own programme, as it did in the 1980s for California.

2   Riparian water rights originate from the English Common Law, which California adopted upon receiving statehood in 1850. It gives landowners the right to use a cor-relative share of the water passing their property. In dry years, all landowners adjacent to a stream are required to share water use reductions equally. Riparian rights do not allow for water storage or the diversion of water outside the respective watershed.

3 Appropriative water rights (also referred to as prior appropriation water rights) emerged during the state's gold rush and reflect a "first in time, first in rights" approach. The principle gained legal recognition in 1851 via the California Supreme Court case of *Irwin v. Phillips* and allowed miners, among others, to stake a claim to water for their mining operations (or some other deemed beneficial use) and thus earn priority over its usage. Ensuing claimants could use the remaining water for their own beneficial uses, insofar as they did not infringe on the rights of preceding users. Accordingly, later users were the first required to reduce or cease their water use in times of scarcity. Unlike riparian rights, appropriative rights allow for water diversion and storage.

4 Overlying rights were established as a result of the California Supreme Court case of *Katz v. Walkinshaw* (1903). They refer to groundwater associated with the land underneath which the groundwater flows. Overlying rights, like riparian rights, are also correlative: landowners must share the groundwater percolating below their properties. However, even though it is well known that surface water and groundwater are intrinsically linked within a watershed, groundwater remained unregulated in California for decades, except in adjudicated basins.

5 Prescriptive water rights are rights conferred to a water user if they access and use a water source for at least five years without being legally challenged by the designated riparian or appropriative right holder. For example, prescriptive rights allow for public access to lake shores, creeks or other waterbodies as a result of hiking trails and other recreational enjoyment by the public.

6 Groundwater aquifers used by multiple parties can be adjudicated by a court. The court assigns water rights to the respective parties and can compel them to cooperate. Watermasters are typically appointed to ensure that the parties comply with the ruling of the court.

7 "The common law Public Trust Doctrine protects sovereign lands, such as tide and submerged lands and the beds of navigable waterways, for the benefit, use and enjoyment of the public. These lands are held in trust by the State of California for the statewide public and for uses that further the purposes of the trust. The hallmark of the Public Trust Doctrine is that trust lands belong to the public and are to be used to promote publicly beneficial uses that connect the public to the water." (California State Lands Commission, www.slc.ca.gov/About/Public_Trust.html, accessed 25 July 2017).

8 Approximately 4,000 farmers, individuals, corporations, limited liability partnerships, agencies and other registered entities hold "senior" water rights as prescribed under California's system of riparian water rights. Another 9,000, many of whom are farmers in the Central Valley, hold "junior" rights.

9 These Priority Pollutants are divided into four classes: (1) heavy metals (also referred to as trace elements or trace metals) and cyanide; (2) volatile organic compounds (VOC); (3) semi-volatile organic compounds; and (4) pesticides and polychlorinated biphenyls (PCBs).

10 Water districts are organisations in California that were founded after the passage of the 1913 County Water District Law and the California Water District Law, which permitted the creation of districts serving drainage, reclamation and securing and distributing water for domestic and irrigation purposes.

11 California Senate Bill 4 (Bill SB-4) (2014). Oil and gas: well stimulation. https://leginfo.legislature.ca.gov/faces/billNavClient.xhtml?bill_id=201320140SB4.

Acknowledgements

The author wishes to thank Louis Spanias for his helpful comments and background research contributions to this chapter.

References

Bamberger, M. and Oswald, R.E. (2014). "Unconventional oil and gas extraction and animal health". *Environmental Science: Processes & Impacts*, vol 16, no 8, pp 1860–1865.

Benko, K.L. and Drewes, J.E. (2008). "Produced water in the Western United States: Geographical distribution, occurrence, and composition". *Environmental Engineering Science*, vol 25, no 2, pp 239–246.

California Department of Conservation, Division of Oil, Gas and Geothermal Resources. (2018). *Underground Injection Control.* [Online]. [Accessed 30 November 2018]. Available from: www.conservation.ca.gov/dog/general_information/Pages/Undergroun dinjectionControl(UIC).aspx.

(State of) California, Department of Finance. (2018). *Gross State Product* [Online]. [Accessed 30 November 2018]. Available from: www.dof.ca.gov/Forecasting/Econom ics/Indicators/Gross_State_Product/.

California Department of Food and Agriculture. (2017). *California Agricultural Production Statistics.* [Online]. [Accessed 30 November 2018]. Available from: www.cdfa.ca. gov/statistics/.

California Department of Water Resources. (2018). *SGMA Groundwater Management.* [Online] [Accessed 30 November 2018]. Available from: https://water.ca.gov/Program s/Groundwater-Management/SGMA-Groundwater-Management.

California Regional Water Boards. (2018). *California Code of Regulations, Title 27 Section 20090.* [Online]. [Accessed 30 November 2018]. Available from: www.wa terboards.ca.gov/water_issues/programs/land_disposal/docs/exemptions.pdf.

California Water Boards, Central Valley-R5. (2018). *Irrigated Lands Regulatory Program.* [Online]. [Accessed 30 November 2018]. Available from: www.waterboards.ca. gov/centralvalley/water_issues/irrigated_lands/.

California Water Boards, Central Valley RWQCB. (2018). *Recycled Oilfield Water for Crop Irrigation.* Food Safety Expert Panel Fact Sheet. [Online]. [Accessed 30 November 2018]. Available from: www.waterboards.ca.gov/centralvalley/water_issues/oil_ fields/food_safety/data/fact_sheet/of_foodsafety_fact_sheet.pdf.

California Water Boards, Los Angeles-R4. (2018). *Oil and Gas Operation – Water Quality.* [Online]. [Accessed 30 November 2018]. Available from: www.waterboards. ca.gov/losangeles/water_issues/programs/Oil_and_Gas/.

California Water Boards, State Water Resources Control Board. (2008). *Overview of California Water Law.* [Online]. [Accessed 30 November 2018]. Available from: www.waterboards.ca.gov/board_reference/docs/wq_law.pdf.

California Water Boards, State Water Resources Control Board. (2018a). *Mission Statement.* [Online]. [Accessed 30 November 2018]. Available from: www.waterboards.ca. gov/about_us/water_boards_structure/mission.html.

California Water Boards, State Water Resources Control Board. (2018b). *The Reasonable Use Doctrine and Agricultural Water Use Efficiency.* [Online]. [Accessed 30 November 2018]. Available from: www.waterboards.ca.gov/board_info/agendas/2011/ jan/011911_12_reasonableusedoctrine_v010611.pdf.

California Water Boards, State Water Resources Control Board. (2018c). "The water rights process". [Online]. [Accessed 30 November 2018]. Available from: www.swrcb. ca.gov/waterrights/board_info/water_rights_process.shtml.

CBS Local San Francisco. (2017). "California farmer sues oil companies for allegedly contaminating water supply, killing crops". [Online]. 1 May. [Accessed 30 November

2018]. Available from: https://sanfrancisco.cbslocal.com/2017/05/01/california-farm er-sues-oil-companies-for-allegedly-contaminating-water-supply-killing-crops/.

Center for Biological Diversity. (2016). "Californians deliver 350,000 signatures calling on state, Gov. Brown to stop irrigation of crops with oil wastewater". [Online]. Press release, 9 August 2016. [Accessed 30 November 2018]. Available from: www.biologica ldiversity.org/news/press_releases/2016/oil-waste-08-09-2016.html.

Chittick, E.A. and Srebotnjak, T. (2017). "An analysis of chemicals and other con- stituents found in produced water from hydraulically fractured wells in California and the challenges for wastewater management". *Journal of Environmental Management*, vol 204, pp 502–509.

Clean Water Action, Clean Water Fund. (2014). *In the Pits: Oil and Gas Wastewater Disposal into Open Unlined Pits and the Threat to California's Water and Air*. [Online]. [Accessed 30 November 2018]. Available from: www.cleanwaterfund.org/ files/publications/ca/CA%20Oil%20and%20Gas%20In%20the%20Pits%20Facesheet. pdf.

Colborn, T., Kwiatkowski, C., Schultz, K. and Bachran, M. (2011). "Natural gas operations from a public health perspective". *Human and Ecological Risk Assessment: An International Journal*, vol 17 no 5, pp 1039–1056.

Fliessbach, A., Martens, R. and Reber, H.H. (1994). "Soil microbial biomass and microbial activity in soils treated with heavy metal contaminated sewage sludge". *Soil Biology and Biochemistry*, vol 26, no 9, pp 1201–1205.

Food and Water Watch (2014). "California farmers band together to fight fracking". [Online] [Accessed 30 November 2018]. Available from: www.foodandwaterwatch. org/news/california-farmers-band-together-fight-fracking.

Hundley, N. (2001). *The Great Thirst: Californians and water*. Berkeley: University of California Press.

Khan, A.G., Kuek, C., Chaudhry, T.M., Khoo, C.S. and Hayes, W.J. (2000). "Role of plants, mycorrhizae and phytochelators in heavy metal contaminated land remedia- tion". *Chemosphere*, vol 41, no 1–2, pp 197–207.

Khan, S., Cao, Q., Zheng, Y.M., Huang, Y.Z. and Zhu, Y.G. (2008). "Health risks of heavy metals in contaminated soils and food crops irrigated with wastewater in Beijing, China". *Environmental Pollution*, vol 152, no 3, pp 686–692.

Los Angeles County Economic Development Corporation (2017). "Oil and gas in Cali- fornia: The industry and its economic impact". [Online]. [Accessed 30 November 2018]. Available from: https://laedc.org/2017/06/08/oil-gas/.

Martin, P.L., Hooker, B., Akhtar, M. and Stockton, M. (2016). "How many workers are employed in California agriculture?" *California Agriculture*, vol 71, no 1, pp 30–34.

Olson-Raymer, G. (2014). *California's Water Policies: Who controls, distributes, and consumes this scarce resource?* Discussion Guide, Department of History, Humboldt State University. [Online]. [Accessed 30 November 2018]. Available from: http://users. humboldt.edu/ogayle/hist383/Water.html.

Otton, J.K. and Mercier, T. (2018) *Produced Water Brine and Stream Salinity*. U.S. Geological Survey. [Online]. [Accessed 30 November 2018]. Available from: https://wa ter.usgs.gov/orh/nrwww/Otten.pdf.

Owsianiak, M., Holm, P.E., Fantke, P., Christiansen, K.S., Borggaard, O.K. and Haus- child, M.Z. (2015). "Assessing comparative terrestrial ecotoxicity of Cd, Co, Cu, Ni, Pb, and Zn: The influence of aging and emission source". *Environmental Pollution*, vol 206, pp 400–410.

Owsianiak, M., Rosenbaum, R.K., Huijbregts, M.A. and Hauschild, M.Z. (2013). "Addressing geographic variability in the comparative toxicity potential of copper and nickel in soils". *Environmental Science and Technology*, vol 4, no 7, pp 3241–3250.

Public Policy Institute of California. (2011). *Managing California's Water: From conflict to reconciliation. Executive summary.* [Online]. [Accessed 30 November 2018]. Available from: www.ppic.org/content/pubs/rb/RB_211EHRB.pdf.

Public Policy Institute of California. (n.d.). *Water Use in California.* [Online]. [Accessed 30 November 2018]. Available from: www.ppic.org/publication/water-use-in-california/.

Reig, P., Shiao, T. and Gassert, F. (2013). *Aqueduct Water Risk Framework.* Working Paper. Washington, DC: World Resources Institute.

The Guardian (2018). "Sinking land, poisoned water: The dark side of California's mega farms". [Online]. 18 July. [Accessed 30 November 2018]. Available from: www.thegua rdian.com/environment/2018/jul/18/california-central-valley-sinking-arsenic-water-farmi ng-agriculture.

The Mercury News (2018). "Farmers protest Delta water plan, say protecting salmon hurts agriculture". [Online]. 20 August. [Accessed 30 November 2018]. Available from: www.mercurynews.com/2018/08/20/farmers-protest-delta-water-plan-say-protec ting-salmon-hurts-agriculture/.

The National Academies of Sciences, Engineering and Medicine (1996). *Use of Reclaimed Water and Sludge in Food Crop Production.* Washington, DC: National Academy Press.

Thompson, A. (2015). "Drought takes $2.7-billion toll on California agriculture". *Scientific American.* [Online] [Accessed 30 November 2018]. Available from: www.scien tificamerican.com/article/drought-takes-2-7-billion-toll-on-california-agriculture/.

Tiedeman, K., Yeh, S., Scanlon, B.R., Teter, J. and Mishra, G.S. (2016). "Recent trends in water use and production for California oil production". *Environmental Science and Technology*, vol 50, no 14, pp 7904–7912.

U.S. Environmental Protection Agency (EPA) (1979). *Effluent Guidelines and Standards, Oil and Gas Extraction Point Source Category.* Federal Register, vol 44, no 73.

U.S. Environmental Protection Agency (EPA) (1984). *Environmental Regulations and Technology. Use and Disposal of Municipal Wastewater.* Washington, DC: U.S. Environmental Protection Agency.

U.S. Environmental Protection Agency (EPA) (2018a). *Section 404 of the Clean Water Act.* [Online]. [Accessed 30 November 2018]. Available from: www.epa.gov/cwa-404/ exemptions-permit-requirements.

U.S. Environmental Protection Agency (EPA) (2018b). *Effluent Guidelines: Oil and gas extraction effluent guidelines documents for 1979 rule.* [Online]. [Accessed 30 November 2018]. Available from: www.epa.gov/eg/oil-and-gas-extraction-effluent-guid elines-documents-1979-rule.

U.S. Geological Service, California Water Science Center (2018). *California Water Use, 2010.* [Online]. [Accessed 30 November 2018]. Available from: https://ca.water.usgs. gov/water_use/2010-california-water-use.html.

9 Integrating the water-energy-food (WEF) nexus in the environmental governance of a metropolitan city in a developing economy

A case study of Lima, Peru

Viachaslau Filimonau

Introduction

The assessment of the world's progress towards the goal of sustainability should be underpinned by a systems thinking approach and by considerations of the water-energy-food (WEF) nexus (Biggs et al., 2015). The global demand for water, food and energy resources is rapidly intensifying which is, in part, driven by the on-going population rise, especially in developing and transitional economies, with the related changes in the quantity and quality of food consumed (Khan and Hanjra, 2009). The sector of agriculture strives to respond to these changes in demand by supplying more food, which results in the increasing pressures imposed by the food production systems on water and energy resources (Allan et al., 2015).

The complexity of inter-linkages between water, energy and food suggests that the global societal challenge of sustainability should be approached from a truly holistic perspective (Liu et al., 2015). This is to ensure the integration of water, energy and food into the practices of environmental governance with the concurrent engagement of all relevant stakeholders as facilitators of successful integration (Leck et al., 2015). Such an integrated, nexus-based approach can aid in better understanding how global water, energy and food security could be enhanced, thus improving societal well-being and building local community resilience around the world (Biggs et al., 2015).

The WEF nexus is of particular relevance to the rapidly developing and transitional economies in Asia, Africa and South America (White et al., 2018). This is not only because these regions host the largest proportion of the global population with increased patterns of (water, energy and food) consumption, but also because they are characterised by the unequal distribution of natural resources and high levels of social segregation (Pretty et al., 2003). Further, these are the regions where the population grows quickly, especially in cities, with urbanised areas representing the ever significant concentrations of diverse communities of people (Cohen, 2006). Urbanised areas in developing and transitional economies rely increasingly on the supply of food from peri-urban and rural areas, known as the hinterlands, thus competing with them for (often already limited) natural resources (Allen, 2003). This competition enlarges the gap in social inequality and disadvantages rural communities, many of which live in poverty and do not always have access to a sustained supply of water and energy (Aguilar et al., 2003). This underlines the need for better understanding of how the WEF nexus could be integrated into the environmental governance of cities in developing and transitional economies as a means of building more sustainable and equitable local, urban and rural, communities (Zhang et al., 2019).

Although the importance of integrating the WEF nexus into environmental governance in cities in developing and transitional economies has been repeatedly recognised, there is limited evidence of this integration in practice (Chirisa and Bandauko, 2015; Williams et al., 2018; Zhang et al., 2019). The opportunities and challenges of applying the WEF nexus in this context remain poorly understood as a result (Williams et al., 2018). Further, there are no examples of "good business" practice in applying the WEF nexus for the environmental governance of urban areas that could be generalised for the broader adoption across cities in Asia, Africa and South America, subject to accounting for the variations in the national, political and socio-economic conditions (Zhang et al., 2019).

This study contributes to knowledge by analysing how the WEF nexus has been considered within the policies of the environmental governance in Lima, a major metropolitan centre in Peru and South America. It highlights the challenges of applying the WEF nexus when managing the natural resources of a mega-city in a rapidly developing economy with emerging patterns of democratic governance. Lastly, it discusses the determinants of the effective integration of the WEF nexus for environmental decision-making in the geographical context of Peru and South America, drawing on first-hand practitioner experience and expert knowledge.

Literature review

Defining the WEF nexus

Although water, energy and food are closely inter-linked and should therefore be considered as the elements of a single system, rather than as "silos", it was not until recently that the need to view them as a nexus has been recognised (Mujtaba et al., 2017). However, within this more holistic and integrated approach, there is still no agreement on what element (if any) of the nexus can or should be prioritised, as this is dependent on a number of different factors. These factors include the political, socio-economic and environmental contexts of analysis, the chosen method of assessment, as well as the analytical objectives themselves (Endo et al., 2017; Mannan et al., 2018; Williams et al., 2018). In addition, it has been argued that, in its current version of conceptualisation, the WEF nexus does not necessarily capture the complexity and the totality of environmental and socio-economic interactions within the global, regional and local ecosystems. It therefore cannot be considered complete unless it encompasses land and climate (weather) as the indispensable factors of production (Ringler et al., 2013), but also environmental pollution as an inevitable consequence of production and consumption (Kumar and Saroj, 2014). Kibler et al. (2018) posit, for instance, that food waste should become an integral element of the WEF nexus given resource wastage represents a major social issue with ever-lasting environmental consequences. As a result, different variations in the name of the WEF concept have been proposed and are currently being used, often interchangeably, throughout the literature. A useful comprehensive overview of the various WEF definitions alongside the geographical scope of their application in academic research to date can be found in Endo et al. (2017).

Drawing upon the debate in conceptualising the WEF nexus, it is fair to suggest that water represents a core attribute of any living system on Earth which may, in part, justify the view of water as being a leading concept within the nexus compared to energy and land (World Economic Forum, 2011). This holds true for the food systems in the context of which the WEF nexus is often considered. Indeed, given the on-going technological developments, natural energy (for example, sunlight) can now be substituted with human-made sources of energy and food can be grown on floating platforms in the ocean and even directly in or under the ocean (see, for instance, McEachran, 2015), thus eliminating the need for land, while water as a core factor of food production cannot be replaced. This explains why the bulk of research on the WEF nexus has been undertaken in the context of (global and national) water security to date (see, for instance, Allan et al., 2015; Endo et al., 2017; Stijn et al., 2017). Concurrently, given the dependence of food production on water, energy and land supply, the WEF nexus has become a popular concept within the domain of food studies (FAO, 2014). Within this domain, food is considered a central element of the nexus, although not necessarily in terms of its overall importance, but rather in relation to its ultimate dependency on the other elements of the nexus, namely water and energy. All in all, despite its relative theoretical novelty and the need for further conceptualisation (Zhang et al., 2019), the WEF nexus represents a significant step forward in the promotion of a systems thinking approach and the integrated environmental governance vision to solving the global sustainability challenges (Albrecht et al., 2018; Biggs et al., 2015; Williams et al., 2018). This is because it enables better understanding of the complex relationships between water, energy and food, thus underlining the need to engage numerous stakeholders for more effective management of these precious natural resources to aid in global progress towards sustainability (Stijn et al., 2017).

The WEF nexus and environmental governance

Given its ability to uncover the complexity of inter-linkages between environmental, socio-economic and management systems, the WEF nexus represents a cornerstone of integrated resource management and environmental governance (Lamia et al., 2017). Indeed, the WEF nexus enables a (more) holistic assessment of water, energy and food, but also increasingly land resources, resource wastage and the social capital, in the context of a specific geography, thus highlighting the critical networks of stakeholders and underlining the scope for synergies and trade-offs across these networks (Ringler et al., 2013). The value of integrating the WEF nexus in environmental decision-making goes further in that it aids in mapping the key social stakeholders whose involvement is instrumental in addressing the water, energy and food related challenges (Scott et al., 2011). The WEF nexus can thus disclose the entry points for intervention that are necessary to facilitate (closer) stakeholder collaboration in more effective management of natural resources. Next, by integrating the WEF nexus into environmental governance, existing environmental policies can be reinforced and made more inclusive and better fit for purpose (Cairns and Krzywoszynska, 2016). Lastly, there is growing evidence to suggest that the adoption of the WEF nexus in environmental decision-making can reveal the scope for business opportunities in conserving water, food and energy and reducing waste generation (Kibler et al., 2018). In the long-term perspective, this can contribute to sustained business growth and provide local businesses with a competitive advantage in the national and global trade market, thus facilitating the transition of a specific geography towards a green and circular economy (Abaza, 2017).

The WEF nexus and environmental governance in cities

The majority of the global population resides in cities. Many of these cities grow rapidly, for a long time raising numerous concerns about the long-term, environmental and socio-economic, sustainability of such growth (Cohen, 2006). The issue is particularly pronounced in developing and transitional economies where the rapid urban sprawl consumes excessive amounts of (often scarce) natural resources (Chirisa and Bandauko, 2015). In many cases, cities compete for these resources with peripheral (rural) areas, thus accelerating societal tension within the region or even the entire nation. To ensure more environmentally benign and equitable urban development, it is critical that cities strive to integrate the principles of environmental governance and follow these principles in practice (Zhang et al., 2019). Most importantly is that, for better effectiveness, the environmental governance in cities should be underpinned by the consideration of the WEF nexus (Walker et al., 2014).

The need to (more closely) integrate the WEF nexus into environmental governance in urban areas in developing and transitional economies has been recognised (Kumar and Saroj, 2014). The challenges and the opportunities of such integration have been discussed (see, for example, a comprehensive review in Zhang et al., 2019), and a number of case studies have been made available to understand the extent to which the environmental policies in cities underpinned by the WEF nexus have been successful. The case studies have looked at urban areas in South-East Asia (Stijn et al., 2017), Africa (Chirisa and

Bandauko, 2015), China (Biba, 2016) and India (Kumar and Saroj, 2014). With reports of both (relative) failures and successes in the integration of the WEF nexus in environmental decision-making of cities, there is a need to develop more case studies in various geographies around the world in order to assess the determinants of the effective integration of the WEF nexus in the environmental governance of cities within different political and socio-economic contexts. The comparative analysis can aid in the selection of "good business practice" examples and case studies with a view to adjusting these for the broader application in urban areas across the globe.

Existing case studies on the WEF nexus and its adoption for environmental governance in the cities of developing and transitional economies have identified a number of determinants of effective integration. These have been effectively summarised as a policy brief by Abaza (2017) and the practical feasibility of many of these determinants has been further exemplified in the case studies reported in Stijn et al. (2017). First of all, it is paramount to have a strong (political) governance system in place as a means of promoting transparency, ensuring accountability, and encouraging the wider stakeholder engagement in adopting and implementing the WEF nexus for environmental decision-making in cities. This is closely related to the necessity to build the institutional capacity within the city/region/country which is often seen as a main driver of positive political and societal transformations in developing and transitional economies (Bazilian et al., 2011). The "mature" political governance system is further essential in the sense that it should strive to facilitate interactions across the different governing bodies, but also within the wider pool of stakeholders and across the various economic sectors, thus enabling an unrestricted flow of information and the (more effective) redistribution of resources, if necessary (Chirisa and Bandauko, 2015). Further, it is critical that the political governance system is underpinned by an effective regulatory framework which, again, should be transparent and, most importantly, whose implementation should be reinforced on the ground (Biba, 2016). Next, market incentives should be given to local businesses to encourage their active participation in environmental conservation (Bizikova et al., 2013). Coupled with that, public awareness should be raised on the scarcity of natural resources and the need for their (more) effective management (Abaza, 2017). Disseminating relevant information to the public represents a short-term instrument in achieving this goal, while public awareness should further be harnessed by integrating the WEF nexus into the national systems of public education, such as, for instance, in school and/or university curricula. All in all, investing in people is essential in making a qualitative shift towards more inclusive environmental policy-making in pursuit of sustainable development goals (Abaza, 2017). Lastly, the overall success of the project will depend on the ability of all stakeholders involved to monitor the progress of the integration of the WEF nexus into environmental policies, with evaluations being undertaken regularly and underpinned by a set of meaningful and transparent evaluation criteria and performance measurement indicators (Bazilian et al., 2011).

Research on the integration of the WEF nexus into the environmental governance of cities in countries of South America is limited. Aside from the notable exceptions of Mexico City in Mexico (Delgado-Ramos, 2015) and Sao Paolo in Brazil (Kraftl et al., 2018), the literature review returned no results when searching for WEF nexus related studies on the urban areas in the continent in question. This justifies the focus of this research on Lima, Peru, which is introduced next.

The case of Lima

Lima has an (officially registered) population of circa 10 million which makes it the fifth largest metropolitan area in South America, after Sao Paolo (Brazil), Buenos Aires (Argentina), Rio de Janeiro (Brazil) and Bogota (Columbia) (World Population Review, 2019). The share of unregistered residents living in informal settlements in Lima is considered high, meaning the city can potentially outdo Bogota on the list of the largest metropolitan areas in South America. The population of Lima increases rapidly, at an average annual growth rate of about two per cent (World Population Review, 2019). Although no data are available to accurately quantify the poverty levels of the residents of Lima, it is recognised that a substantial share of the urban population is represented by the impoverished communities living informally on the city's slopes. These informal settlements do not always have electricity or a centralised water supply and their food provision is often dependent on what is grown nearby and/or purchased in the local markets. This food is often of poor quality and of low nutritional value.

Due to its location in the tropical desert, the water resources of Lima are limited and the city is under the constant threat of water crisis (Collyns, 2015). A substantial portion of Lima sits on slopes and this is where continuous water supply represents a major issue, especially given that the slopes are dominated by informal settlements. Furthermore, this is where the populations are endangered by the constant threat of landslides, often caused by extreme weather events, due to the structural instability of the slopes as well as the lack of urban planning. Water is brought to Lima from the hinterlands implying increased competition for this precious resource between the city, the national sector of agriculture and also rural communities (Collyns, 2015).

The energy resources in Lima are restricted and some of the city's energy is imported. The country's energy balance is dominated by fossil fuels while renewable energy accounts for a small proportion (Feron and Cordero, 2018). The use of biomass as a fuel prevails in the impoverished communities. Combined with the dominant use of old vehicles for intra-city transportation, the burning of biomass for cooking and heating purposes contributes substantially to outdoor and indoor air pollution, thus contributing to the deterioration of public health in Lima (Energypedia, 2018).

Lima has access to one of the world's most productive fishing areas but faces the on-going challenge of food (in)security (OECD, 2016). This is attributed to the over-exploitation of coastal marine ecosystems, but also to the popularity of meat in the diet of its residents. The growing urban population imposes extra pressures on the food supply chain within the city and intensifies its complexity as a large proportion of food comes to Lima from the hinterlands (OECD, 2016).

Research design

The study adopted the qualitative research paradigm to conduct a critical evaluation of the extent to which the (local, regional and national) policies in Peru have integrated the WEF nexus into their discourse. To this end, semi-structured interviews (n=10) with main stakeholders in Lima were conducted. The stakeholders were selected based on their familiarity with the 1) Lima-related policies on the environmental governance in Peru; and 2) the concept of the WEF nexus alongside the opportunities it offers for more inclusive and effective environmental governance in cities. To this end, the participants were recruited from among 1) academics who have written on the topics of water, energy and food (and other natural resources) management and policy in Lima/Peru (n=4); 2) local and regional policy-makers involved in the design of urban and national policies, but also in the political debate on the above issues in the context of Lima/Peru (n=3); and 3) representatives of third sector organisations (including not-for-profit and community groups) engaged in activities on water, energy and food security in the local communities in Lima (n=3). To protect their anonymity, only the professional description of the interview participants (i.e. "academic", "policy maker" and "civil society representative") was used when analysing and writing up the outcome of this study, which is in line with the approach adopted by Cairns and Krzywoszynska (2016).

The initial themes for the interview schedule were extracted from the literature review. These were primarily underpinned by the determinants of integrating the WEF nexus into environmental policies as summarised by Abaza (2017). The interviews were conducted face-to-face in May to August 2018. The interviews were in Spanish and subsequent translation was made by a professional interpreter. The interviews lasted between 30 minutes and 1 hour and were digitally recorded and transcribed. Thematic analysis was applied to the collected qualitative data and NVivo was utilised for mapping the themes.

The thematic analysis was conducted through the lens of the relational equity approach (Sawhney and Zabin, 2002). This approach offers an opportunity to better understand the role of different stakeholders in facilitating the adoption of the concept of the WEF nexus for environmental governance in Peru and enabling its integration into extant environmental policies. This approach to analysis was further favoured due to its established ability to provide a more holistic outlook on the (political, socio-economic and environmental) system of interest, thus not only revealing the complex inter-linkages between the different actors, but also identifying the areas where these inter-linkages could be reinforced while their complexity is reduced (Ansell and Gash, 2008). This, as

Abaza (2017) suggests, is crucial for the effective integration of the WEF nexus into environmental governance. In essence, the relational equity approach enables better understanding of the determinants of corporate/institutional governance in pursuit of a specific goal which, in the context of this study, is the effective integration of the WEF nexus into environmental decision-making in Lima. The next section discusses the study's findings by revisiting the main themes to emerge from the interviews.

Findings and discussion

Evaluating extant policies on the environmental governance in Lima

The interviews started with exploratory questions aiming to understand what policies have been put in place to shape the approaches to environmental governance in Lima. According to the majority of participants, there are a number of policies in Peru which are either directly related to sustainability or integrate some of the elements of sustainability in their vision, for instance the dedicated policies on agriculture, energy generation and fishing. The major issue is not only that the policies are fairly generic but, most importantly, that they are disjointed and do not work together in an integrated, cohesive manner:

> *There are many policies [on sustainability], but that's not the main problem. The real problem is that they simply do not work together! And the politicians do not care as they probably do not even understand how or why they [policies] have been designed to help us overcome the [environmental] crisis in the city. They could not care less as they [politicians] are well paid and not affected [by the problem] directly.*
>
> (Civil sector representative)

This finding is in line with Gutierrez (2012) who identifies that the environmental policies in Peru lack consolidation and that the authorities in charge do not always understand the need to adopt a holistic vision when managing such a complex challenge as the inter-play of water, energy and food in Lima. This problem persists in cities of other developing and transitional countries (Chirisa and Bandauko, 2015), suggesting the truly universal scope of its significance. Even in the context of developed economies, such as the UK (Cairns and Krzywoszynska, 2016), there is evidence of diverse understanding of the WEF nexus and its implications for the integrated management of natural resources within cities.

Institutional capacity as a determinant of integrated environmental governance in Lima

The lack of interaction and collaboration across the different governmental bodies was identified as a major barrier towards the successful integration of the WEF nexus in the environmental governance of Lima. The relational equity approach (Sawhney and Zabin, 2002) suggests that (all) stakeholders should understand the benefits of collaborative work. Limited collaboration has important implications for the case of Lima given that governmental bodies represent the core stakeholder within the city. Indeed, most interview participants agreed that the local authorities do not collaborate effectively and can even engage in activities that run in parallel but are contradictory in terms of the anticipated outcomes. Institutional capacity represents a key success factor of integrated environmental governance (Abaza, 2017). Its lack however was identified in this study in line with the view expressed by Gutierrez (2012) and confirming the conclusions drawn by Liebenthal and Salvemini (2011). The study by Liebenthal and Salvemini (2011) is interesting in that it reports on the outcome of the World Bank Group's experience of working on the issues of environmental governance in Peru. The study posits that, although the Peruvian government has made a number of positive changes to its governance structure and working flows since 2002 in an attempt to consolidate the in-house resources and capitalise upon available internal competencies, thus reducing the detrimental effect of the institutional disintegration, these changes did not result in any significant improvements to environmental decision-making, with the exception of the domain of solid waste management. As this study found, the lack of institutional capacity in Lima/Peru remains a substantial barrier towards the effective environmental governance of the city.

The challenges of assigning the right priorities and monitoring progress in policy implementation

Most participants further claimed that the local and national authorities, being a core stakeholder in the implementation of these policies, tend to prioritise short-term economic gains over long-term, socio-cultural and environmental, benefits. This is despite certain evidence of the potential integration of the WEF nexus into many environmental policies in Lima/Peru, and in pursuit of improved economic development of the city and of some personal, financial benefits from the facilitated commercial activities. Further, even if there is a genuine intention among the local authorities to make the policy work, the practical application of the policies is not always reinforced, thus diminishing its potential positive effect.

A related problem was seen in the lack of monitoring the impact of policy implementation on the ground, which is considered a major omission according to Abaza (2017). The lack of practical reinforcement of environmental policies was further identified in Liebenthal and Salvemini (2011), meaning that little has changed in Peru for the last six years. Importantly, the issue persists across the world, as demonstrated by the research on the integration of the WEF nexus in the environmental governance of urban areas conducted outside Peru (Chirisa and Bandauko, 2015; White et al., 2018). The lack of reinforcement and monitoring is well articulated by an academic who participated in the study:

The policies are well written and they are often well intended. The lack of skills of those who are authorised to apply these policies in the field can damage their success ... It's also difficult to monitor how the policies work and there is no real monitoring mechanism in place which, I'd say, definitely works.

Trust as a cornerstone of effective environmental governance in Lima

More importantly, given the lack of practical reinforcement of environmental policies on the ground, the study identified the growing distrust of the public in the governmental bodies. As articulated by the representative of the third sector below, public authorities in Lima have repeatedly failed to evaluate the effectiveness of the implementation of environmental policies that were designed to benefit the local communities.

They had so many chances to apply the policies right but they failed and they did not care less ... To make them [policies] work, they [policies] need to be monitored but the officials are incapable of doing that. Best would be to find an organisation from outside the government and brief them on the monitoring of the policy applications in Lima. The officials would then be accountable to that organisation which can prompt them to work better.

This suggests that, in the future, the monitoring should be outsourced to organisations that are not directly affiliated with the government. This will not only add transparency to the monitoring process, but may also potentially increase the accountability of public authorities, thus encouraging more focused work of this key stakeholder towards the implementation of environmental policies in Lima. The need for accountability and continuous monitoring of policy implementation has been emphasised in the literature as a determinant of effective integration of the WEF nexus in the environmental governance (Abaza, 2017). Hence, for Lima to excel in this regard, it is paramount to ensure that an effective monitoring system is put in place and run by organisations that are trusted by the public.

The role of stakeholder collaboration

The relational equity approach suggests that the success of (pro-environmental) interventions is highly dependent on the ability of all stakeholders to work collaboratively towards a mutual goal (Sawhney and Zabin, 2002). This was not found to be the case for Lima which confirms the findings from Gutierrez (2012). The local authorities in Lima do not always engage with academics, third sector organisations and/or the general public. In turn, the ability of all these stakeholders to influence local authorities is limited which is in part due to their insufficient (time and labour) resources, but also partially due to the unavailability and poor accessibility of the governmental representatives. To ensure effective integration of the WEF nexus into environmental policies in Lima/Peru, it is critical to facilitate collaboration among the main stakeholders. To achieve this the, both national and local, government is seen as instrumental in enabling and maintaining this collaboration given the power and resources it holds.

Conclusions

There is a growing body of academic literature which suggests that, to enable global progress towards sustainability, it is important to integrate the WEF nexus into the environmental policies of cities in developing and transitional economies. This is because such integration can facilitate a truly holistic analysis of the main environmental issues that affect urban development, thus revealing more inclusive, and therefore arguably more effective, approaches to management of (limited) natural resources in cities and in their hinterlands. It is further necessary to evaluate the extent to which such integration has been effective and identify the determinants of effective integration. This can aid in the policy (re)design to facilitate more integrated urban governance in various consumption and production contexts.

This study contributed to knowledge with an evaluation of the effectiveness of integration of the WEF nexus in the environmental governance of Lima, a rapidly growing metropolitan area in South America. This contribution is timely given the lack of research on the WEF nexus in this emerging economy. Interviews with key stakeholders revealed that it is not the number of environmental policies, but the effectiveness of their practical implementation and the "right" allocation of (long-term environmental as opposed to short-term economic) priorities, which determines the success of the environmental governance framework underpinned by the WEF nexus in Lima. In the future, the environmental policies in Lima/Peru should be revisited and re-evaluated with a view to enhance and better align their focus and objectives and to develop a mechanism to ensure effective application and monitoring of these policies on the ground.

Drawing upon the relational equity approach (Sawhney and Zabin, 2002) the study further found that for more effective implementation of the WEF nexus-underpinned environmental policies in Lima, the stakeholders need to collaborate better and this collaboration should be grounded on mutual trust. Trust building is therefore necessary to bring the main stakeholders on board and ensure they collaborate effectively. Given the power of the national government of Peru and the local authorities in Lima, these stakeholders can play a key role in applying measures to build and maintain trust, thus initiating and sustaining stakeholder collaboration for the purpose of integrated environmental governance in the city.

Lastly, the work of the government in relation to policy implementation on the ground should be closely monitored by stakeholders who are not directly affiliated with the official governing bodies. This is to ensure transparency and enhance the government's accountability to the public and other stakeholders, but also to establish and sustain the trust of local residents in the environmental policies developed and implemented by the government. Representatives of non-governmental organisations/the third sector in Lima/Peru were identified as being best positioned to monitor the performance of the government and local authorities in integrating the WEF nexus into environmental policies and implementing them practically. This is due to higher levels of trust assigned to third sector representatives by other stakeholders.

This study made use of a small, but carefully selected, sample of interviews. Although data saturation was reached, the sample could have been extended to give voice to other stakeholders, thus offering more material for analysis. The main limitation of this study is the absence of representatives from the business sector in the sample of interviewed stakeholders. Abaza (2017) posits that local companies are instrumental in the effective integration of the WEF nexus in the environmental governance in cities; unfortunately, the study was unable to recruit them for participation. The local businesses approached with an interview request declined to participate referring to lack of time, but also their unfamiliarity with the topic in question. It was however felt that some businesses were unwilling to discuss the issue of environmental governance in Lima because of the perception that it is a sensitive topic. Future research should strive to capture the opinion of local businesses in the discourse on the WEF nexus and its integration in the environmental governance in Lima/Peru. This is in line with the relational equity approach (Sawhney and Zabin, 2002) which highlights the need for inclusive stakeholder collaboration in the context of the WEF nexus-underpinned environmental governance of cities. Future research should also target other geographies where the issues of integrated environmental governance in the context of urban areas are of importance, such as the major metropolitan centres in South America and South East Asia. Subsequent comparative analysis would enable the identification of "good business practices" and case studies on the effective integration of the WEF nexus in the environmental governance of cities in different parts of the globe. This would, in turn, provide evidence in support of the (re)design of national environmental policies whilst accounting for the variations in the political and socio-economic (consumption and production) contexts across the world.

References

Abaza, H. (2017). *Mainstreaming the Nexus Approach in Water, Food and Energy Policies in the MENA Region*. European Institute of the Mediterranean. [Online]. [Accessed 23 November 2018]. Available from: www.iemed.org/observatori/arees-da nalisi/arxius-adjunts/quaderns-de-la-mediterrania/qm25/water_energy_policies_Hussein _Abaza_QM25_en.pdf/.

Aguilar, A.G., Ward, P.M. and Smith, C.B.Sr. (2003). "Globalization, regional development, and mega-city expansion in Latin America: Analyzing Mexico City's peri-urban hinterland". *Cities*, vol 20, no 1, pp 3–21.

Albrecht, T.R., Crootof, A. and Scott, C.A. (2018) "The water-energy-food nexus: A systematic review of methods for nexus assessment". *Environmental Research Letters*, vol 13, no 4, 043002. doi:10.1088/1748-9326/aaa9c6.

Allan, T., Keulertz, M. and Woertz, E. (2015). "The water–food–energy nexus: An introduction to nexus concepts and some conceptual and operational problems". *International Journal of Water Resources Development*, vol 31, no 3, pp 301–311.

Allen, A. (2003). "Environmental planning and management of the peri-urban interface: Perspectives on an emerging field". *Environment and Urbanisation*, vol 15, no 1, pp 135–148.

Ansell, C. and Gash, A. (2008). "Collaborative governance in theory and practice". *Journal of Public Administration Research and Theory*, vol 18, pp 543–571.

Bazilian, M., Rogner, H., Howells, M., et al. (2011). "Considering the energy, water and food nexus: Towards an integrated modelling approach". *Energy Policy*, vol 39, no 12, pp 7896–7906.

Biba, S. (2016). "The goals and reality of the water–food–energy security nexus: The case of China and its southern neighbours". *Third World Quarterly*, vol 37, no 1, pp 51–70.

Biggs, E.M., Bruce, E., Boruff, B. et al. (2015). "Sustainable development and the water–energy–food nexus: A perspective on livelihoods". *Environmental Science & Policy*, vol 54, pp 389–397.

Bizikova, L., Roy, D. and Swanson, D. (2013). *The Water–Energy–Food Security Nexus: Towards a practical planning and decision-support framework for landscape investment and risk management*. Winnipeg: International Institute for Sustainable Development. [Online]. [Accessed 23 November 2018]. Available from: www.cilt.uct.ac.za/sites/default/files/image_tool/images/91/Bizikova%20et%20al.%20wef_nexus_2013%20OIISD.pdf.

Cairns, R. and Krzywoszynska, A. (2016). "Anatomy of a buzzword: The emergence of 'the water-energy-food nexus' in UK natural resource debates". *Environmental Science & Policy*, vol 64, pp 164–170.

Chirisa, I. and Bandauko, E. (2015). "African cities and the water-food-climate-energy nexus: An agenda for sustainability and resilience at a local level". *Urban Forum*, vol 26, no 4, pp 391–404.

Cohen, B. (2006). "Urbanization in developing countries: Current trends, future projections, and key challenges for sustainability". *Technology in Society*, vol 28, no 1–2, pp 63–80.

Collyns, D. (2015). "Peru harnesses ancient canal system to tackle Lima water shortage". *The Guardian*. [Online]. 22 June. Available from: www.theguardian.com/global-development/2015/jun/22/peru-harnesses-ancient-canal-system-to-tackle-lima-water-shortage.

Delgado-Ramos, G.C. (2015). "Water and the political ecology of urban metabolism: The case of Mexico City". *Journal of Political Ecology*, vol 22, no 1, pp 98–114.

Endo, A., Tsurita, I., Burnett, K., and Orencio, P.M. (2017). "A review of the current state of research on the water, energy, and food nexus". *Journal of Hydrology: Regional Studies*, vol 11, pp 20–30.

Energypedia. (2018). "Peru energy situation". Energypedia. [Online]. [Accessed 23 November 2018]. Available from: https://energypedia.info/wiki/Peru_Energy_Situation.

FAO (Food and Agriculture Organisation). (2014). *The Water-Energy-Food Nexus. A new approach in support of food security and sustainable agriculture*. Rome: FAO.

Feron, S. and Cordero, R.R. (2018). "Is Peru prepared for large-scale sustainable rural electrification?". *Sustainability*, vol 10, no 5, pp 1–20.

Gutierrez, W.B. (2012). "Towards the environmental governance consolidation in Peru". *Apuntes de Ciencia & Sociedad*, June. doi:10.18259/acs.2012001.

Khan, S., and Hanjra, M.A. (2009). "Footprints of water and energy inputs in food production – Global perspectives". *Food Policy*, vol 34, no 2, pp 130–140.

Kibler, K.M., Reinhart, D., Hawkins, C., et al. (2018). "Food waste and the food-energy-water nexus: A review of food waste management alternatives". *Waste Management*, vol 74, pp 52–62.

Kraftl, P., Balastieri, J.A.P., Campos, A.E.M., et al. (2018). "(Re)thinking (re)connection: Young people, 'natures' and the water–energy–food nexus in São Paulo State, Brazil". *Transactions of the Institute of British Geographers*. [Online]. doi:10.1111/tran.12277.

Kumar, P. and Saroj, D.P. (2014). "Water–energy–pollution nexus for growing cities". *Urban Climate*, vol 10, part 5, pp 846–853.

Lamia, M., Kramer, A., Abaza, H., et al. (2017). *National Policy Guidelines for Mainstreaming the Water-Energy-Food Nexus*. Bonn: Deutsche Gesellschaft für Internationale Zusammenarbeit (GIZ) GmbH.

Leck, H., Conway, D., Bradshaw, M., and Rees, J. (2015). "Tracing the water–energy–food nexus: Description, theory and practice". *Geography Compass*, vol 9, no 8, pp 445–460.

Liebenthal, A., and Salvemini, D. (2011). *Promoting Environmental Sustainability in Peru: A review of the World Bank Group's experience (2003–2009)*. IEG Working Paper 2011/No. 1. [Online]. [Accessed 23 November 2018]. Available from: http://ieg.worldbankgroup.org/sites/default/files/Data/reports/WP_2011-1_environmental_sustainability_peru.pdf.

Liu, J., Mooney, H., Hill, V., et al. (2015). "Systems integration for global sustainability". *Science*, vol 347, no 6225, 1258832.

Mannan, M., Al-Ansari, T., Mackey, H.R. and Al-Ghamdi, S.G. (2018). "Quantifying the energy, water and food nexus: A review of the latest developments based on life-cycle assessment". *Journal of Cleaner Production*, vol 193, pp 300–314.

McEachran, R. (2015). "Under the sea: The underwater farms growing basil, strawberries and lettuce". *The Guardian*. [Online]. 13 August. Available from: www.theguardian.com/sustainable-business/2015/aug/13/food-growing-underwater-sea-pods-nemos-garden-italy.

Mujtaba, I.M., Srinivasan, R. and Elbashir, N.O. (eds) (2017). *The Water-Food-Energy Nexus: Processes, technologies, and challenges*. Florida: CRC Press.

OECD (Organisation for Economic Cooperation and Development) (2016). *Environmental Performance Reviews. PERU. Highlights and recommendations*. OECD Report. [Online]. [Accessed 23 November 2018]. Available from: www.oecd.org/environment/country-reviews/16-00312-environmental%20performance%20review-peru-web.pdf.

Pretty, J.N., Morison, J.I.L. and Hine, R.E. (2003). "Reducing food poverty by increasing agricultural sustainability in developing countries". *Agriculture, Ecosystems and Environment*, vol 95, no 1, pp 217–234.

Ringler, C., Bhaduri, A. and Lawford, R. (2013). "The nexus across water, energy, land and food (WELF): Potential for improved resource use efficiency?". *Current Opinion in Environmental Sustainability*, vol 5, no 6, pp 617–624.

Sawhney, M. and Zabin, J. (2002). "Managing and measuring relational equity in the network economy". *Journal of the Academy of Marketing Science*, vol 30 no 4, pp 313–332.

Scott, C.A., Pierce, S.A., Pasqualetti, M.J., et al. (2011). "Policy and institutional dimensions of the water–energy nexus". *Energy Policy*, vol 39, no 10, pp 6622–6630.

Stijn, R., Verhagen, J., Wolters, W. and Ruben, R. (2017). *Water-Food-Energy Nexus: A quick scan*. Wageningen, Wageningen Economic Research, Report 2017–2096.

Walker, R.V., Beck, M.B., Hall, J.W., et al. (2014). "The energy-water-food nexus: Strategic analysis of technologies for transforming the urban metabolism". *Journal of Environmental Management*, vol 141, pp 104–115.

White, D.J., Hubacek, K., Feng, K., Sun, L. and Meng, B. (2018). "The water-energy-food nexus in East Asia: A tele-connected value chain analysis using inter-regional input-output analysis". *Applied Energy*, vol 210, pp 550–567.

Williams, J., Bouzarovski, S. and Swyngedouw, E. (2018). "The urban resource nexus: On the politics of relationality, water–energy infrastructure and the fallacy of integration". *Environment and Planning C, Politics and Space*. [Online]. doi:10.1177%2F0263774X18803370.

World Economic Forum. (2011) *Water Security. The water-food-energy-climate nexus*. [Online]. [Accessed 21 November 2018]. Available from: www3.weforum.org/docs/WEF_WI_WaterSecurity_WaterFoodEnergyClimateNexus_2011.pdf.

World Population Review. (2019). "Lima population 2019". [Online]. Available from: http://worldpopulationreview.com/world-cities/lima-population/.

Zhang, P., Zhang, L., Chang, Y., et al. (2019). "Food-energy-water (FEW) nexus for urban sustainability: A comprehensive review". *Resources, Conservation and Recycling*, vol 142, pp 15–224.

Part III
Conclusion

10 The water-energy-food nexus

Lessons for governance

Nikolai Mouraviev and Anastasia Koulouri

Introduction

The book offered a novel conceptualisation of collaborative governance of the WEF nexus, in which the participants are in a network setting, and made an original contribution to the literature by highlighting the principles that would guide relational equity management within the network. Although the principles might stay the same across the nations, networks and contexts, the exact models for collaboration and implementation arrangements might vary, allowing for flexibility and innovation.

This chapter draws the learning points from the selected nations' experience in integrating the nexus conceptualisation in governing the water, energy and food sectors. The principal aim is to identify lessons for nexus governance. The chapter also summarises the book's core argument and makes suggestions for future research.

Lessons for nexus governance

The book chapters have drawn a broad range of lessons for nexus governance stemming from many scales (international, interregional, regional and local) and contexts. Although some nexus challenges, such as users' competition for water and energy, are typical for many settings, other challenges to nexus governance are uniquely contextual. Without suggesting that each item applies to all types of nexus problem, this chapter delineates the learning points based on observed commonalities in how the WEF nexus is dealt with across the globe. These are discussed below.

- *Climate change has emerged as a critical factor that must be included in all nexus considerations at all stages, from policy design to implementation.*
There is little doubt that the world is currently experiencing climate change at an accelerated pace, and its impact (e.g. global warming, floods, forest fires) presents significant challenges and risks for the water, energy and agricultural sectors (Al-Saidi and Elagib, 2017). With this in mind, all nexus analyses should incorporate climate change as a factor of critical importance (de Grenade et al.,

2016). Disregarding forces that drive climate change is likely to make nexus problems even more acute and may further accelerate negative alterations of climate conditions.

- *Conceptualisation of security (energy security, water security and food security) should depart from a unidimensional approach and become multidimensional.*

Extensive debates engaging policy-makers, academics, practitioners and activists about each kind of security – water, energy or food – over time have become, to a degree, an impediment to WEF nexus thinking (Mouraviev and Koulouri, 2019). This is because professionals in a certain sector naturally focus on their own sector and pay little or no attention to other industries. To overcome a sector-focused approach, security has to be considered holistically, aligning the conceptualisation of sector-specific security with WEF nexus thinking (Daher et al., 2018).

- *Open and transparent polylogue between all nexus network participants should be present at all stages of policy-making and governance.*

Owing to the strong impact of nexus problems on society, economy and ecology, maintaining an ongoing conversation on what is at stake and how to identify and implement solutions becomes an important task for all those who oversee the network governance. This polylogue should engage all participants, not just major stakeholders (Koulouri and Mouraviev, 2018), which aligns well with relational equity management.

- *Due to the complex, multisectoral and multidimensional nature of the nexus, policy design and recommendations should be based on extensive research, collected data and scientific assessment, comprehensive and detailed evidence to inform policy-making and governance at all levels.*

Although this recommendation might seem obvious, in reality actors may push for their own agenda. For example, agricultural firms, driven by the profit motive, may insist on the use of harmful pesticides, while coal mining companies may downplay the harmful effects of the utilisation of fossil fuels.

- *Securing early on the commitment of participants to the outcomes for the WEF nexus, rather than for a certain sector, is an important step that sets the proper background for the application of the nexus approach and relational equity management.*

To participate in the network, participants need to agree on the basic terms of collaboration. Early agreement that finding nexus equilibrium is a priority within a range of goals helps to shape the participants' collaboration and depart from corporate and sector-specific interests. Furthermore, financing needs to be organised for nexus, rather than for sector-specific, goals. Naturally, sector-focused activities could be included in a work plan that pursues a nexus goal; nonetheless, the task within a sector needs to be linked with and serve the broader nexus governance goals.

- *To work to the guiding principles of relational equity, concerns raised by any nexus network participant should be considered equitably, regardless of whether a participant is a large stakeholder, a small organisation or a small interest group.*

Transparent reviews and prompt responses are required for building trust and maintaining effective relationships within the network (Klijn et al., 2010).

- *Synergies, competing demands (on resources) and trade-offs have to be identified early on.*

This is yet another tool that would permit the alignment of the nexus network participants with each other, form realistic expectations for contributions and results, and avoid controversies in the future.

- *Collaborative governance within a network requires consensus-oriented decision-making.*

This is aligned with the concept of relational equity management in which each participant contributes to solving the nexus problems and each expects benefits in the form of improvements to all three nexus sectors and beyond (Ansell and Gash, 2008).

- *Relationship building in the networks in most cases should be underpinned by a regulatory framework.*

Although the government may not be directly involved in a certain programme or a project, its role for designing a regulatory framework is likely to be significant (Bachmann and Inkpen, 2011). This is one of the most important elements of nexus network governance.

- *Certain critical nexus aspects, such as water rights and property (land) ownership rights, should be shaped by the legislation and take the form of a law.*

This is because citizens view access to water and land as their fundamental right. This is yet another area in which the role of government is crucial.

- *Social dimensions of the nexus problems cannot be separated from the core actions and/or programme activities related to energy, water and/or agriculture.*

In other words, social aspects should be treated as core, rather than additional, tasks in the nexus governance (Stein et al., 2014). In many nexus programmes, actors begin with the sectoral or multi-sectoral problems, and only years later the social dimensions gradually become incorporated in the nexus governance. The international experience suggests that it would be best to address the social concerns from the very beginning, alongside other work on the nexus problems.

It is unrealistic to expect that each network of actors would take on board all suggestions and recommendations. While dealing with the WEF nexus problems is a challenging task, it is worth drawing on world experience and paying spe-cial attention to the governance aspects. The learning points discussed above might significantly contribute to shaping effective governance structures and processes.

Future research

This book discussed only a small number of nexus problems. In terms of geo-graphical scope, it would be useful to investigate how the WEF nexus is dealt with in China and India with their high and rapidly growing demand for water, energy and food. Another opportunity presents itself in resource-rich nations, such as Brazil, Russia and Venezuela where the nexus problems often stem from the dominance of the oil sector. A special study focusing on cities, such as Bangkok, Istanbul, Kuala Lumpur, Mexico City, Moscow and Rio de Janeiro, could shed light on commonalities and differences in urban WEF nexus governance in the context of developing countries.

Although this book has provided answers, at least in part, to certain questions regarding the participation of actors in a network, their contribu-tions to governance and how relationships in WEF nexus could be managed, a significant volume of research and practical work has to be done to iden-tify the effective approaches and best practice. Some salient unanswered questions are:

- What impedes and what might facilitate nexus thinking as a standard approach to addressing water, energy and food challenges? How could corporate interests and sector-focused decision-making be mitigated?
- What should the role of the government be in nexus governance? Is it pos-sible that certain networks can effectively work without the involvement of the government that would underpin organisational arrangements, finance (at least in part) project implementation and play a mobilising role for all those involved? Is this realistic? This looks feasible for a smaller network dealing with a narrow nexus problem, which could be led, for example, by an NGO in partnership with an international donor. However, is this a realistic possibility for a large-scale nexus programme involving dozens of participants? If so, who could be playing a leading role and how could this leadership be legitimised?
- Are there standard (or typical) governance structures, procedures and solutions that permit the organisation of financing and the work of the network actors? As the nexus problems are common across the globe, could at least some of them be addressed with standardised approaches to minimise society's transaction costs and, more importantly, to mitigate climate change and ensure sustainability?
- How could market-based incentives be introduced for the network partici-pants to make sure they implement the assigned tasks? What are the most effective ways to incentivise actors?

- In the context of a certain nation, how could legal, regulatory and institutional frameworks be aligned to mitigate nexus problems? What experience in this field could be borrowed from industrialised economies and developing countries?

This list is non-exhaustive and other, more context-specific questions also require the attention of policy-makers, researchers and practitioners in international, national, regional and local governing bodies. The WEF nexus problems, with their ultimate impact on climate change and sustainable development, are often acute and require effective governance as delays and/or mistakes might have catastrophic consequences. Therefore, building robust governance frameworks is a challenge that needs to be addressed by policy-makers, researchers and practitioners for the benefit of those who are engaged with the three sectors and for society at large. In a search for effective governance, relational equity management might serve as one of the promising approaches that could deliver the desired outcomes.

References

Al-Saidi, M. and Elagib, N.A. (2017). "Towards understanding the integrative approach of the water, energy and food nexus". *Science of the Total Environment*, vol 574, pp 1131–1139.

Ansell, C. and Gash, A. (2008). "Collaborative governance in theory and practice". *Journal of Public Administration Research and Theory*, vol 18, no 4, pp 543–571.

Bachmann, R., and Inkpen, A.C. (2011). "Understanding institutional-based trust building processes in inter-organisational relationships". *Organisation Studies*, vol 32, no 2, pp 281–301.

Daher, B., Lee, S., Mohtar, R., Asaka, J.O. and VanDeveer, S. (2018). "Security, climate change and the nexus". In R. Bleischwitz, H. Hoff, C. Spataru, E. van der Voet and S. VanDeveer (eds) *Routledge Handbook of the Resource Nexus*. New York: Routledge.

de Grenade, R., House-Peters, L., Scott, C.A., Thapa, B., Mills-Novoa, M., Gerlak, A. and Verbist, K. (2016). "The nexus: Reconsidering environmental security and adaptive capacity". *Current Opnion in Environmental Sustainability*, vol 21, August, pp 15–21.

Klijn, E. H., Steijn, B. and Edelenbos, J. (2010). "The impact of network management strategies on the outcomes in governance networks". *Public Administration*, vol 88, no 4, pp 1063–1082.

Koulouri, A. and Mouraviev, N. (2018). "Governance of the clean energy sector in Kazakhstan: Impediments to investment". *International Journal of Technology Intelligence and Planning*, vol 12, no 1, pp 6–23.

Mouraviev, N. and Koulouri, A. (eds) (2019). *Energy Security: Policy challenges and solutions for resource efficiency*. London: Palgrave Macmillan.

Stein, C., Barron, J. and Moss, T. (2014). *Governance of the Nexus: From buzz words to a strategic action perspective*. The Nexus Network. [Online]. 1 April. [Accessed on 19 February 2019]. www.thenexusnetwork.org/wp-content/uploads/2014/08/Stein-Barron-and-Moss-Strategic-Action-Perspective-Nexus-Thinkpiece-2014-page-numbers.pdf.

Index

agricultural 4, 6, 14, 17–20, 23–4, 35–6,
    52–3, 60, 64–72, 100, 106, 109, 120–2,
    125–30, 132–5, 137, 161–2
agriculture 13–18, 20–5, 37–8, 40–2, 52–3,
    56, 64, 66, 68–9, 96, 98–9, 103–4, 110,
    112–5, 120–1, 125, 127–30, 133–8, 143,
    148, 150, 163
appropriative doctrine 53–4
Aral Sea 4, 20, 26, 95–116

biodiversity 21, 52, 79, 96
Bonn (Climate Change) Conference(s) 12,
    31, 49

California 4, 26, 35, 120, 121, 122–36,
    137–9
Canada 34–5, 37–41, 111
Central Asia 4, 17–18, 20, 24, 59, 95–6,
    98–9, 102, 109–10, 113–6,
Chile 34, 36–8, 40–3, 54
China 17–8, 66, 132, 147, 164–5
climate change 1, 4, 21, 31, 35, 37–40,
    48–51, 58–9, 65–7, 78, 82–4, 88, 90,
    98, 107, 116, 122–5, 161, 164
collaborative 4, 11–3, 15, 17, 24, 39, 45,
    48–9, 51, 58–61, 67, 69–71, 77–8, 81,
    87, 89–90, 96, 102–3, 107, 121, 133–4,
    136, 151–2, 161
Common Agricultural Policy (also: CAP)
    66, 68
community 2, 4, 14, 43, 55–6, 68, 79–81,
    83, 86–7, 98–9, 115, 130, 132, 135,
    143, 149
conflict 12, 32, 38, 44, 50, 53, 55, 67–8, 77,
    80, 82, 84–6, 88–90, 107, 135–7;
    management 86; resolution 53
consumptive 51–7, 60
co-production of knowledge 67, 69–71
corruption 2, 83–4

Department of Environment, Food and
    Rural Affairs (also: DEFRA) 64, 66–67,
    70–71
desertification 20–21, 96, 98, 100
desiccation 96, 100, 106

ecological 1, 21, 45, 48, 54, 56–7, 59, 61,
    79, 96–8, 100, 104, 108, 112, 113–4, 120,
    124; justice 61; system(s) 1, 21, 45
ecology 52, 112–4, 162
ecosystem(s) 35–6, 58, 67, 145, 149
Ecuador 34, 36–40, 42
electricity generation 3
emerging economy 153
energy: consumption 19; efficiency 19,
    69; generation 17, 19, 67–8, 150;
    policy 3, 66; production 4, 19, 44, 50,
    52, 55, 57, 106, 113, 120–2, 125, 136;
    resource(s) 38, 78, 83, 85, 143, 148;
    sector 15, 17, 19, 21, 25, 31, 51, 97,
    101, 125, 133, 136, 138; security 3, 19,
    22, 162
environmental: consequences 100, 145;
    conservation 147: damage 58, 133;
    decision-making 144, 146–7, 150–1;
    governance 4, 64, 111, 143–54; impact(s)
    59; policy(ies) 64–5, 146–7, 149–54;
    pollution 145; protection 101–3, 105,
    115–16, 122–3, 127; security 79, 81;
    sustainability 96, 107–8
equity mobilisation 5
Europe 59, 65, 69, 71, 113–15
European Commission 68–69
European Union (EU) 6, 64, 66–71,
    102, 104

fishery(ies) 35, 96, 104, 106, 108, 110
food: production 3, 21, 23, 35, 44, 49, 52,
    55, 64, 67–8, 121, 137, 143, 145; sector

3–5, 12, 17, 21, 67, 161; security 12,
  20–1, 23–5, 31, 49, 69–70, 79–80,
  102, 143, 149, 162; supply chain 149;
  waste 145
Food and Agriculture Organisation (FAO)
  64, 66, 69–71, 115
fossil fuel(s) 3, 17–9, 21, 134, 148, 162
freshwater 3, 112, 120, 122, 124–5,
  130–1, 133

global sustainability challenges 145
globalisation 1, 49
governmental agencies 3, 5, 12, 54
Green Economy 12, 23, 49
groundwater 17, 35–7, 120, 122, 124, 126,
  128, 132, 134

health security 79
human security 4, 77–80, 84–90, 107
hydropower 3, 21, 24–5, 52, 54–5,
  59, 97

integrated management 67, 150
Integrated Water Resource Management
  (also: IWRM) 12, 22, 97–8, 101–3,
  105–6, 108, 114, 116
integrative environmental governance 64
integrative water management 120
international 2–5, 12, 15, 22, 26, 31, 36,
  53, 64–6, 68–72, 79, 85, 90, 98–9,
  101–3, 106–112, 114–15, 161, 163–5
Iran 95

Japan 34–5, 37–8, 40, 106

Kazakhstan 3, 11, 16–25, 95–9, 104, 106,
  110–2, 116
Kenya 4, 26, 77–82, 84–90
Kyrgyzstan 3, 17, 24–5, 95–9, 106, 112,
  114–16

land use 21, 24, 36, 64, 67–8, 78, 81–3,
  88, 108
legislative framework 18, 24, 115
Lima 4, 26, 143–4, 148–54

migration 84, 96
mining 35–8, 41, 53, 162
mitigation measure(s) 35

network 13–7, 20, 26, 69, 104, 114, 146,
  161–4
network governance 15–7, 26, 162–3
network participant(s) 14, 16–7, 162–4

nexus: challenges 2, 4, 81, 88–9, 161;
  concept 4, 49–50; conceptualisation 11,
  12, 161; goal 162; governance 2, 2–6,
  11, 13–5, 77, 89, 95, 107–9, 161–4;
  management 96; network 17, 162–3;
  programme(s) 163–4; thinking 2, 4–5,
  16–7, 25, 49–51, 56–7, 64–72, 87, 89,
  162, 164
NGO 2, 5, 12, 15, 90, 164
non-consumptive 51–7
non-governmental 3, 5, 36, 89, 100, 154
North America 65

oilfield produced water (OPW) 120–2,
  127, 129–31, 133, 136–8
oilfield wastewater 127, 134

pastoralism 81, 83, 84, 88
pastoralist communities 81–2
pastureland 77, 82–4, 88
path dependence 1
personal security 79–80
Peru 4, 26, 143–4, 148–51, 153–4
policy: change(s) 31, 34, 39, 42, 44;
  coherence 12, 32, 41–2; design 4,
  11–13, 33, 40–42, 90, 161–2; document
  (s) 23, 38, 68; interventions 3, 50;
  implementation 25, 151–3; linkages 34,
  38; makers 2, 32–5, 37–45, 65, 149, 162,
  165; making 4, 13, 44–5, 64–7, 71,
  109–10, 112, 114, 147, 162;
  recommendations 31–3, 40–1;
  research 5
political security 79–80
poverty 66, 79, 144, 148
price mechanism(s) 50
property rights 4, 6, 48–9, 51–61

relational equity 1–4, 6, 11, 13–6, 26, 43,
  45, 49, 51, 58–61, 70–1, 77–8, 81, 86–7,
  89–90, 95–8, 103–9, 121, 136, 138,
  149–54, 161–3, 165
renewable(s) 3, 17–9, 22–3, 25, 64, 68–9,
  97, 148
residual benefits 49
residual claimancy 49, 54, 56–7, 59–61
resource curse 77, 86
resource efficiency 5, 19, 25, 49
resource management 1–2, 5–6, 12, 22, 24,
  50, 57–60, 87, 97, 101, 109, 146
resource-rich 3, 18, 164
riparian doctrine 53–4
river basin 17, 36, 40, 54, 59, 105
river system(s) 49, 51–5, 57–60

rural 6, 22, 26, 37, 44, 64, 66–7, 69, 112, 114, 144, 146, 148; communities 144, 148; policy 67, 69; services 67
Russia 17, 18, 23, 114, 164

salination 20, 122
socialcost(s) 50, 56, 57, 59
social inequality 144
socio-economic 5, 12, 90, 96, 100–4, 196, 108, 112–14, 144–7, 149, 154; development 5, 101–2, 106, 112–14; sustainability 146
Soviet 16, 22, 24, 96–7
Sri Lanka 54, 59
stakeholder(s) 1–3, 5, 11–2, 16, 25, 35, 38, 41–4, 51, 56, 58–9, 61, 67, 69–71, 86–90, 96–9, 101–9, 115, 121, 123, 133–8, 143, 145–7, 149, 151–4, 162–3; analysis 105; involvement 86, 101; management 16, 103
subsidy(ies) 23, 50–1
Suriname 34–5, 37–40
sustainability 4, 5, 14, 45, 48, 51, 65–6, 69, 96, 102, 107–9, 143, 145–6, 150, 153, 164
Sustainable Development Goals 12, 32, 147
systems modelling 50

Tajikistan 95–100, 106, 110, 112, 114–16
third sector 149, 152, 154
transaction cost(s) 53, 56–7, 60, 164
transboundary 18, 78, 85, 90, 97–8, 102, 112
transnational 4
Turkmenistan 17, 95–9, 106, 111, 113, 116

United Kingdom (also: UK) 6, 64, 66–8, 70, 110, 150
United Nations (also: UN) 12, 65–6, 69, 78, 98–9, 107, 113–5
United Nations Development Programme (also: UNDP) 78–80, 109, 111
United States of America (also: USA) 4, 39, 54, 61, 65, 66, 111, 130, 134
urban 6, 17, 25, 59, 125, 143–4, 146–9, 151, 153–4, 164; planning 148; population 148–9
urbanisation 1, 18, 21, 48, 57, 64
Uzbekistan 17, 25, 95–9, 105–7, 110–1, 113–6

wastewater 121–3, 125, 127–30, 132–5
water: allocation 36, 40, 53–4, 105, 123, 136; availability 18, 19, 20, 35–6, 44, 56, 120; conservation 18, 20, 55–6, 126; quality 3, 110, 120, 123, 126–9, 131–2, 137; management 18, 21–2, 36, 65, 96–8, 101–2, 105–6, 108–9, 111–5, 120, 124–5, 129; resource(s) 3, 12, 17, 22, 24, 35–7, 39–40, 58, 85, 97, 101–3, 109–11, 114–6, 120, 122–4, 126, 129–30, 135, 137, 148; right(s) 52, 54–5, 123–5, 137–9, 163; scarcity 18, 65; sector 12, 22, 84, 97; security 11–2, 84, 145, 162; supply 14, 66, 111–3, 148; system(s) 120; use(s) 22, 25, 36–7, 42, 55, 59, 102–3, 105–6, 108, 121–2, 124–6, 132–3, 138–9; utilisation 14
wildlife conservation 83, 88
World Bank 17, 102, 104, 109–11, 115–6, 151
World Economic Forum 31, 145